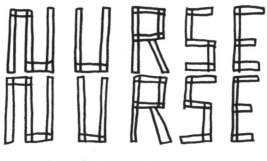

NURSE NURSE

KATIE SKELLY

SPARKPLUG BOOKS

First Edition
ISBN: 978-0-9854150-0-6

Katie Skelly
www.calicocomics.com

This book was printed with care by:
Brown Printing of Portland, OR USA

Published by:
Sparkplug Books
P.O. Box 10952
Portland, OR 97296-0952
www.sparkplugcomicbooks.com

IN MEMORY OF
DYLAN WILLIAMS

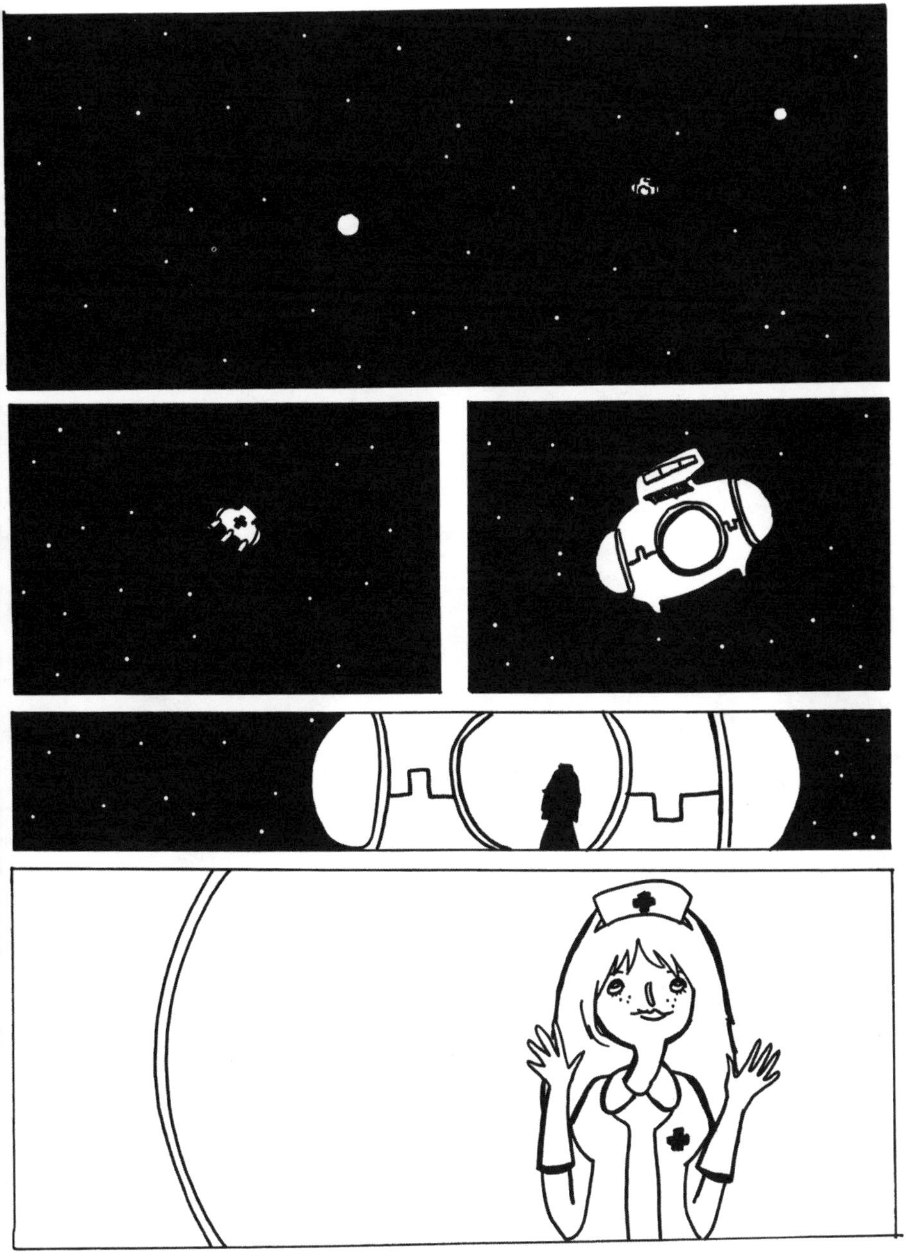

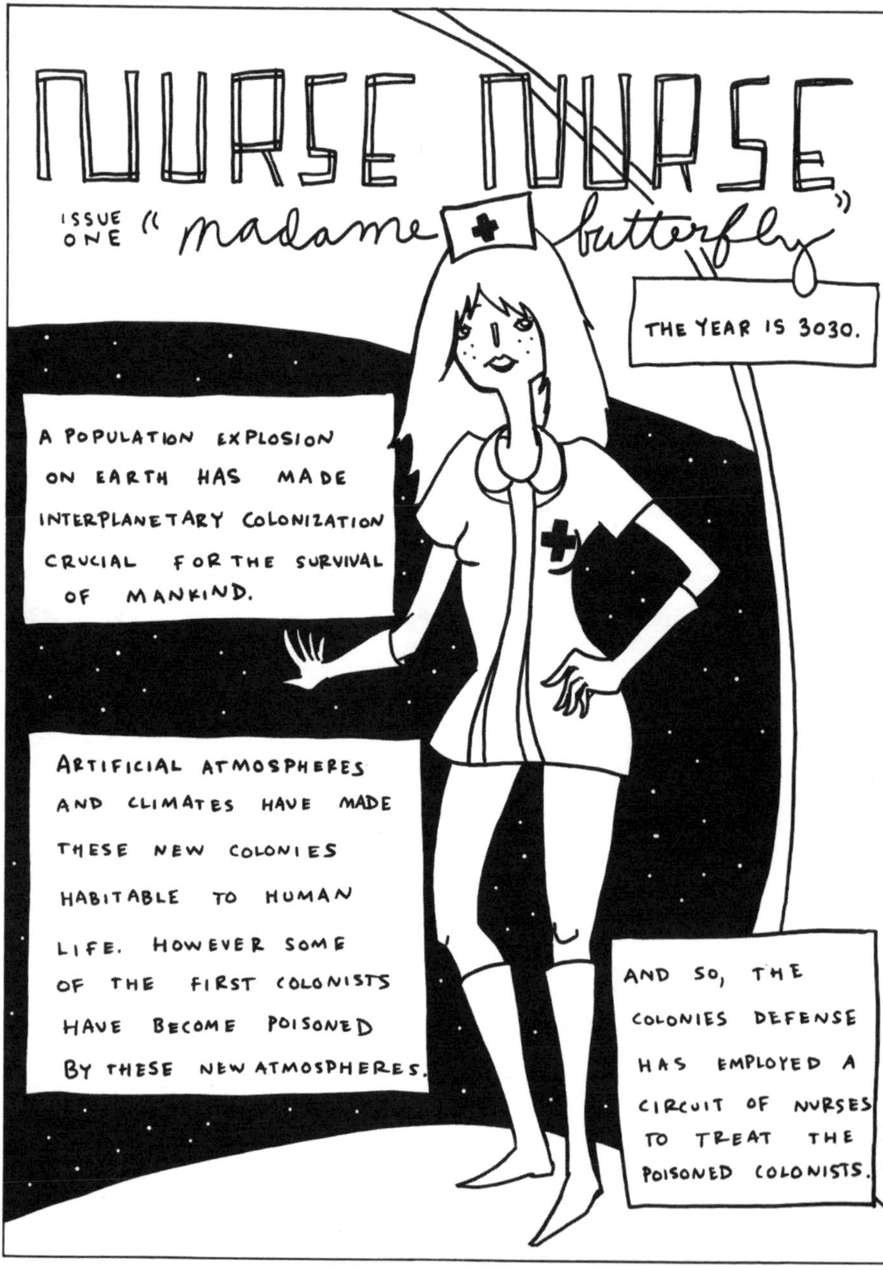
NURSE NURSE
ISSUE ONE "madame butterfly"
THE YEAR IS 3030.
A POPULATION EXPLOSION ON EARTH HAS MADE INTERPLANETARY COLONIZATION CRUCIAL FOR THE SURVIVAL OF MANKIND.
ARTIFICIAL ATMOSPHERES AND CLIMATES HAVE MADE THESE NEW COLONIES HABITABLE TO HUMAN LIFE. HOWEVER SOME OF THE FIRST COLONISTS HAVE BECOME POISONED BY THESE NEW ATMOSPHERES.
AND SO, THE COLONIES DEFENSE HAS EMPLOYED A CIRCUIT OF NURSES TO TREAT THE POISONED COLONISTS.

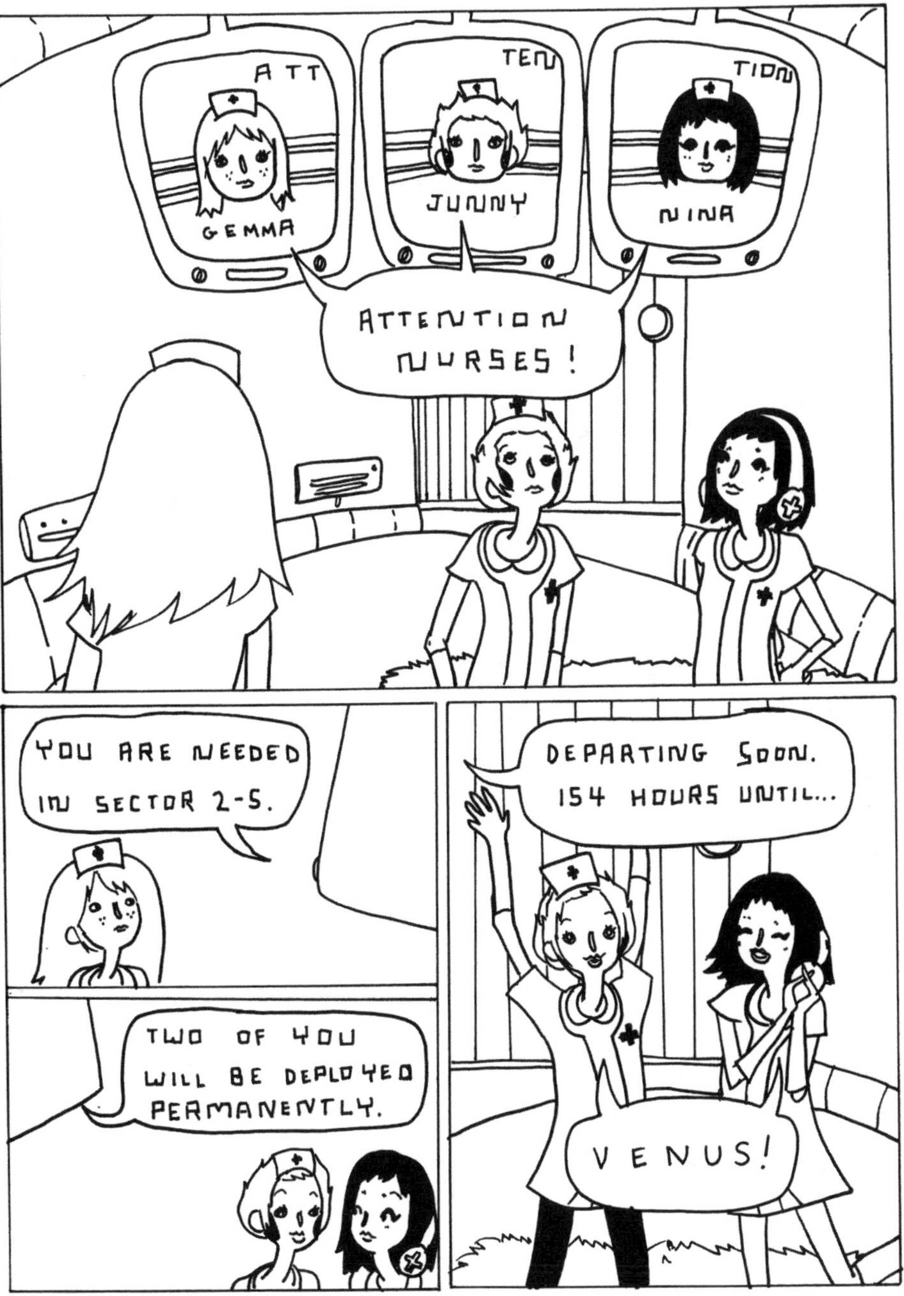
ATT
TEN
TION
GEMMA
JUNNY
NINA
ATTENTION NURSES!
YOU ARE NEEDED IN SECTOR 2-5.
TWO OF YOU WILL BE DEPLOYED PERMANENTLY.
DEPARTING SOON. 154 HOURS UNTIL...
VENUS!

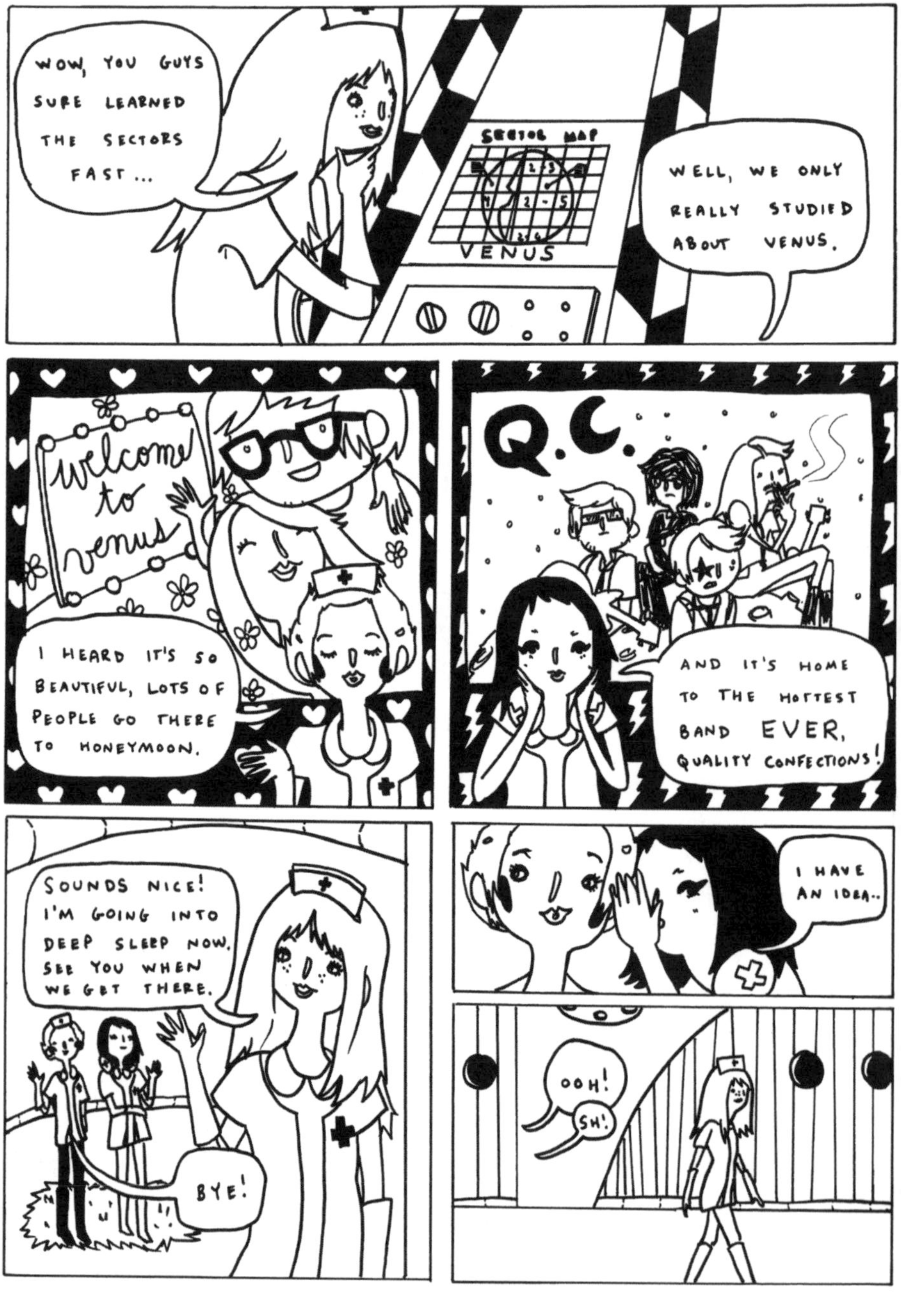
WOW, YOU GUYS SURE LEARNED THE SECTORS FAST...
SECTOR MAP
VENUS
WELL, WE ONLY REALLY STUDIED ABOUT VENUS.
welcome to venus
I HEARD IT'S SO BEAUTIFUL, LOTS OF PEOPLE GO THERE TO HONEYMOON.
Q.C.
AND IT'S HOME TO THE HOTTEST BAND EVER, QUALITY CONFECTIONS!
SOUNDS NICE! I'M GOING INTO DEEP SLEEP NOW. SEE YOU WHEN WE GET THERE.
BYE!
I HAVE AN IDEA...
OOH!
SH!

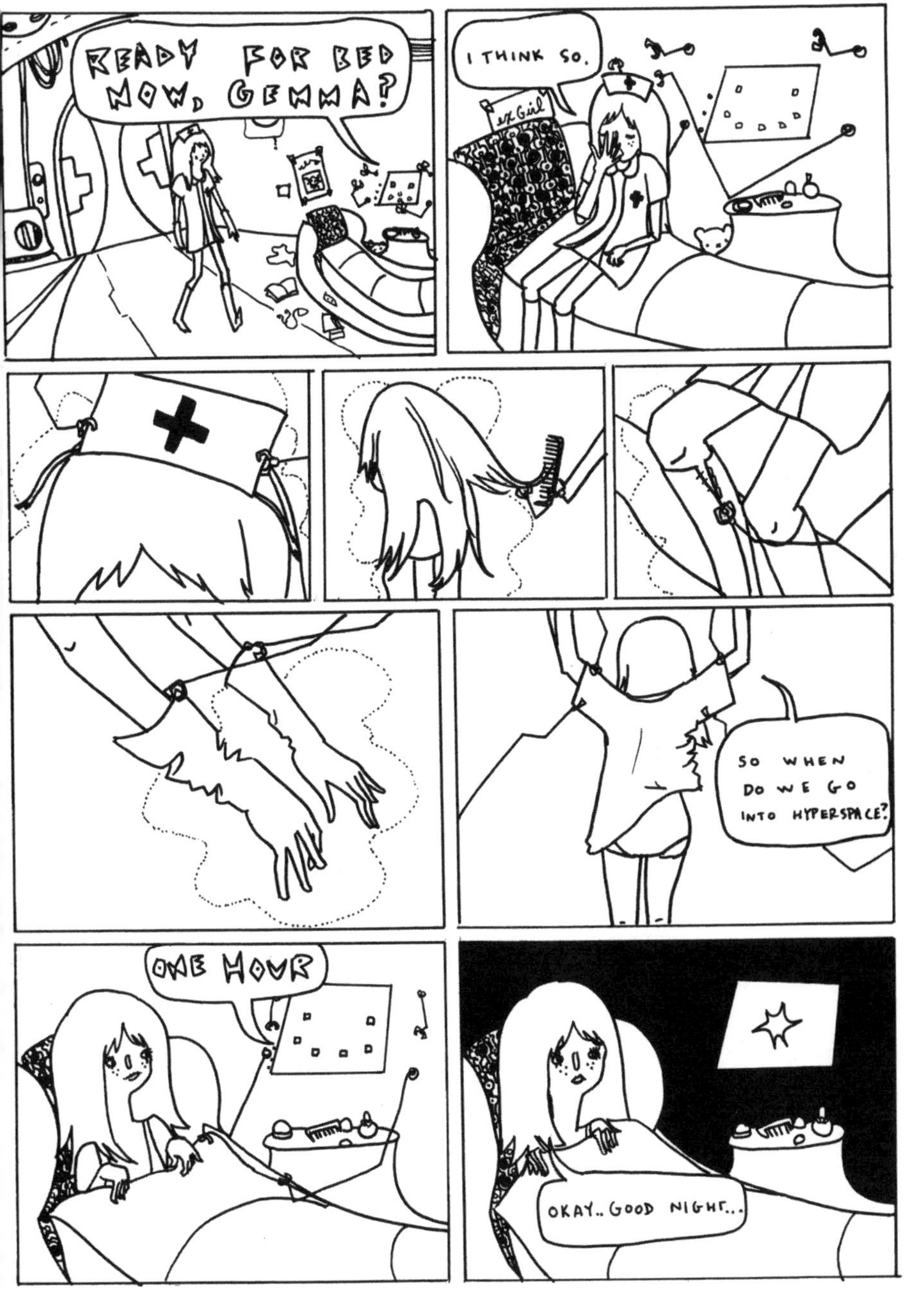
READY FOR BED NOW, GEMMA?
I THINK SO.
exGirl
SO WHEN DO WE GO INTO HYPERSPACE?
ONE HOUR
OKAY.. GOOD NIGHT...

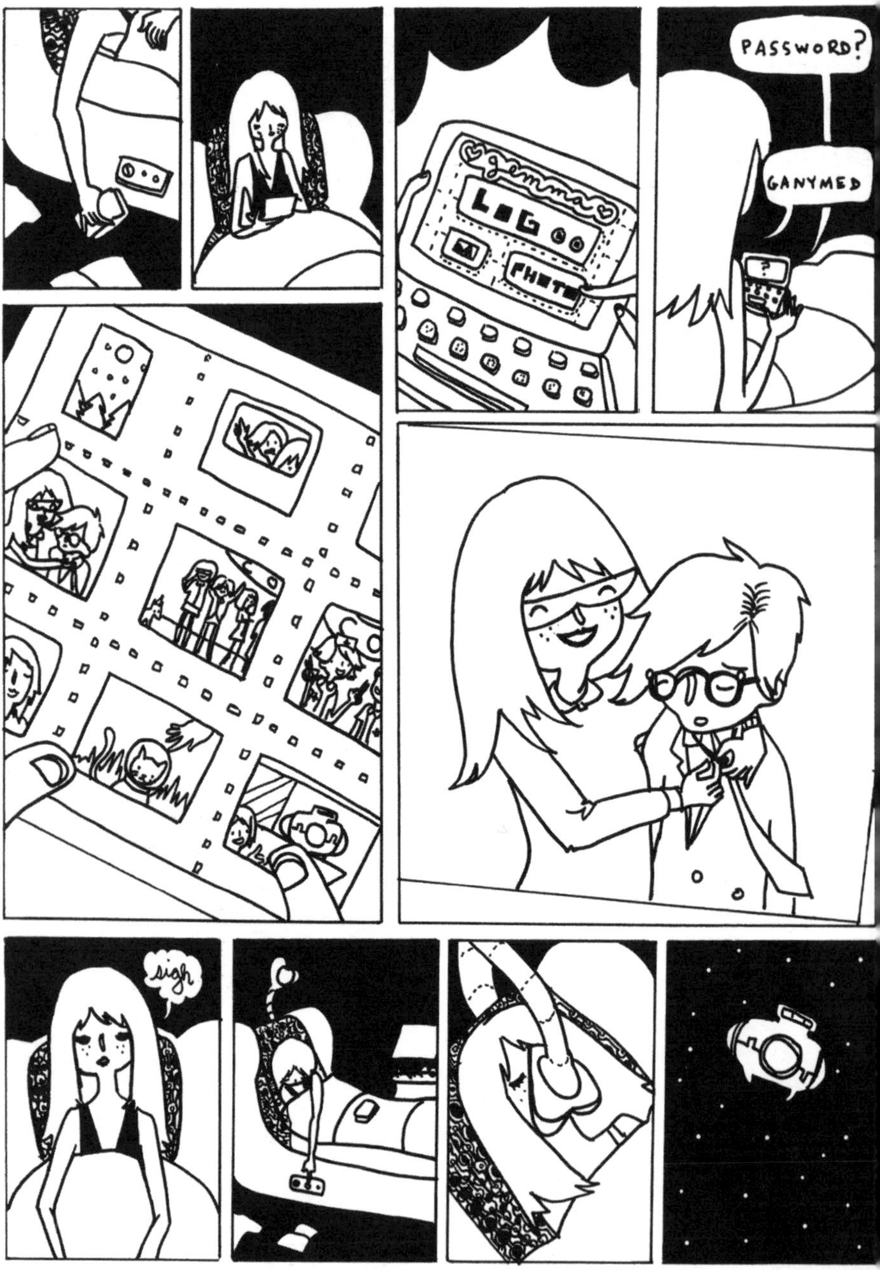
gemma
LOG
PHOTO
PASSWORD?
GANYMED
sigh

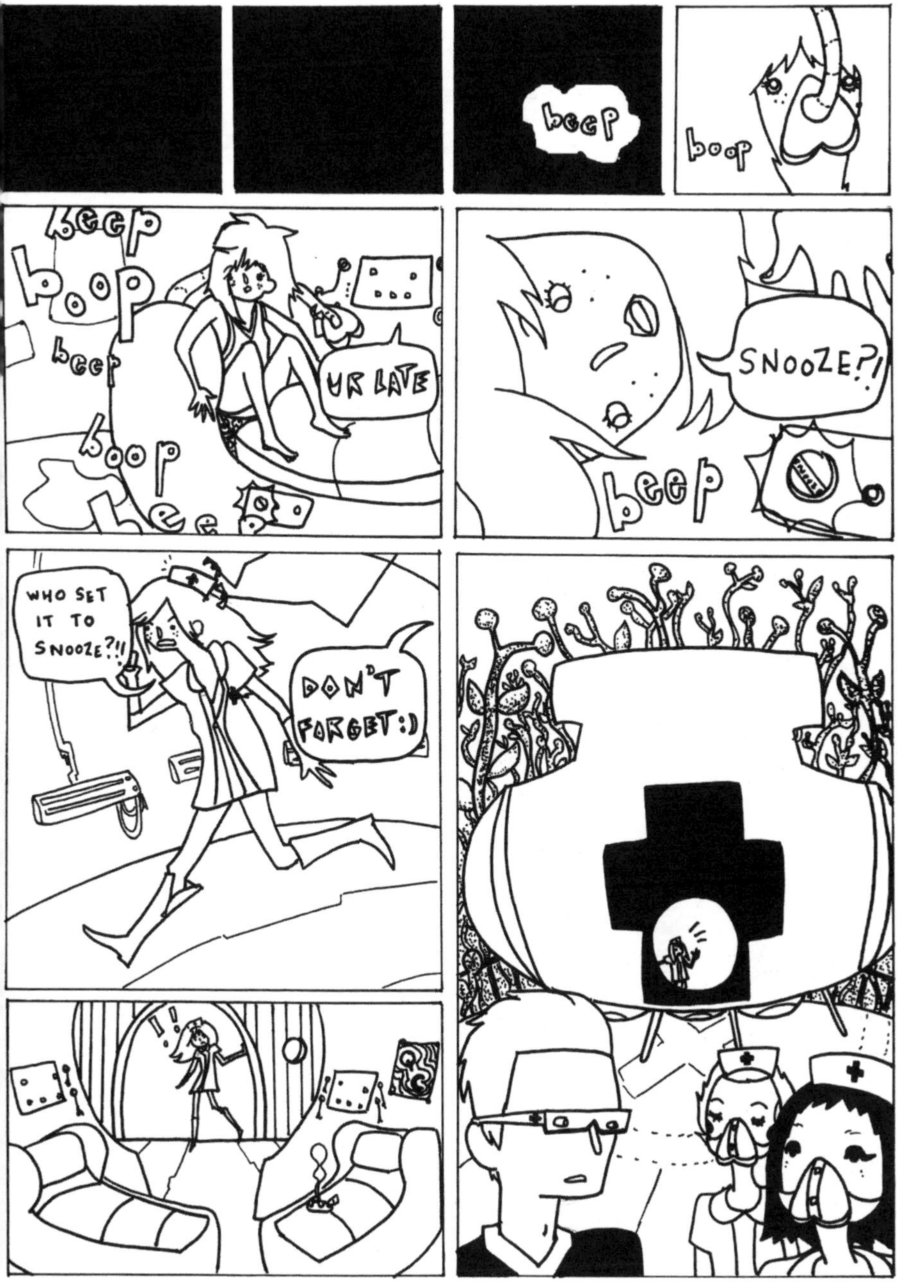
beep
boop
beep
boop
beep
boop
UR LATE
SNOOZE?!
beep
WHO SET IT TO SNOOZE?!!
DON'T FORGET :)

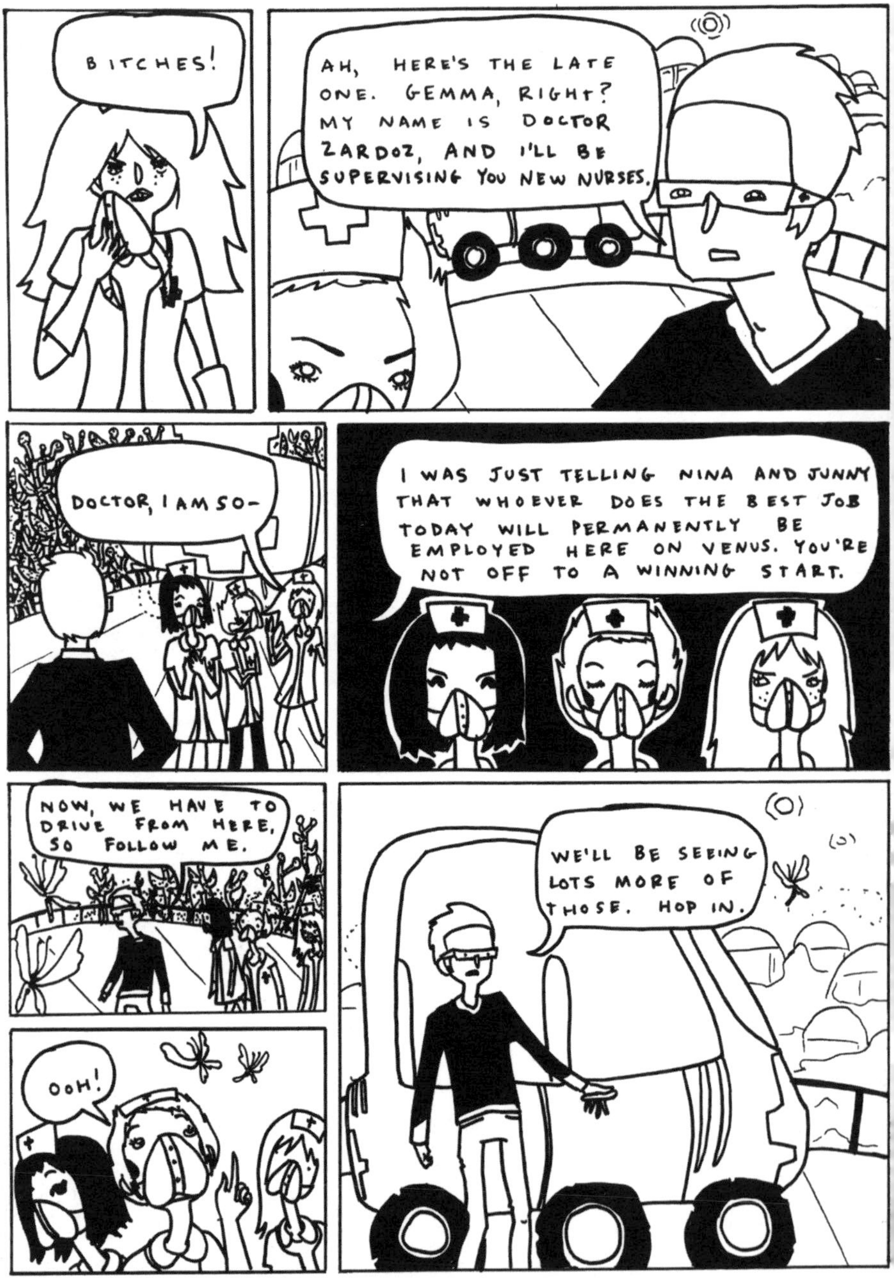
BITCHES!
AH, HERE'S THE LATE ONE. GEMMA, RIGHT? MY NAME IS DOCTOR ZARDOZ, AND I'LL BE SUPERVISING YOU NEW NURSES.
DOCTOR, I AM SO-
I WAS JUST TELLING NINA AND JUNNY THAT WHOEVER DOES THE BEST JOB TODAY WILL PERMANENTLY BE EMPLOYED HERE ON VENUS. YOU'RE NOT OFF TO A WINNING START.
NOW, WE HAVE TO DRIVE FROM HERE, SO FOLLOW ME.
OOH!
WE'LL BE SEEING LOTS MORE OF THOSE. HOP IN.

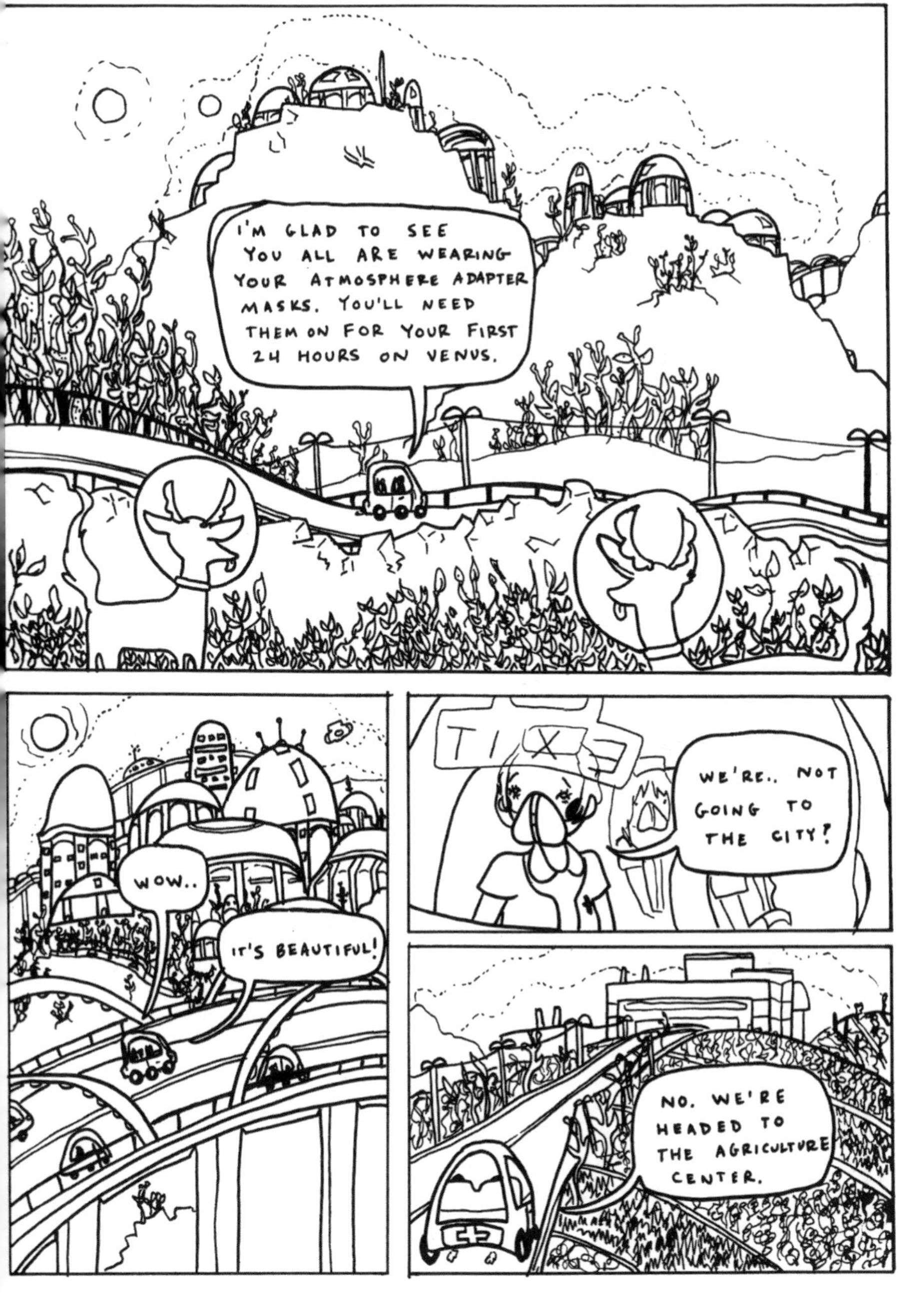
I'M GLAD TO SEE YOU ALL ARE WEARING YOUR ATMOSPHERE ADAPTER MASKS. YOU'LL NEED THEM ON FOR YOUR FIRST 24 HOURS ON VENUS.
WOW..
IT'S BEAUTIFUL!
WE'RE.. NOT GOING TO THE CITY?
NO. WE'RE HEADED TO THE AGRICULTURE CENTER.

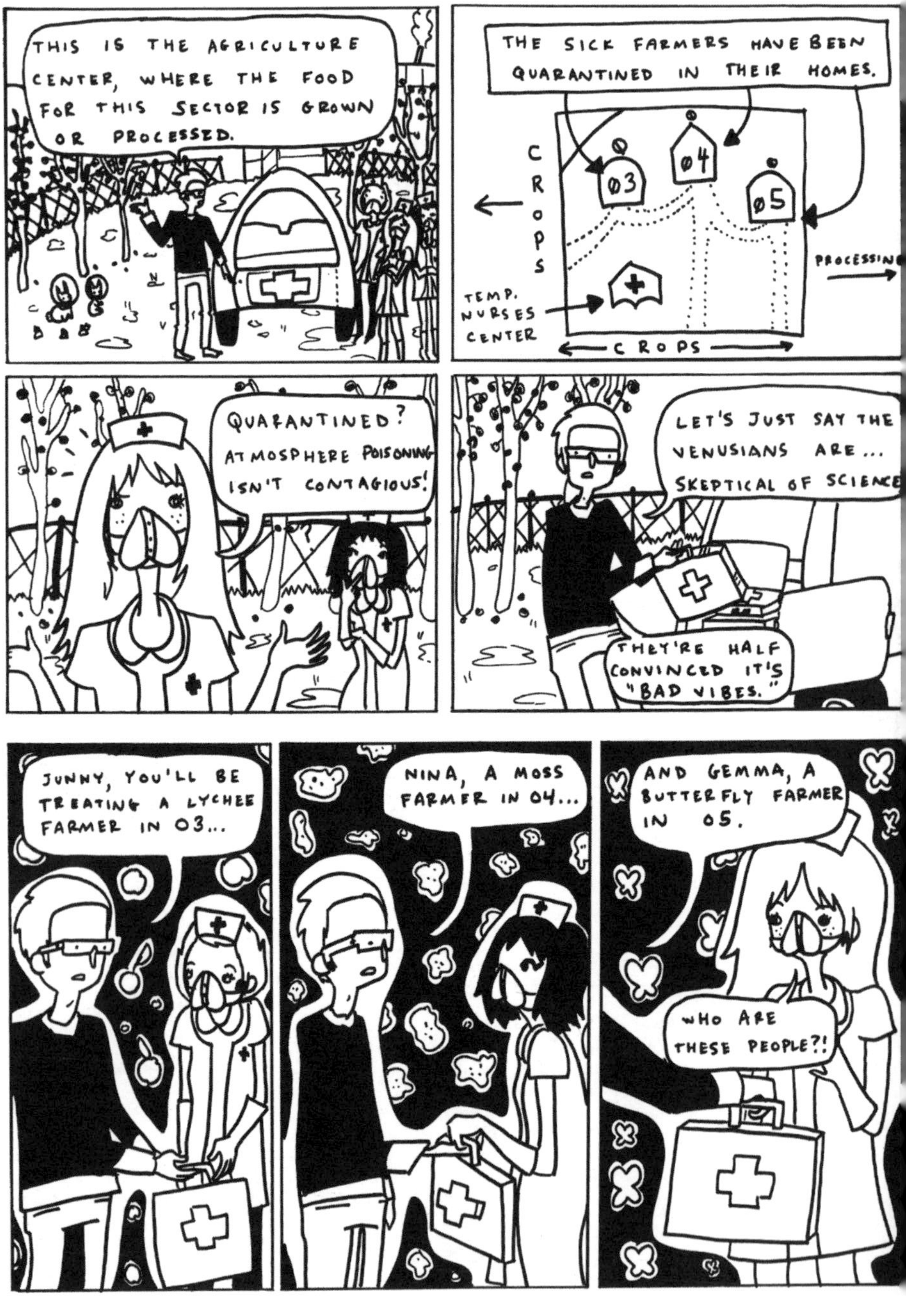
THIS IS THE AGRICULTURE CENTER, WHERE THE FOOD FOR THIS SECTOR IS GROWN OR PROCESSED.
THE SICK FARMERS HAVE BEEN QUARANTINED IN THEIR HOMES.
CROPS
Ø3
Ø4
Ø5
PROCESSING
TEMP. NURSES CENTER
CROPS
QUARANTINED? ATMOSPHERE POISONING ISN'T CONTAGIOUS!
LET'S JUST SAY THE VENUSIANS ARE... SKEPTICAL OF SCIENCE
THEY'RE HALF CONVINCED IT'S "BAD VIBES."
JUNNY, YOU'LL BE TREATING A LYCHEE FARMER IN O3...
NINA, A MOSS FARMER IN O4...
AND GEMMA, A BUTTERFLY FARMER IN O5.
WHO ARE THESE PEOPLE?!

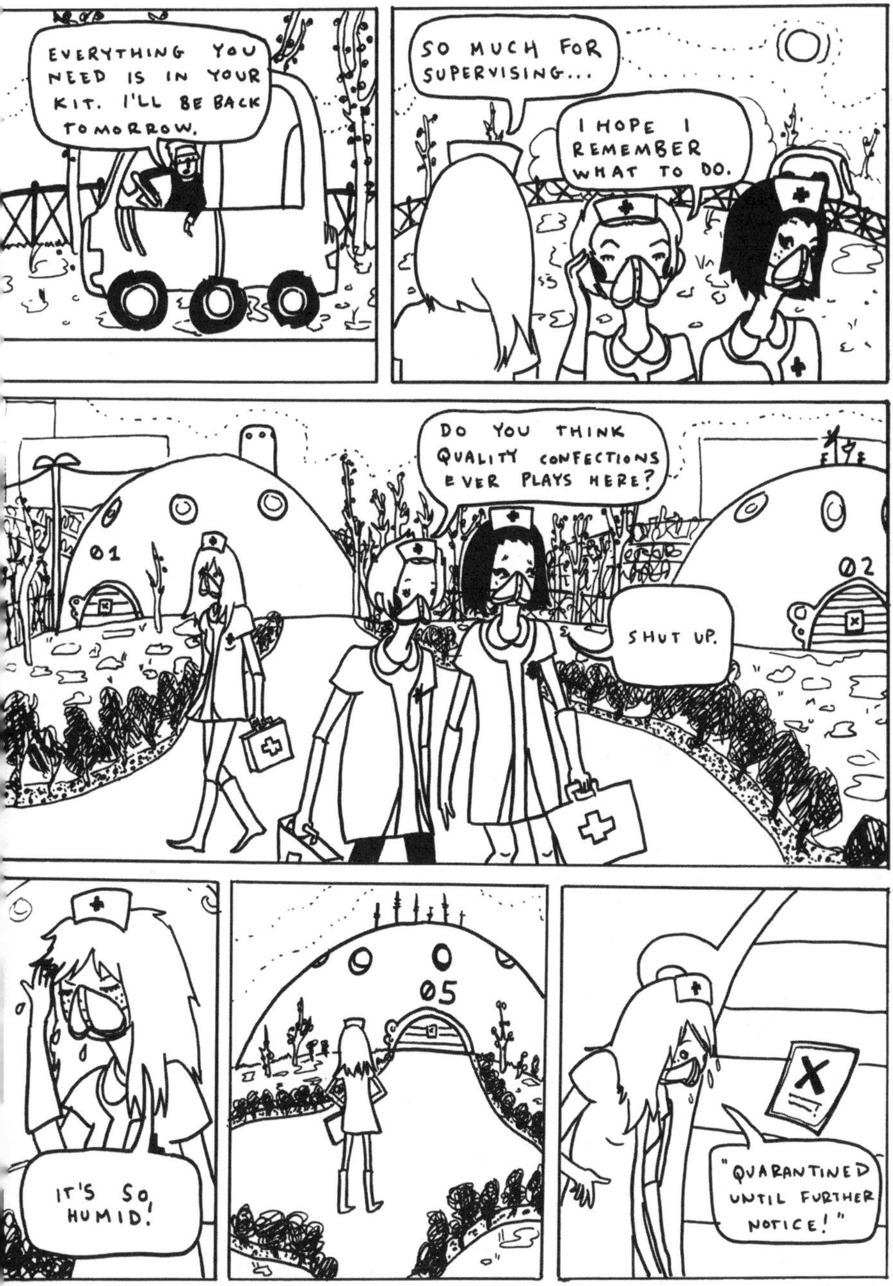
EVERYTHING YOU NEED IS IN YOUR KIT. I'LL BE BACK TOMORROW.
SO MUCH FOR SUPERVISING...
I HOPE I REMEMBER WHAT TO DO.
01
DO YOU THINK QUALITY CONFECTIONS EVER PLAYS HERE?
02
SHUT UP.
IT'S SO HUMID!
05
"QUARANTINED UNTIL FURTHER NOTICE!"

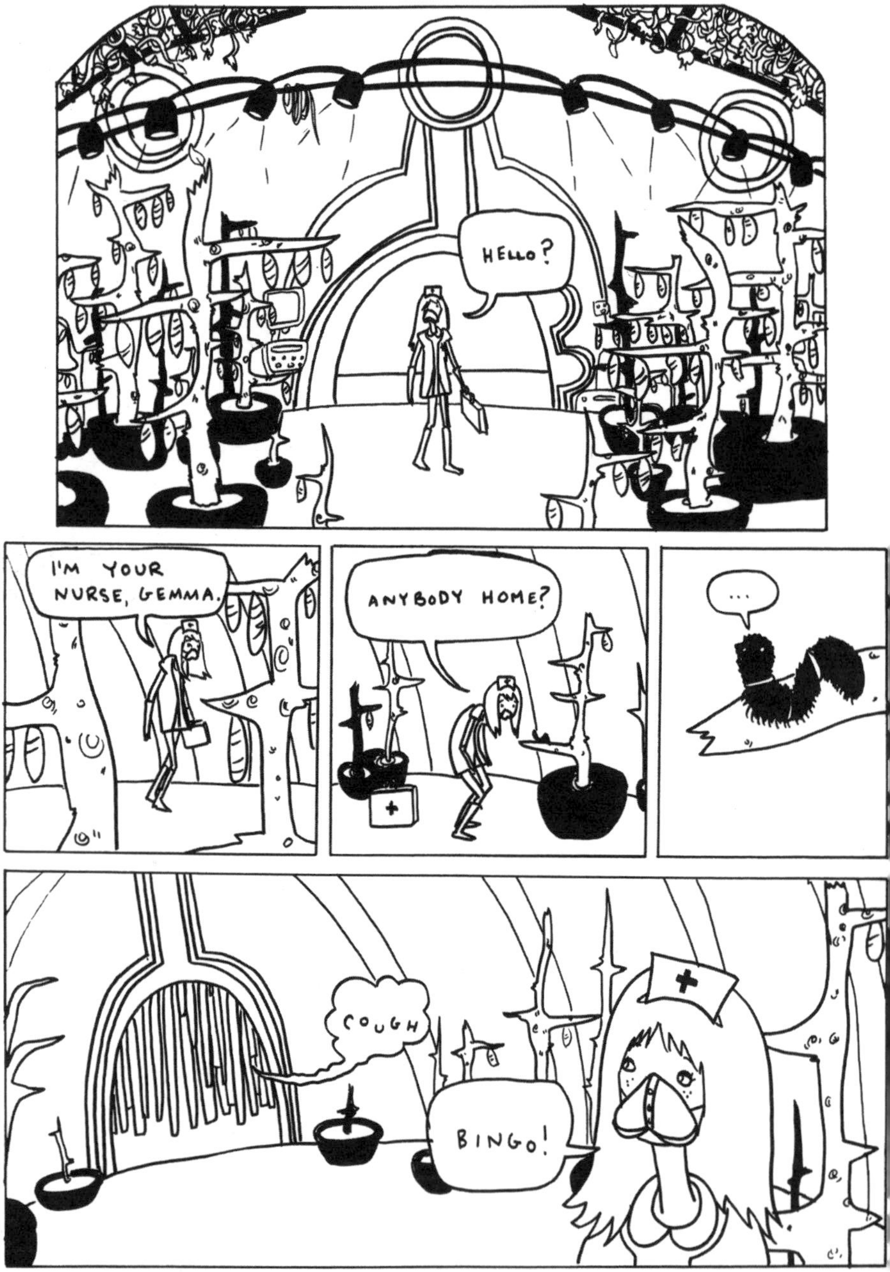
HELLO?
I'M YOUR NURSE, GEMMA.
ANYBODY HOME?
...
COUGH
BINGO!

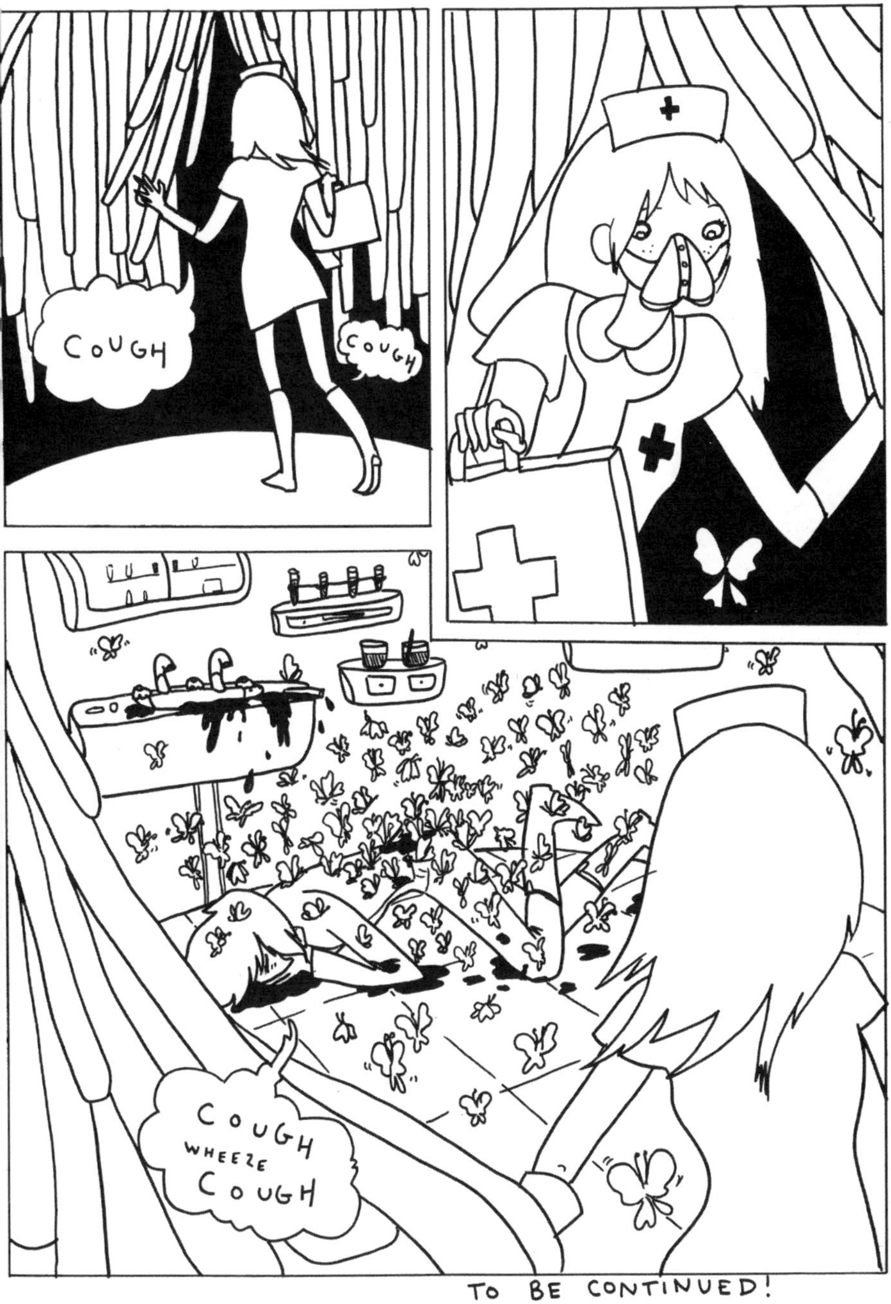
COUGH
COUGH
COUGH
WHEEZE
COUGH

TO BE CONTINUED!

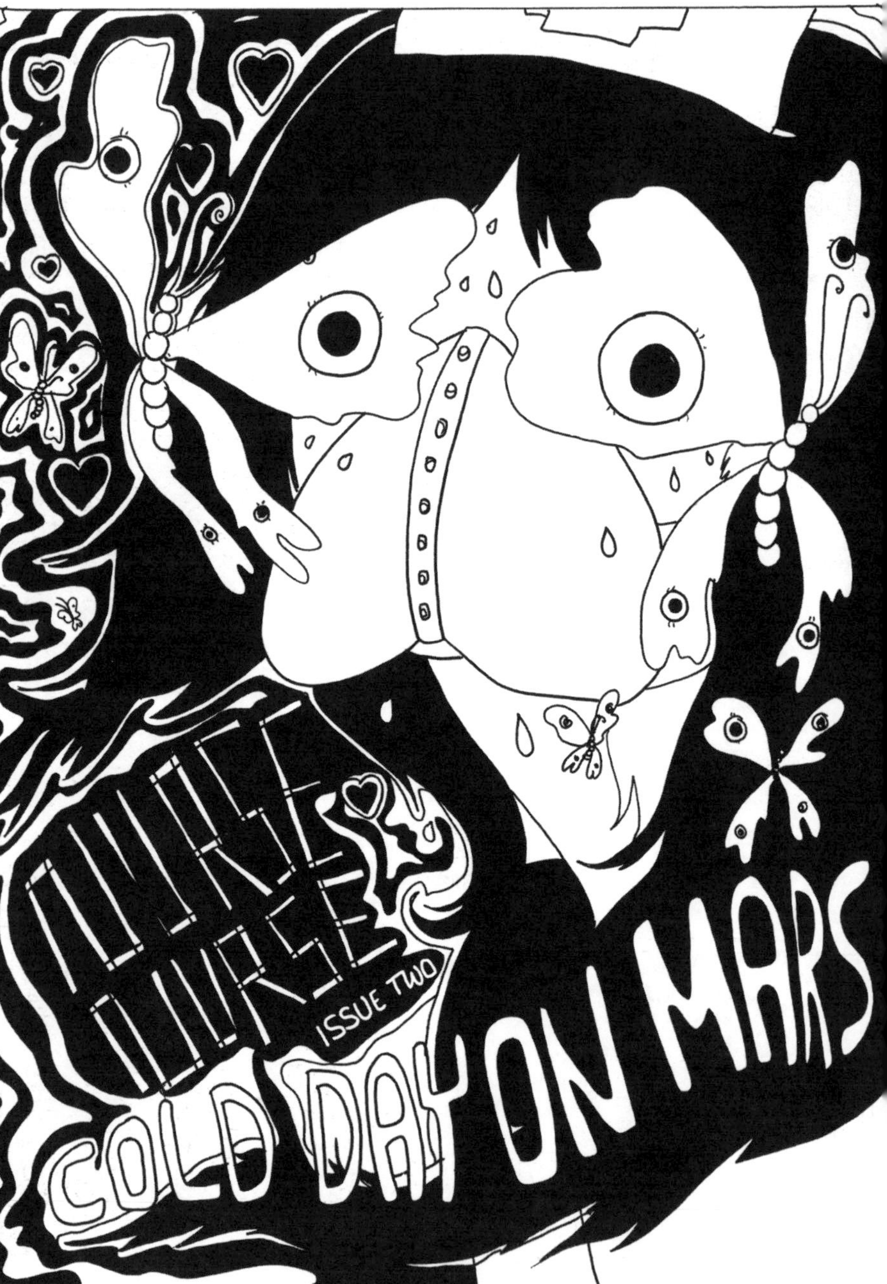
NURSE
NURSE
ISSUE TWO
COLD DAY ON MARS

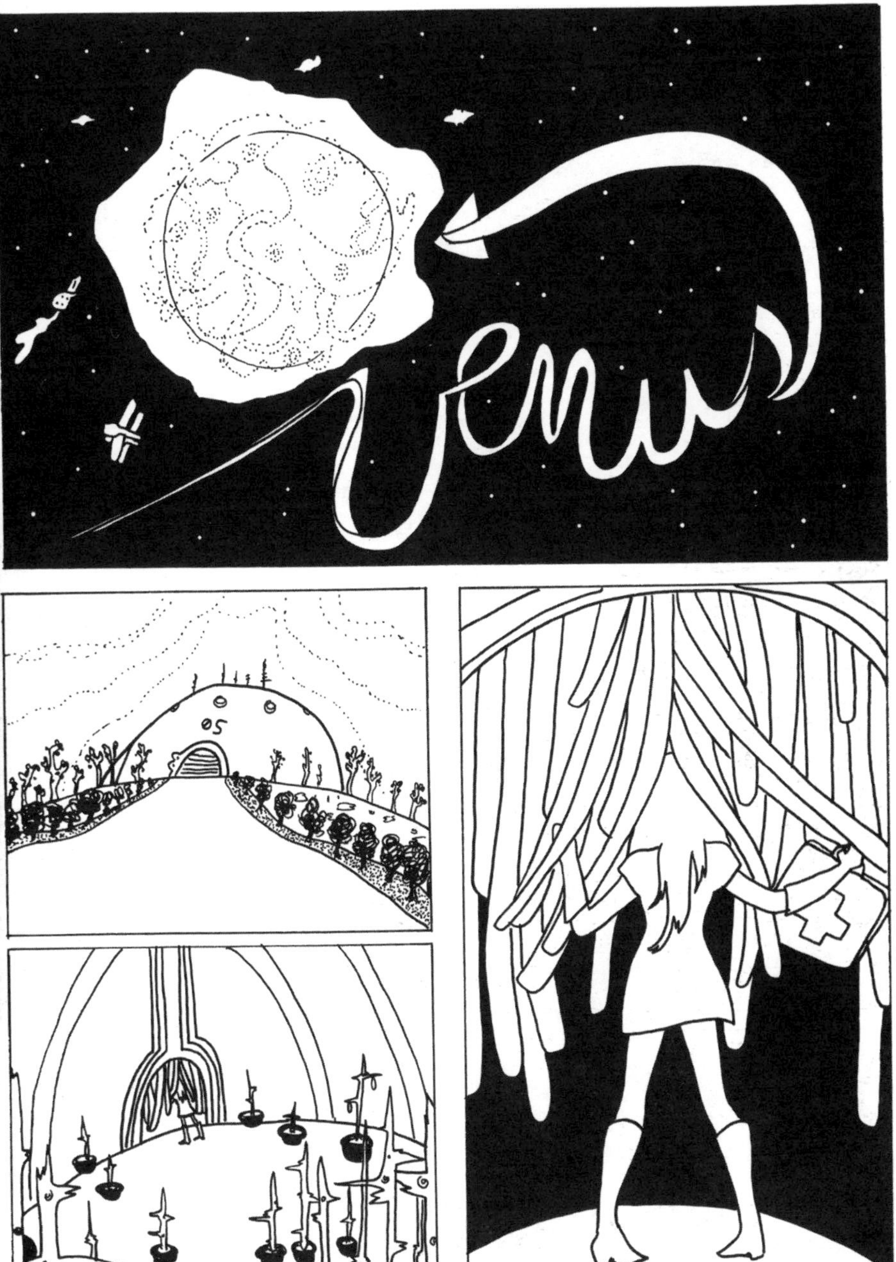
venus
05

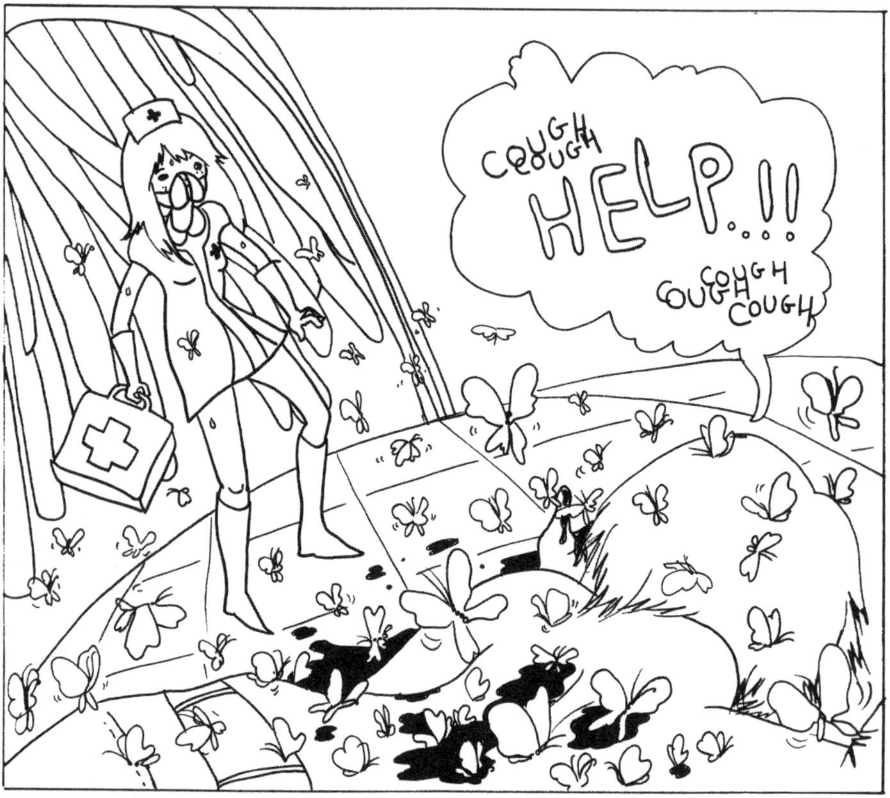
COUGH COUGH
HELP..!!
COUGH COUGH COUGH COUGH

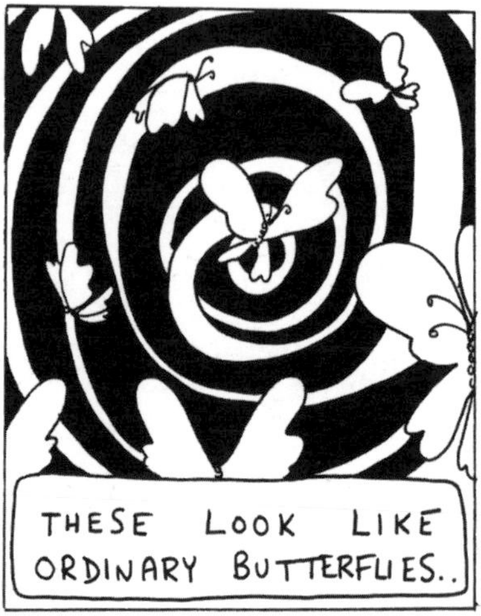
THESE LOOK LIKE ORDINARY BUTTERFLIES..

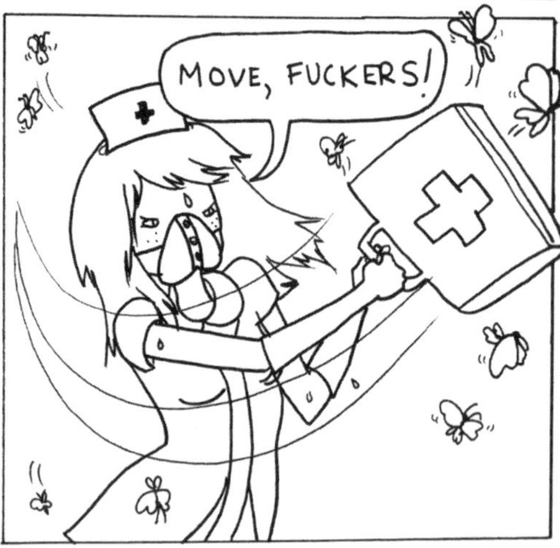
MOVE, FUCKERS!

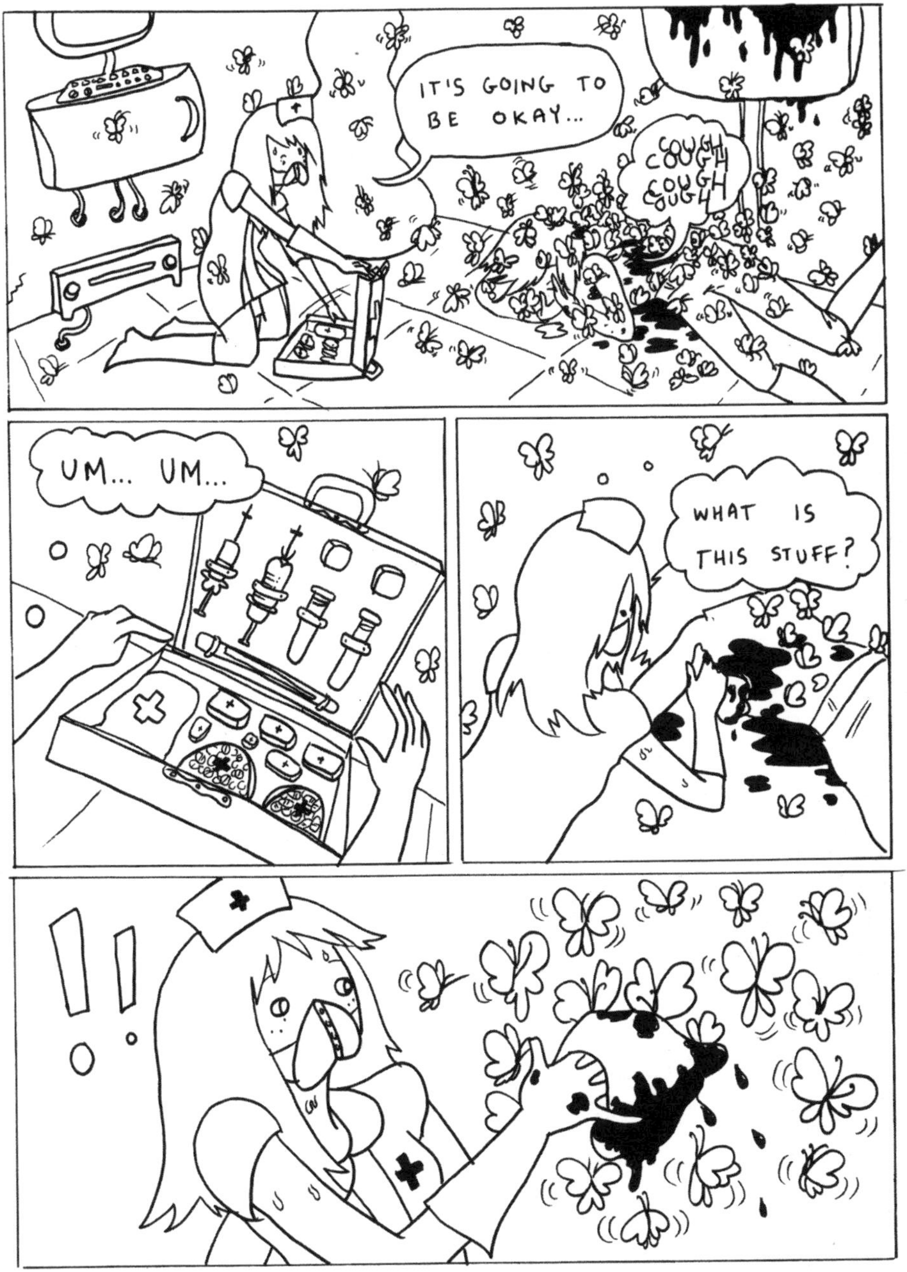
IT'S GOING TO BE OKAY...
COUGH COUGH COUGH COUGH
UM... UM...
WHAT IS THIS STUFF?
!!

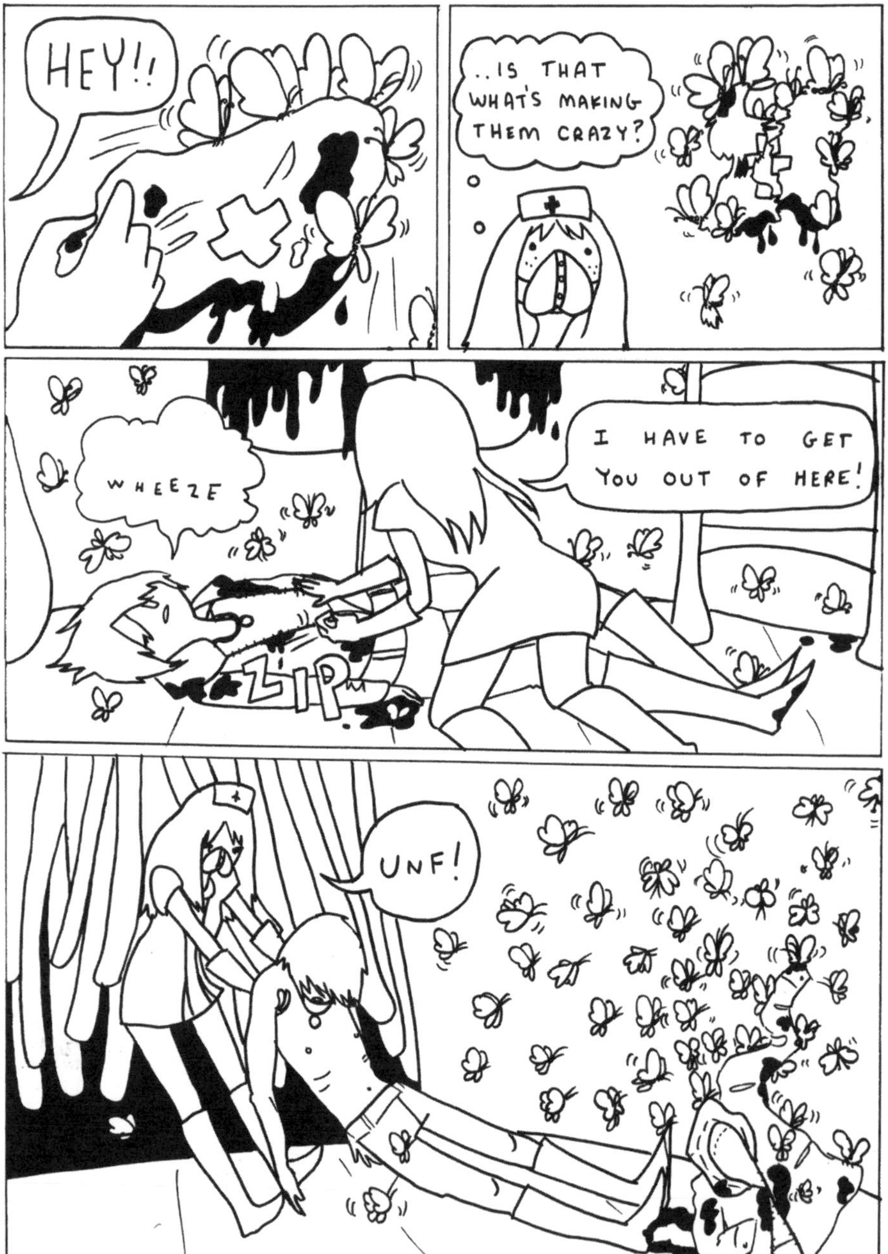
HEY!!
..IS THAT WHAT'S MAKING THEM CRAZY?
WHEEZE
I HAVE TO GET YOU OUT OF HERE!
ZIP
UNF!

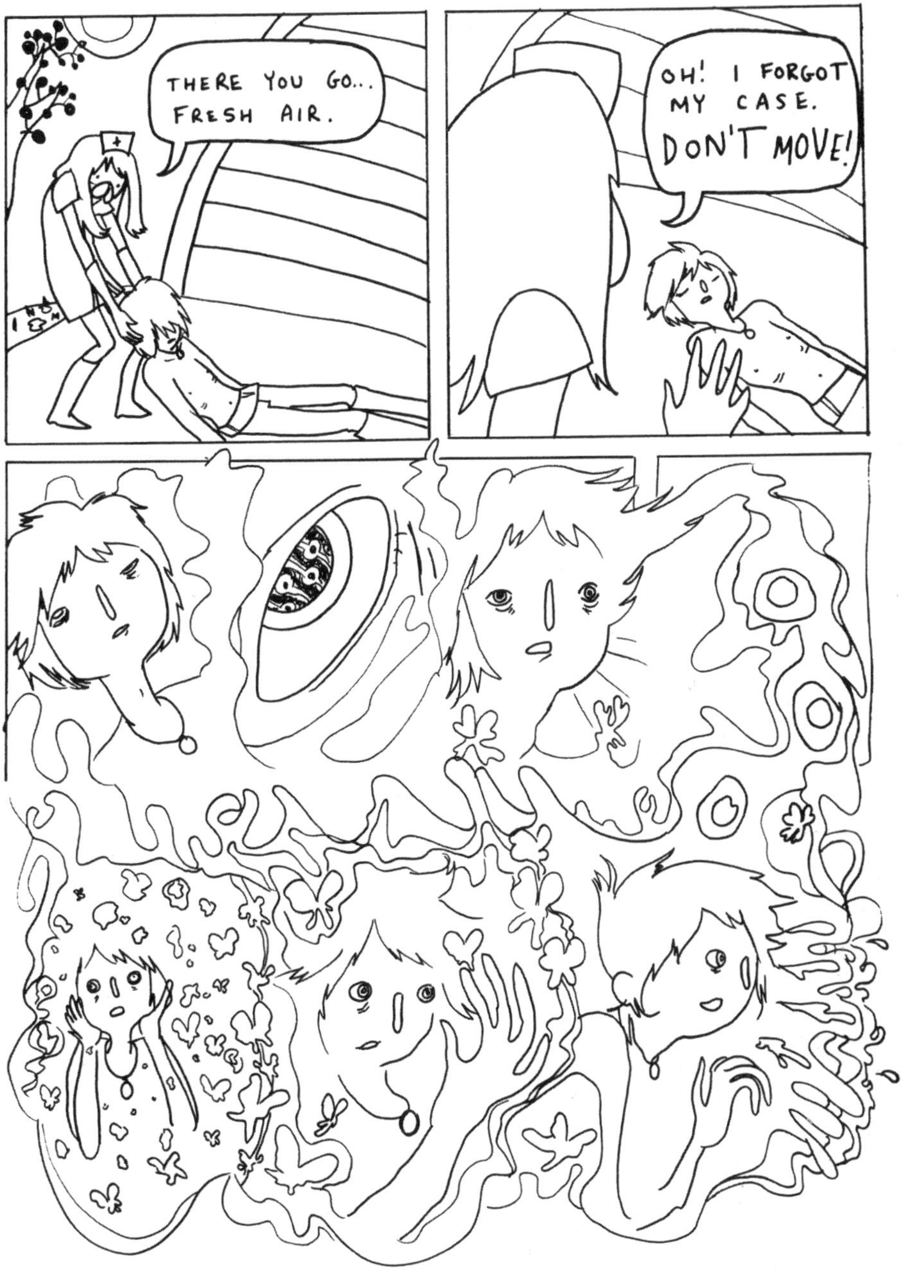
THERE YOU GO... FRESH AIR.
OH! I FORGOT MY CASE. DON'T MOVE!

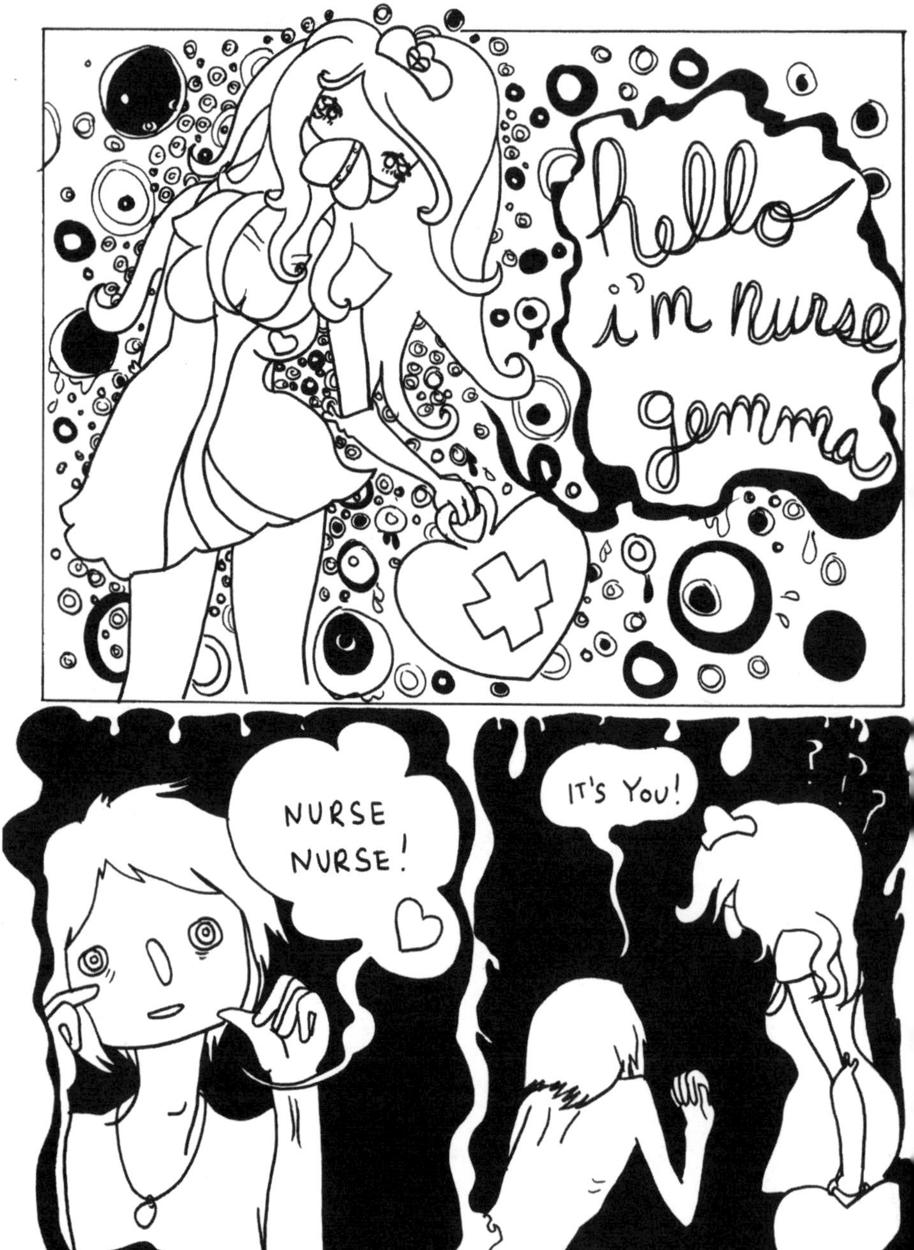
hello i'm nurse gemma
NURSE NURSE!
IT'S YOU!
? ? ?

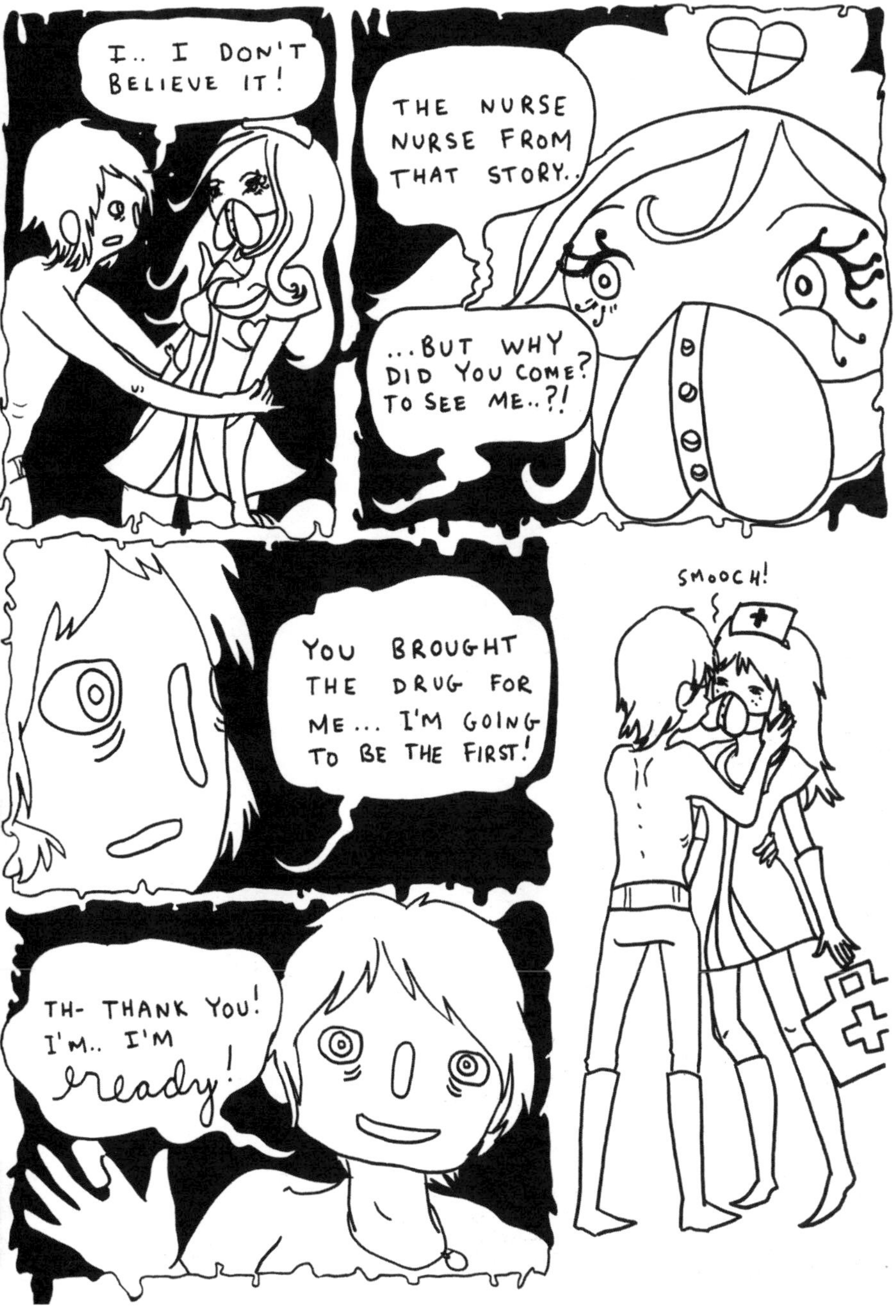
I.. I DON'T BELIEVE IT!
THE NURSE NURSE FROM THAT STORY..
...BUT WHY DID YOU COME? TO SEE ME..?!
YOU BROUGHT THE DRUG FOR ME... I'M GOING TO BE THE FIRST!
TH- THANK YOU! I'M.. I'M ready!
SMOOCH!

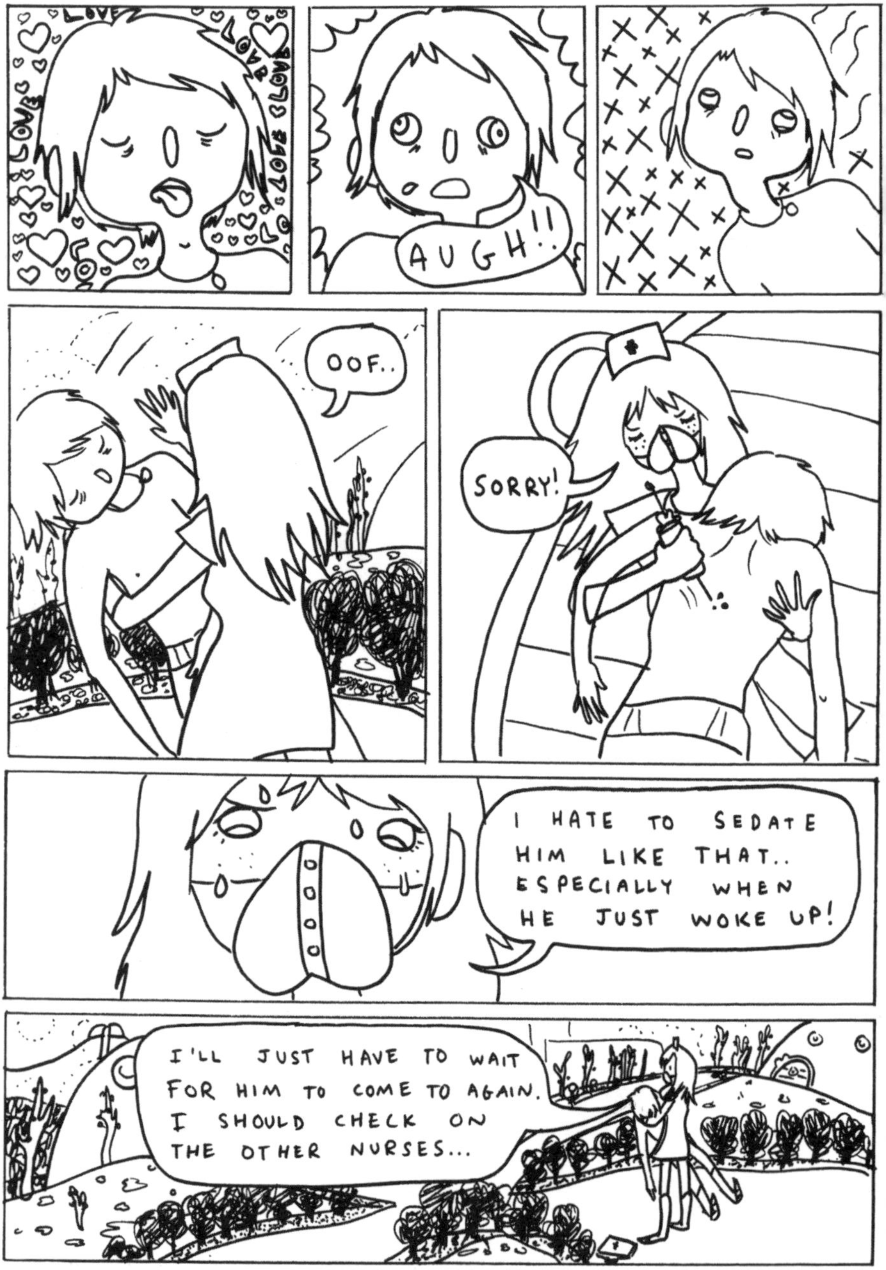
LOVE
LOVE
LOVE
LOVE
LOVE
AUGH!!
OOF..
SORRY!
I HATE TO SEDATE HIM LIKE THAT.. ESPECIALLY WHEN HE JUST WOKE UP!
I'LL JUST HAVE TO WAIT FOR HIM TO COME TO AGAIN. I SHOULD CHECK ON THE OTHER NURSES...

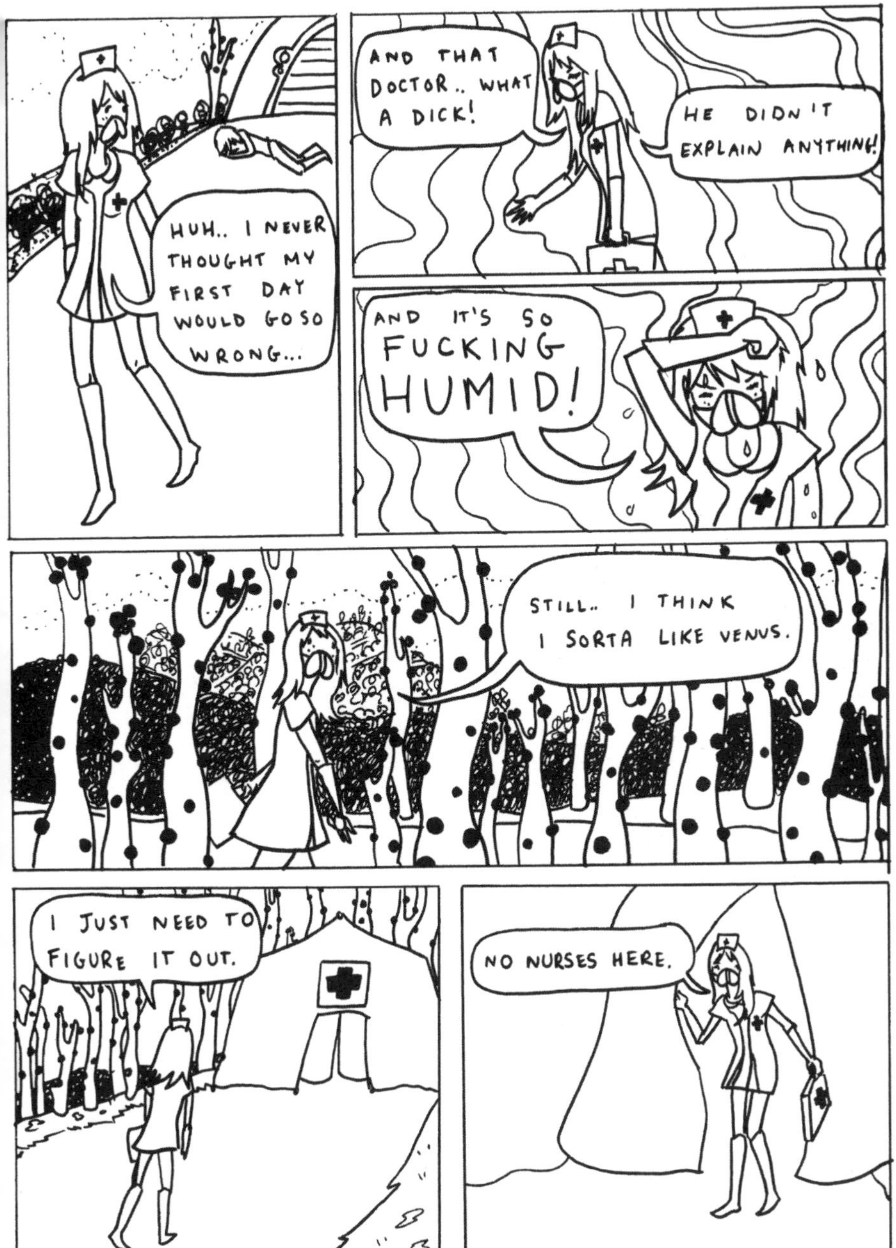
HUH.. I NEVER THOUGHT MY FIRST DAY WOULD GO SO WRONG...
AND THAT DOCTOR.. WHAT A DICK!
HE DIDN'T EXPLAIN ANYTHING!
AND IT'S SO FUCKING HUMID!
STILL.. I THINK I SORTA LIKE VENUS.
I JUST NEED TO FIGURE IT OUT.
NO NURSES HERE.

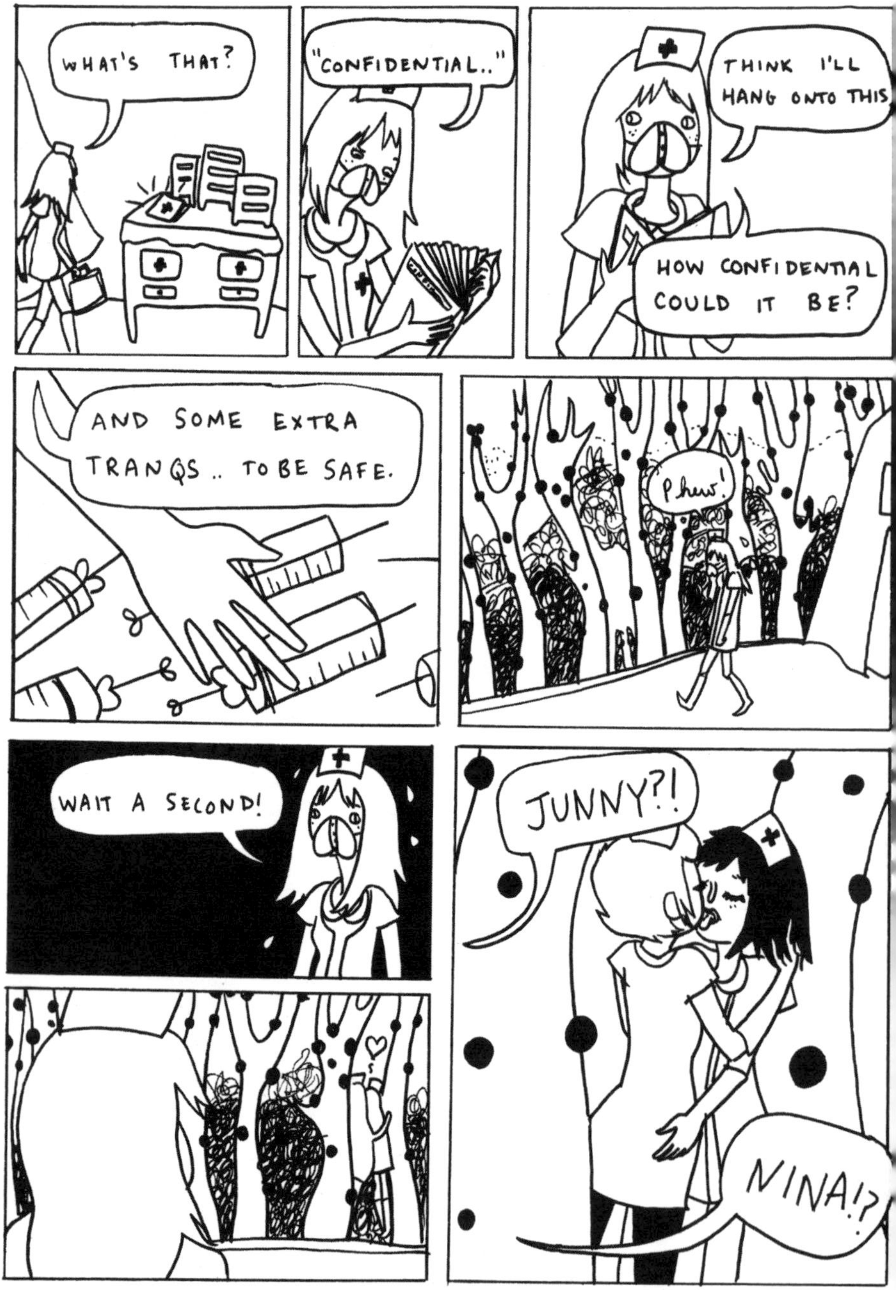
WHAT'S THAT?
"CONFIDENTIAL.."
THINK I'LL HANG ONTO THIS
HOW CONFIDENTIAL COULD IT BE?
AND SOME EXTRA TRANQS .. TO BE SAFE.
Phew!
WAIT A SECOND!
JUNNY?!
NINA!?

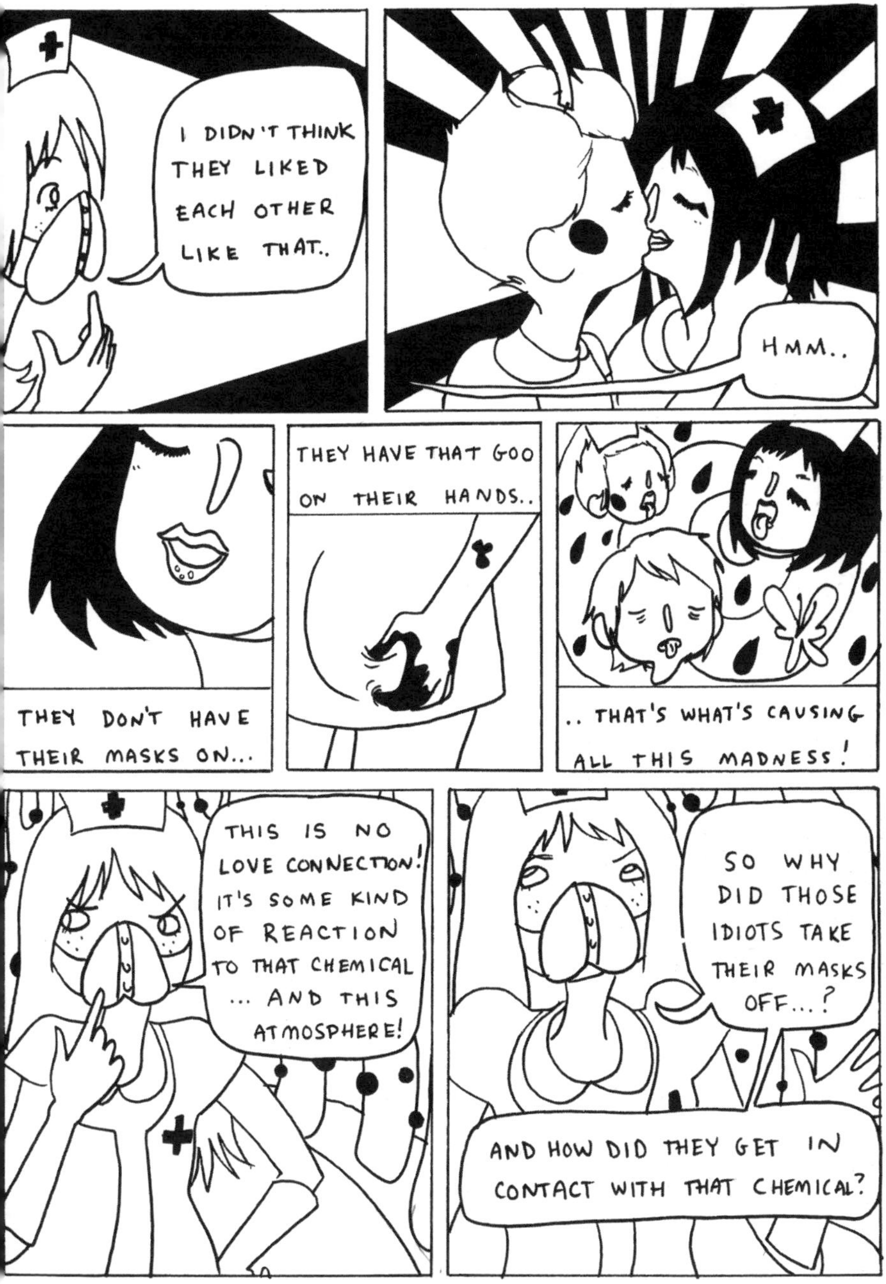
I DIDN'T THINK THEY LIKED EACH OTHER LIKE THAT..
HMM..
THEY DON'T HAVE THEIR MASKS ON...
THEY HAVE THAT GOO ON THEIR HANDS..
.. THAT'S WHAT'S CAUSING ALL THIS MADNESS!
THIS IS NO LOVE CONNECTION! IT'S SOME KIND OF REACTION TO THAT CHEMICAL ... AND THIS ATMOSPHERE!
SO WHY DID THOSE IDIOTS TAKE THEIR MASKS OFF...?
AND HOW DID THEY GET IN CONTACT WITH THAT CHEMICAL?

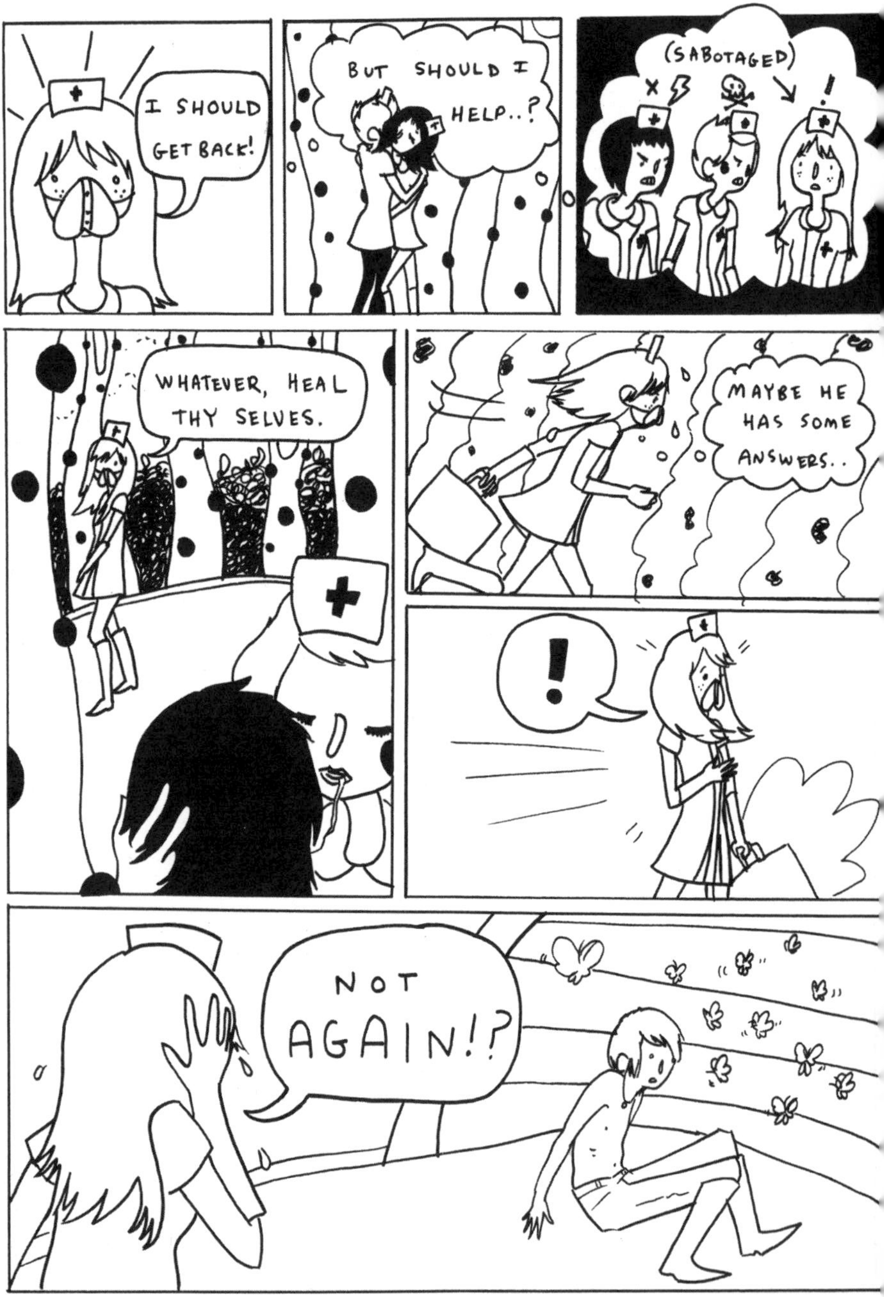
I SHOULD GET BACK!
BUT SHOULD I HELP..?
(SABOTAGED)
WHATEVER, HEAL THY SELVES.
MAYBE HE HAS SOME ANSWERS..
!
NOT AGAIN!?

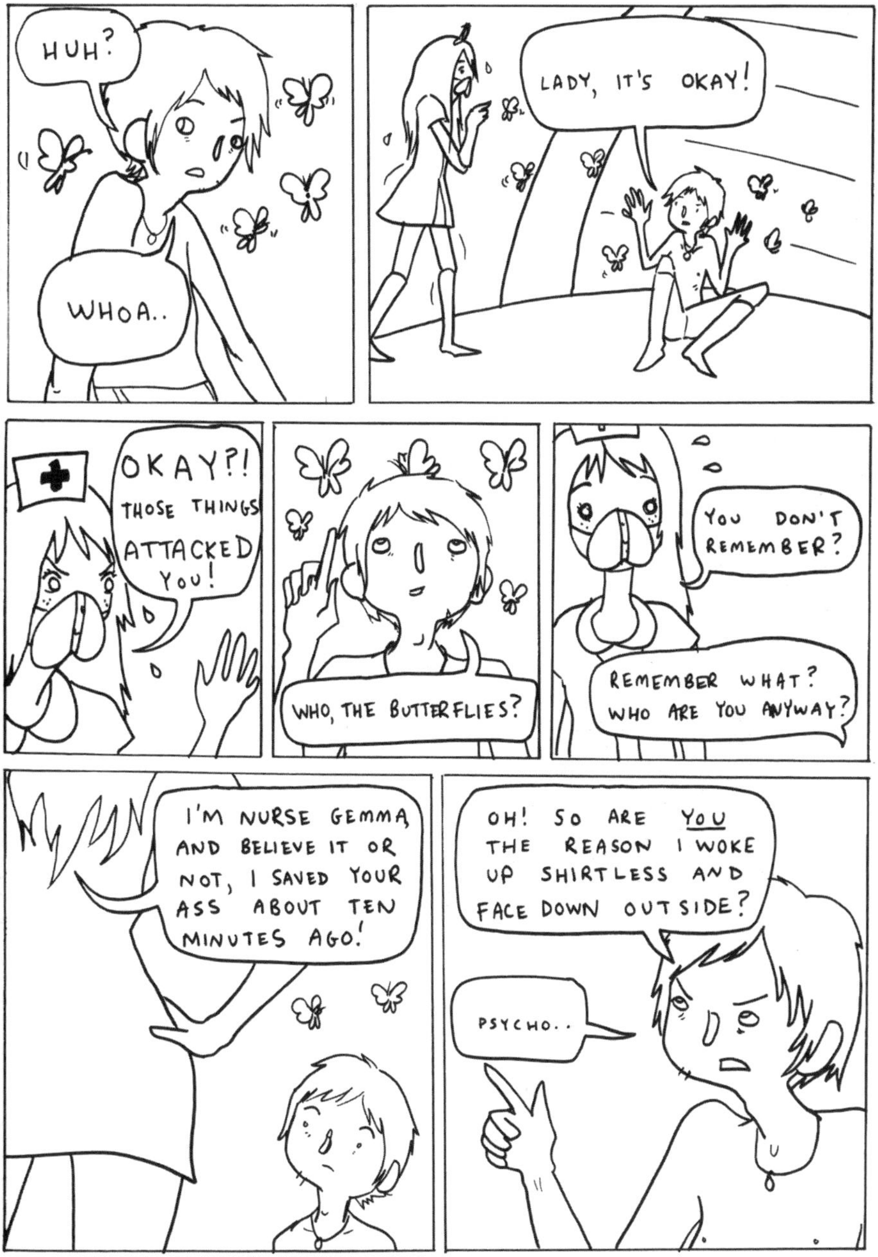
HUH?
WHOA..
LADY, IT'S OKAY!
OKAY?! THOSE THINGS ATTACKED YOU!
WHO, THE BUTTERFLIES?
YOU DON'T REMEMBER?
REMEMBER WHAT? WHO ARE YOU ANYWAY?
I'M NURSE GEMMA, AND BELIEVE IT OR NOT, I SAVED YOUR ASS ABOUT TEN MINUTES AGO!
OH! SO ARE YOU THE REASON I WOKE UP SHIRTLESS AND FACE DOWN OUTSIDE?
PSYCHO..

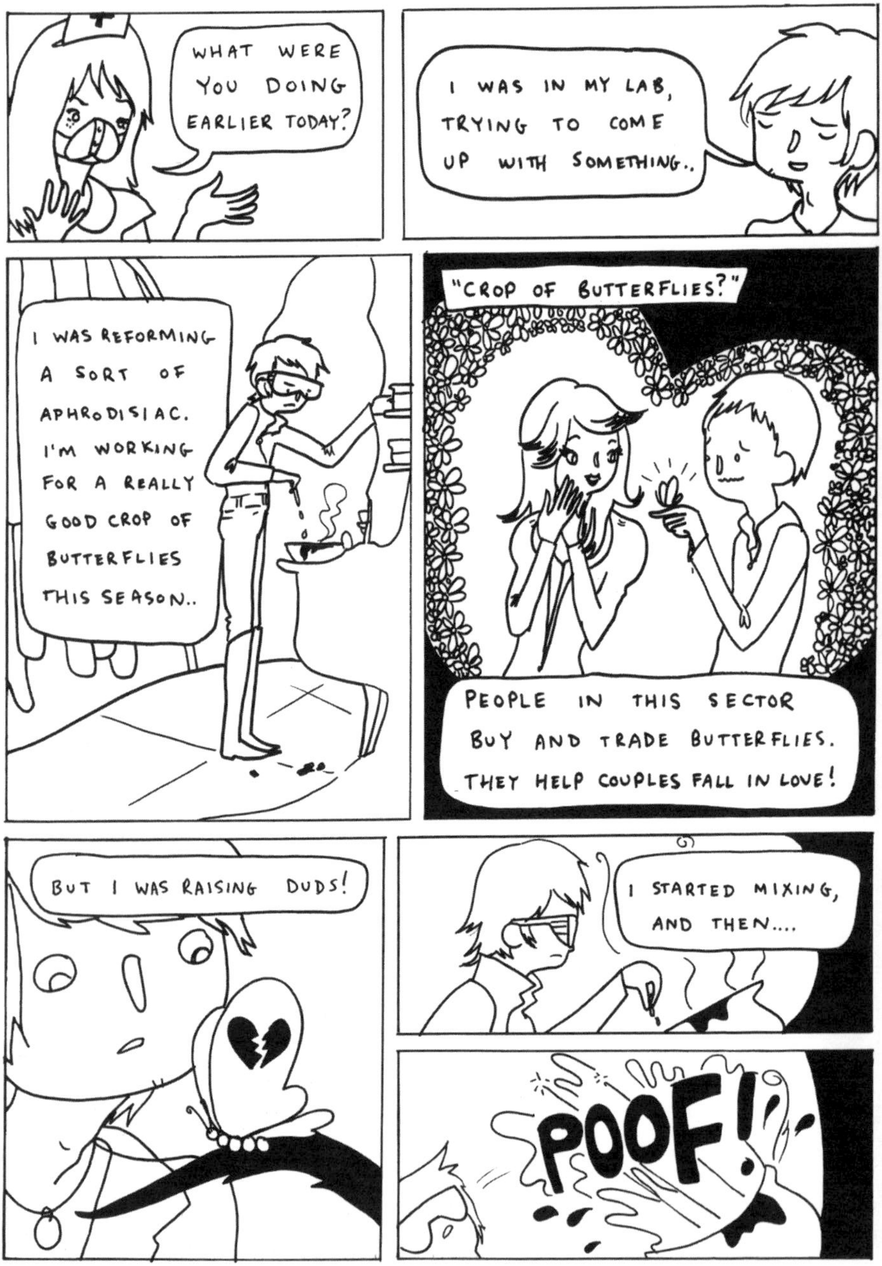
WHAT WERE YOU DOING EARLIER TODAY?
I WAS IN MY LAB, TRYING TO COME UP WITH SOMETHING..
I WAS REFORMING A SORT OF APHRODISIAC. I'M WORKING FOR A REALLY GOOD CROP OF BUTTERFLIES THIS SEASON..
"CROP OF BUTTERFLIES?"
PEOPLE IN THIS SECTOR BUY AND TRADE BUTTERFLIES. THEY HELP COUPLES FALL IN LOVE!
BUT I WAS RAISING DUDS!
I STARTED MIXING, AND THEN....
POOF!

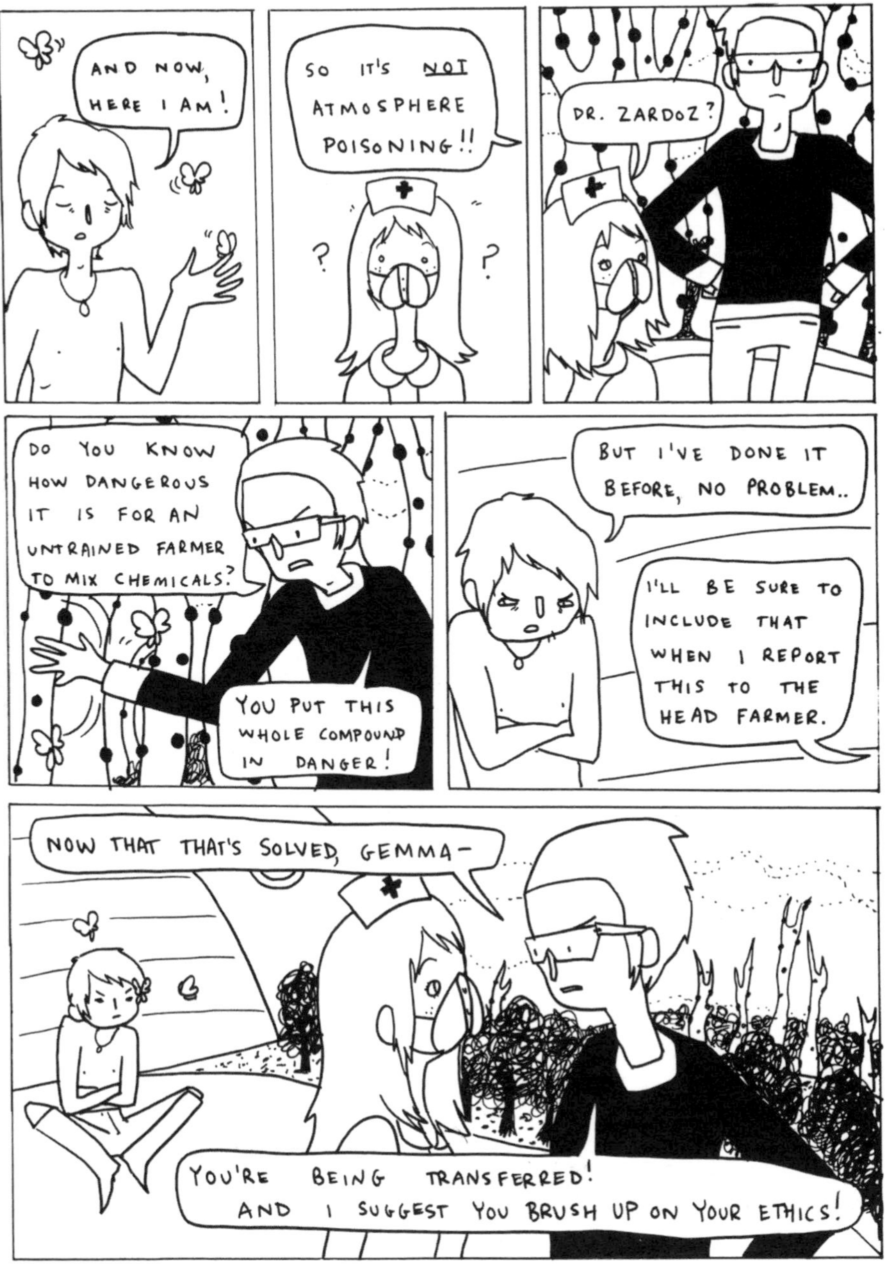
AND NOW, HERE I AM!
SO IT'S NOT ATMOSPHERE POISONING!!
DR. ZARDOZ?
DO YOU KNOW HOW DANGEROUS IT IS FOR AN UNTRAINED FARMER TO MIX CHEMICALS?
YOU PUT THIS WHOLE COMPOUND IN DANGER!
BUT I'VE DONE IT BEFORE, NO PROBLEM..
I'LL BE SURE TO INCLUDE THAT WHEN I REPORT THIS TO THE HEAD FARMER.
NOW THAT THAT'S SOLVED, GEMMA-
YOU'RE BEING TRANSFERRED! AND I SUGGEST YOU BRUSH UP ON YOUR ETHICS!

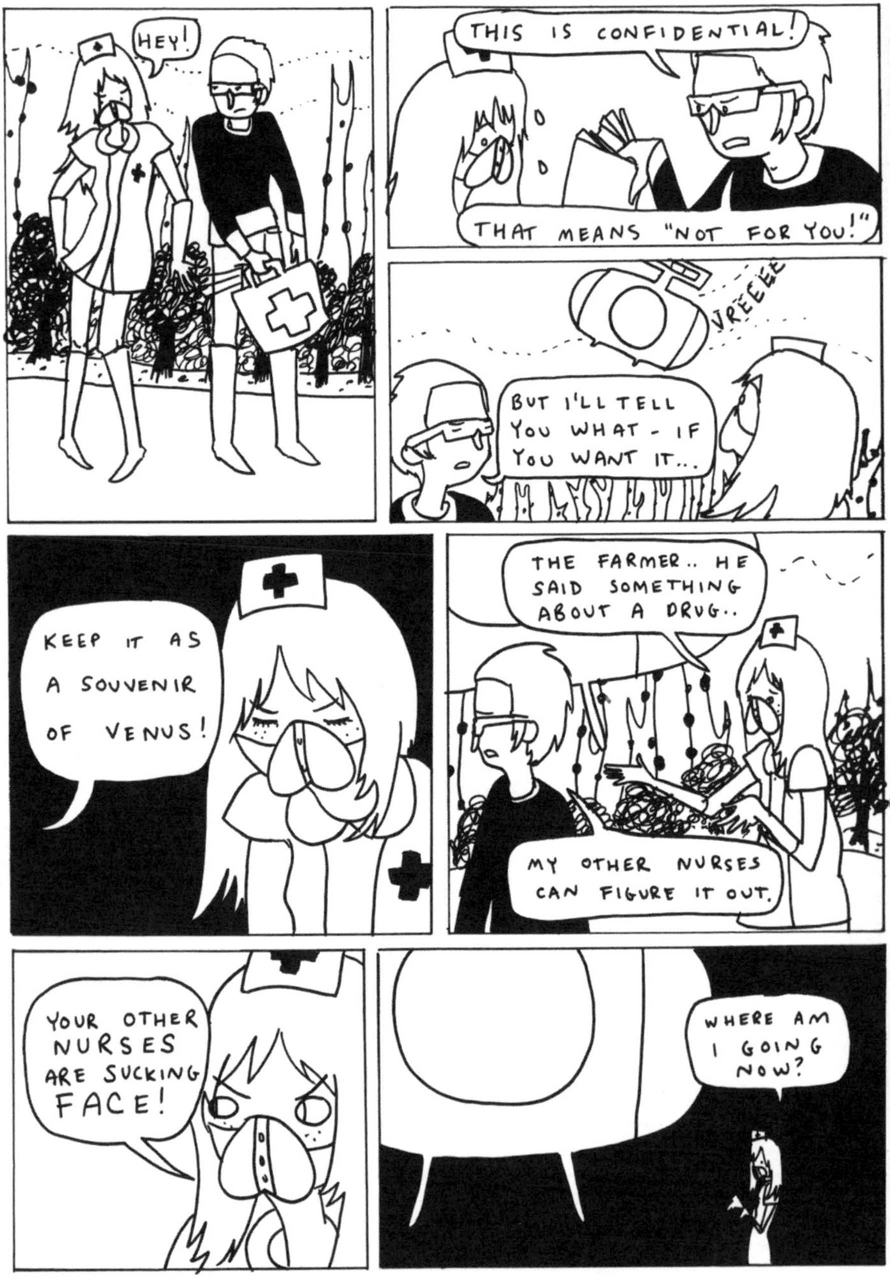
HEY!
THIS IS CONFIDENTIAL!
THAT MEANS "NOT FOR YOU!"
VREEEE
BUT I'LL TELL YOU WHAT - IF YOU WANT IT...
KEEP IT AS A SOUVENIR OF VENUS!
THE FARMER.. HE SAID SOMETHING ABOUT A DRUG..
MY OTHER NURSES CAN FIGURE IT OUT.
YOUR OTHER NURSES ARE SUCKING FACE!
WHERE AM I GOING NOW?

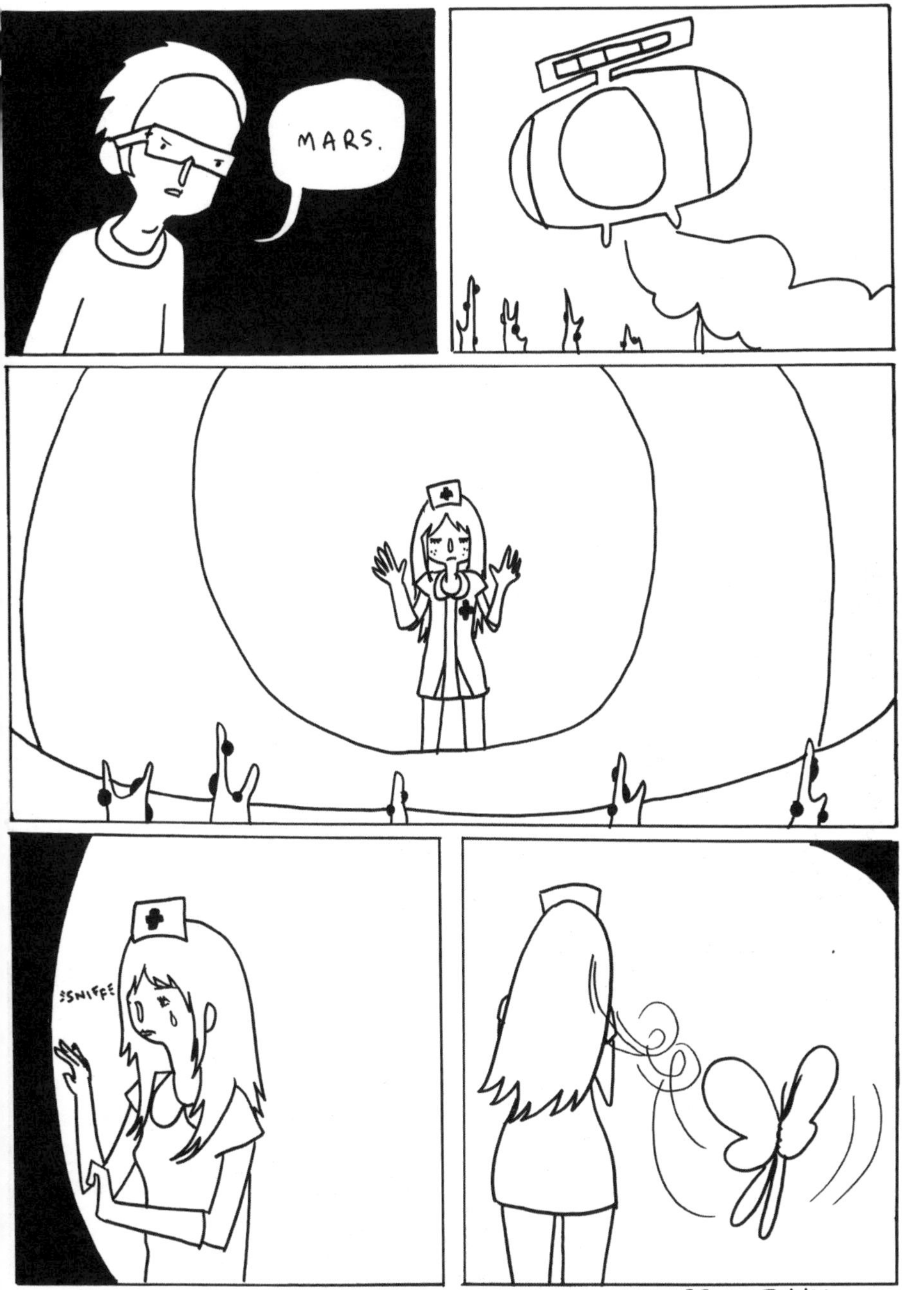
MARS.
SNIFF

TO BE CONTINUED...

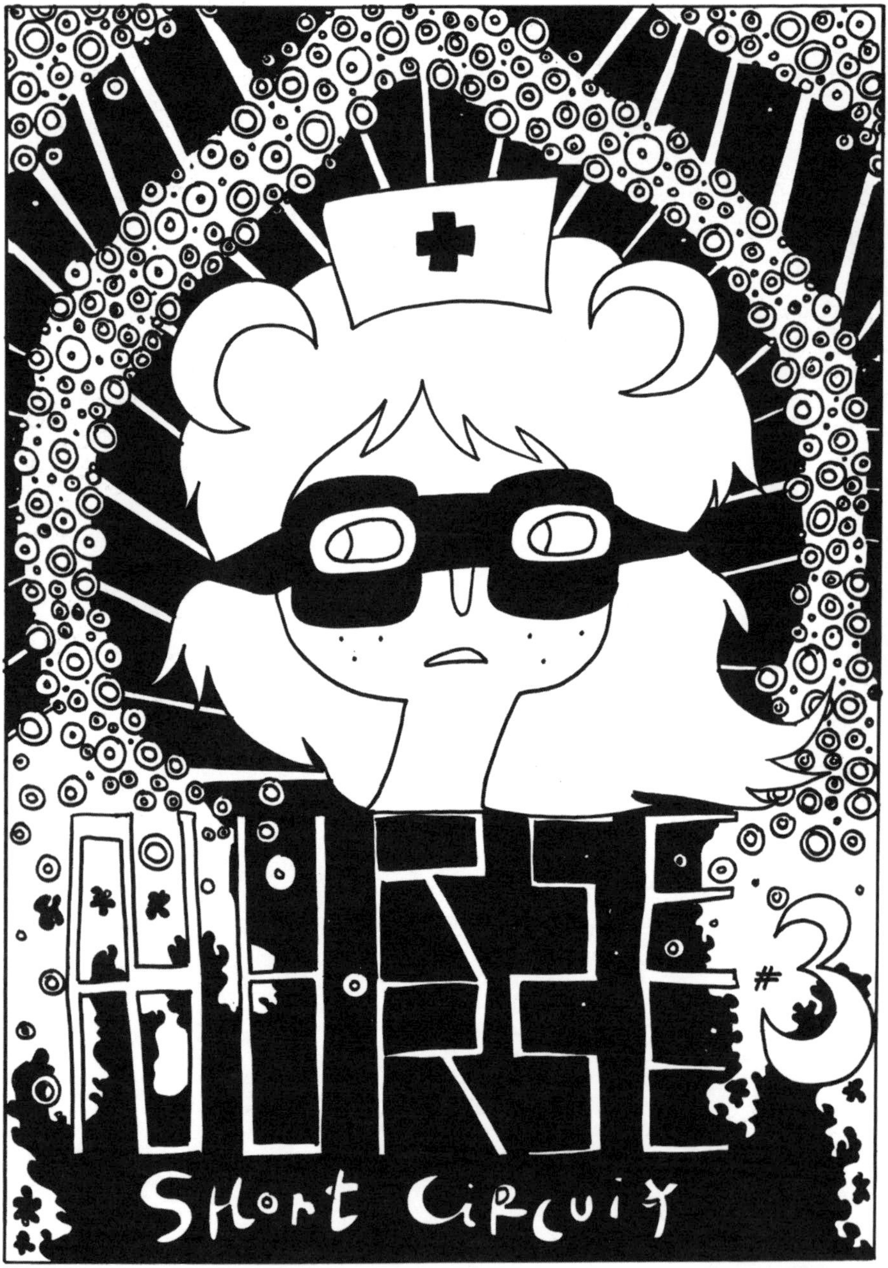
NURSE #3
Short Circuit

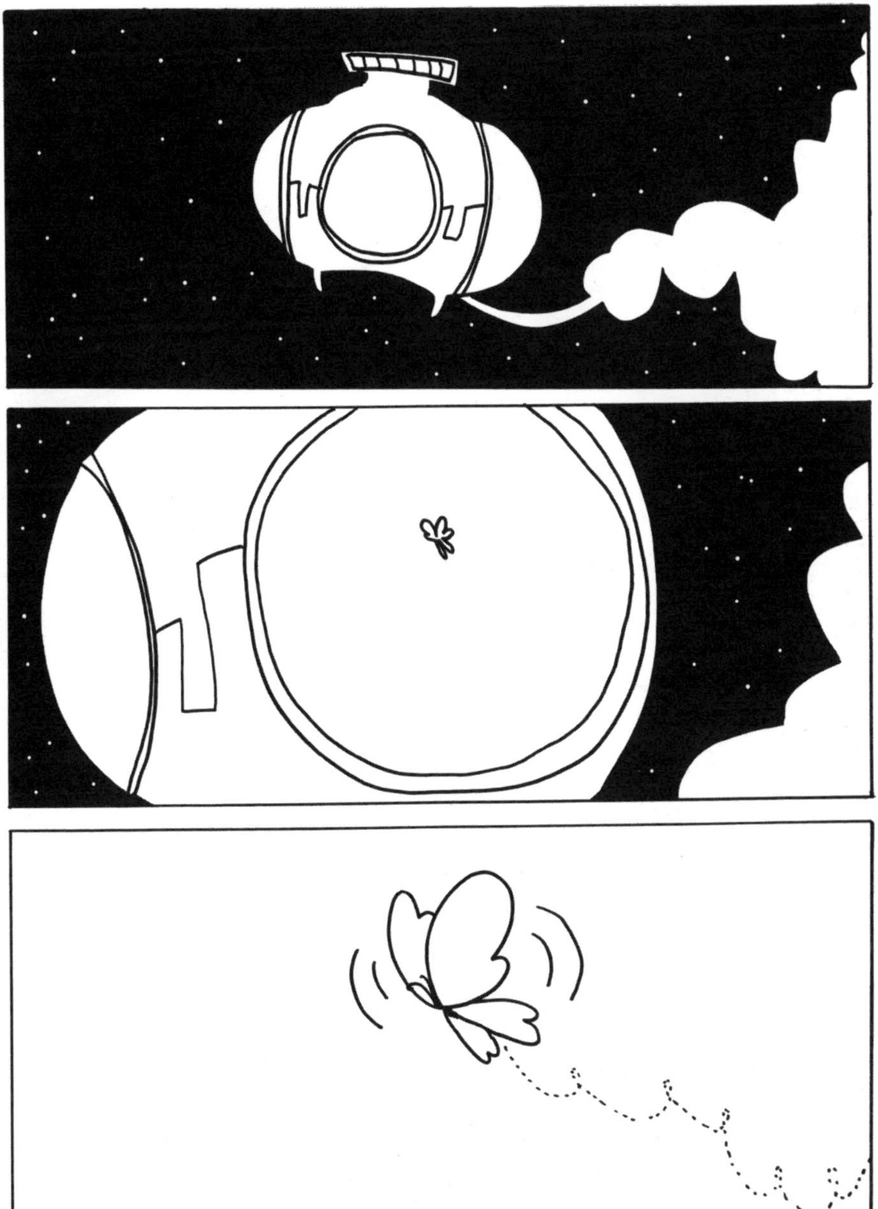

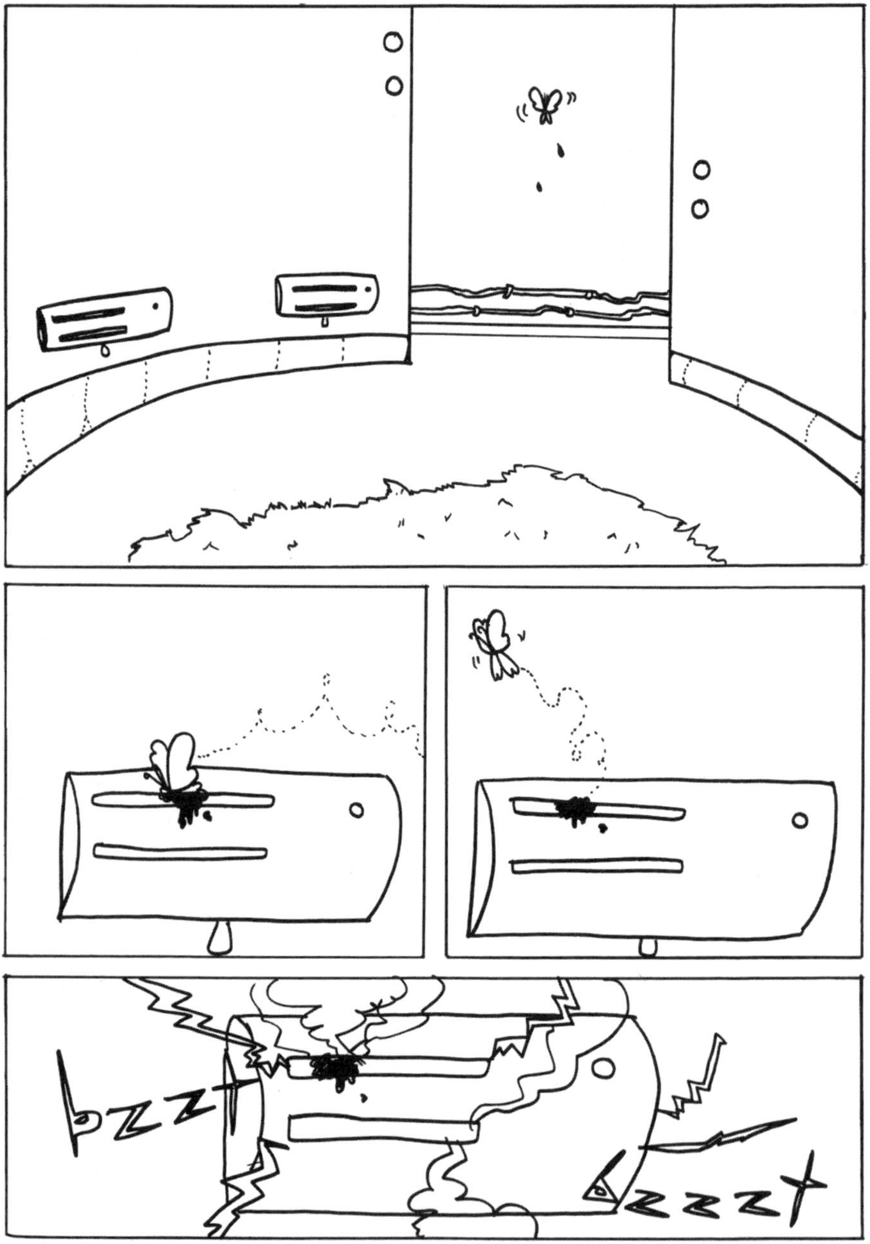
bzzzt
bzzzt

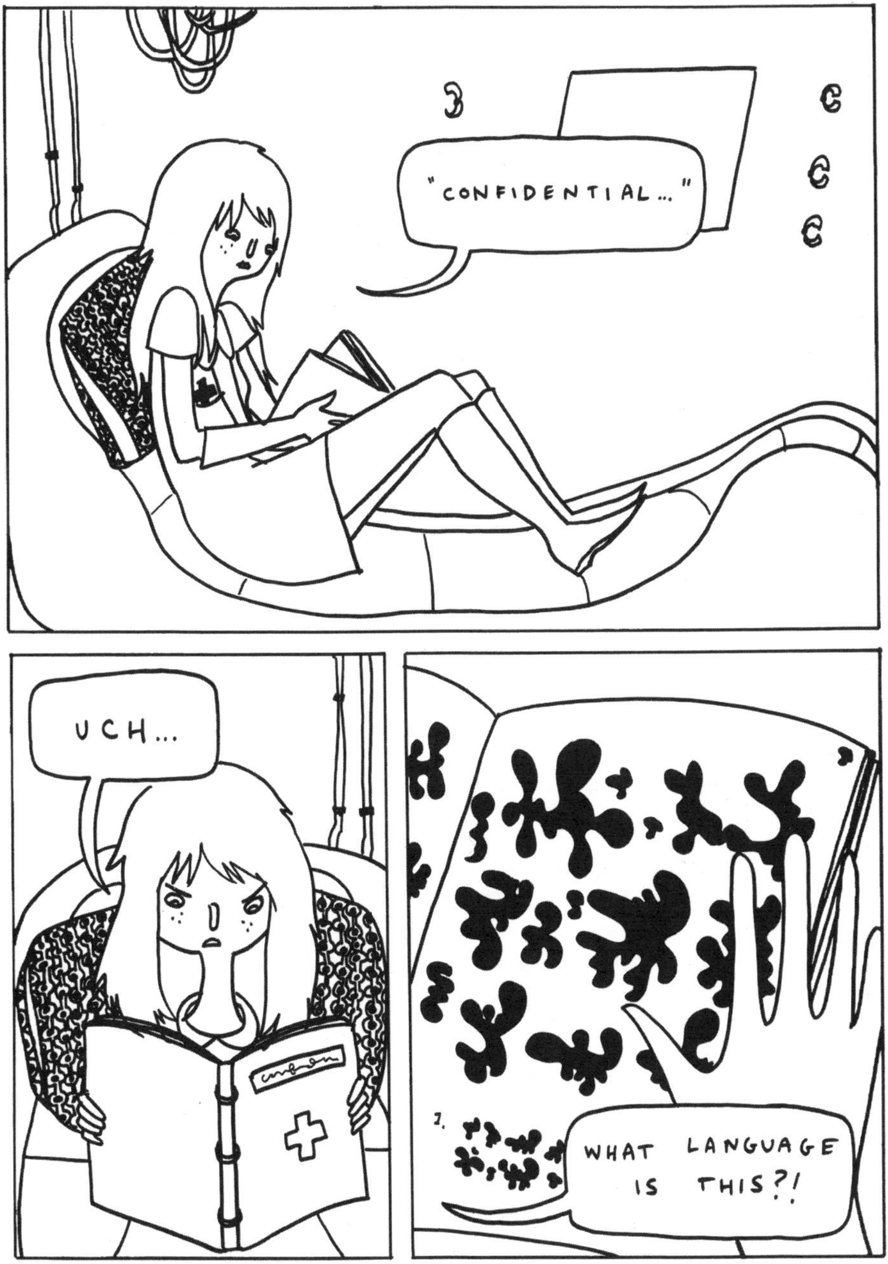
"CONFIDENTIAL..."
UCH...
WHAT LANGUAGE IS THIS?!

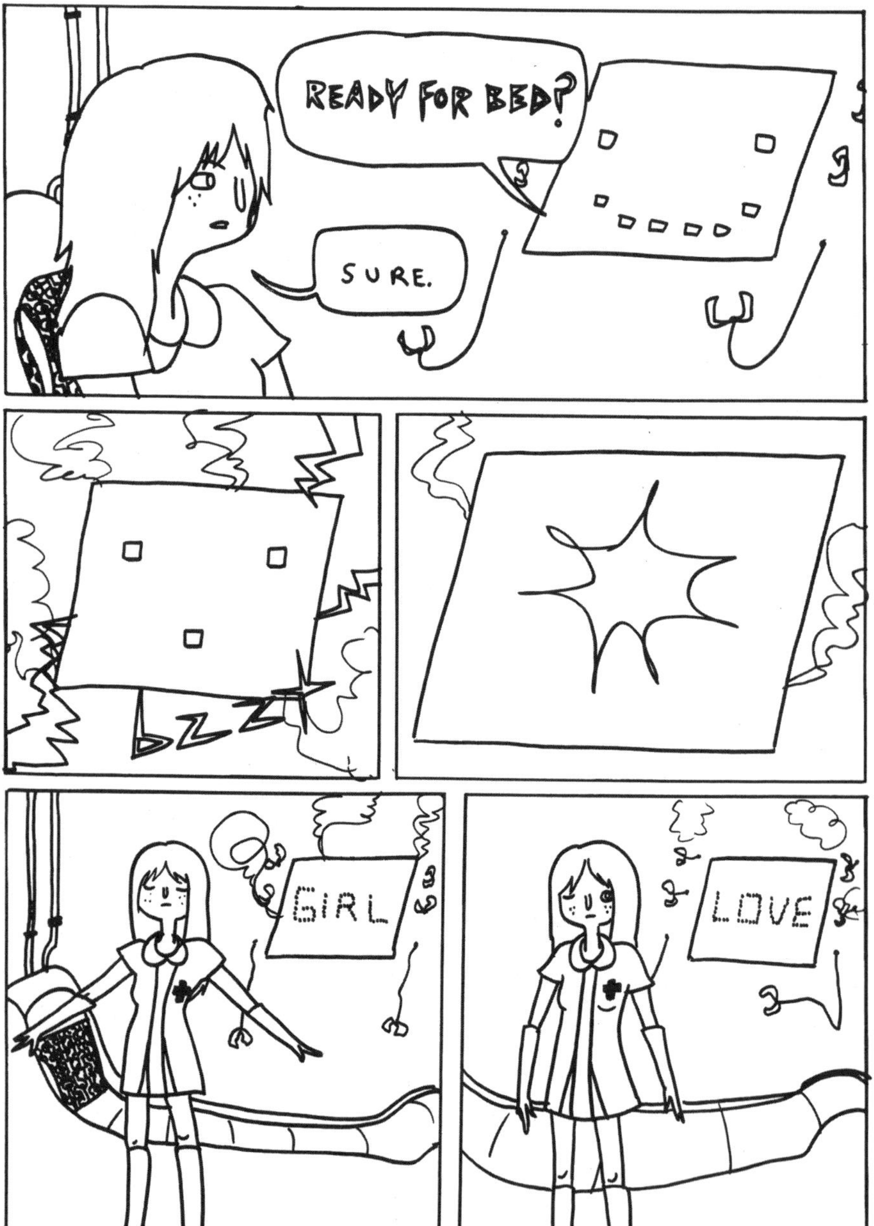
READY FOR BED?
SURE.
BZZZT
GIRL
LOVE

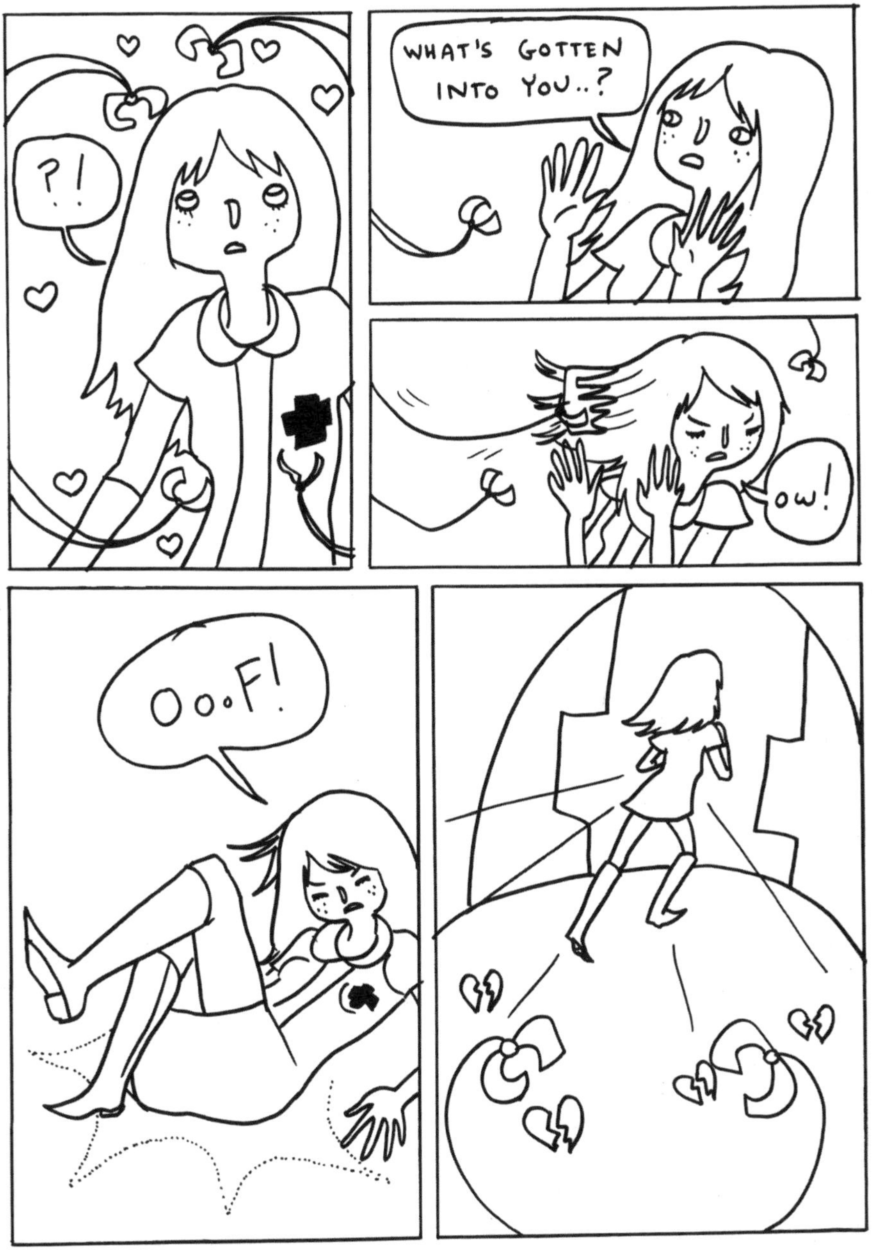
?!
WHAT'S GOTTEN INTO YOU..?
OW!
OooF!

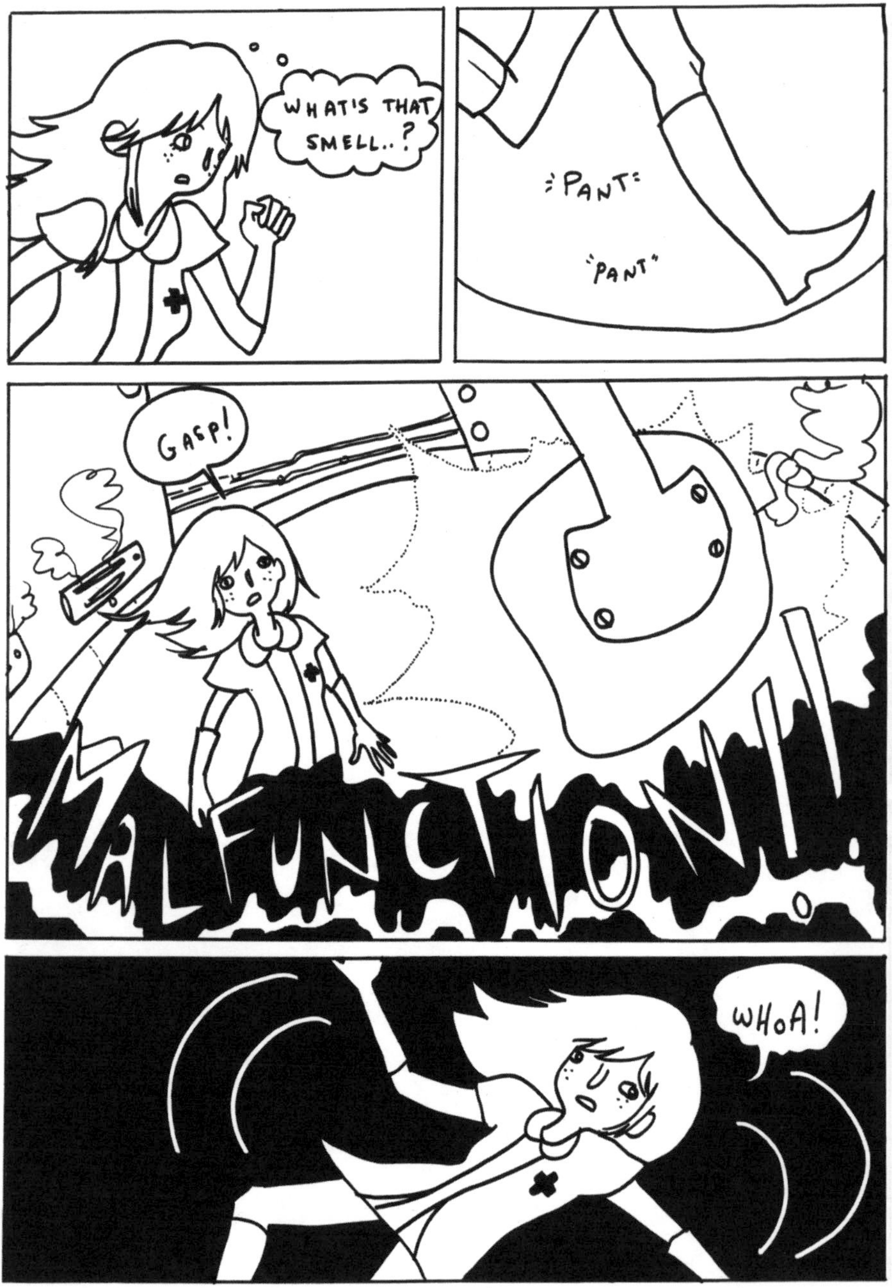
WHAT'S THAT SMELL..?
PANT
PANT
GASP!
MALFUNCTION!!
WHOA!

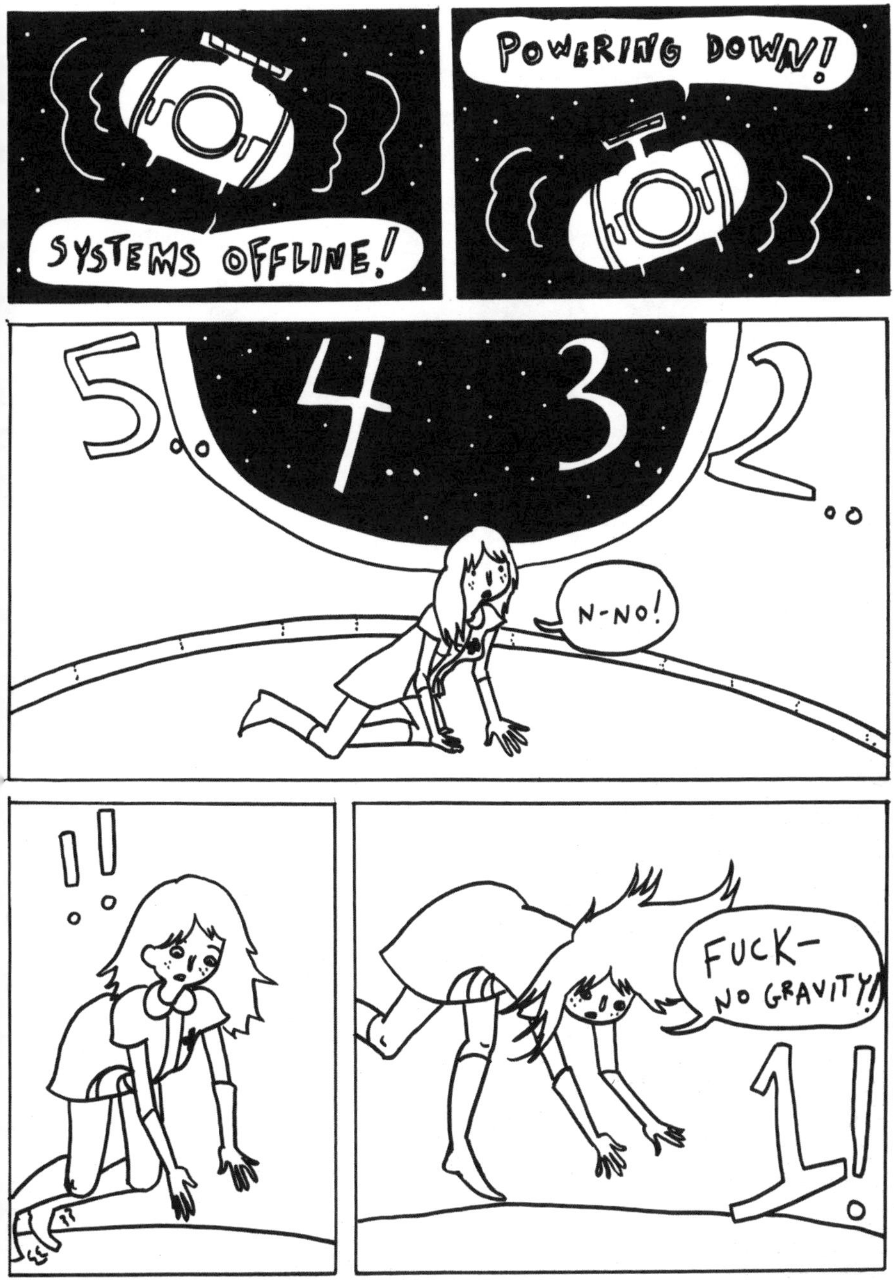
SYSTEMS OFFLINE!
POWERING DOWN!
5..
4..
3
2..
N-NO!
!!
FUCK-
NO GRAVITY!
1!

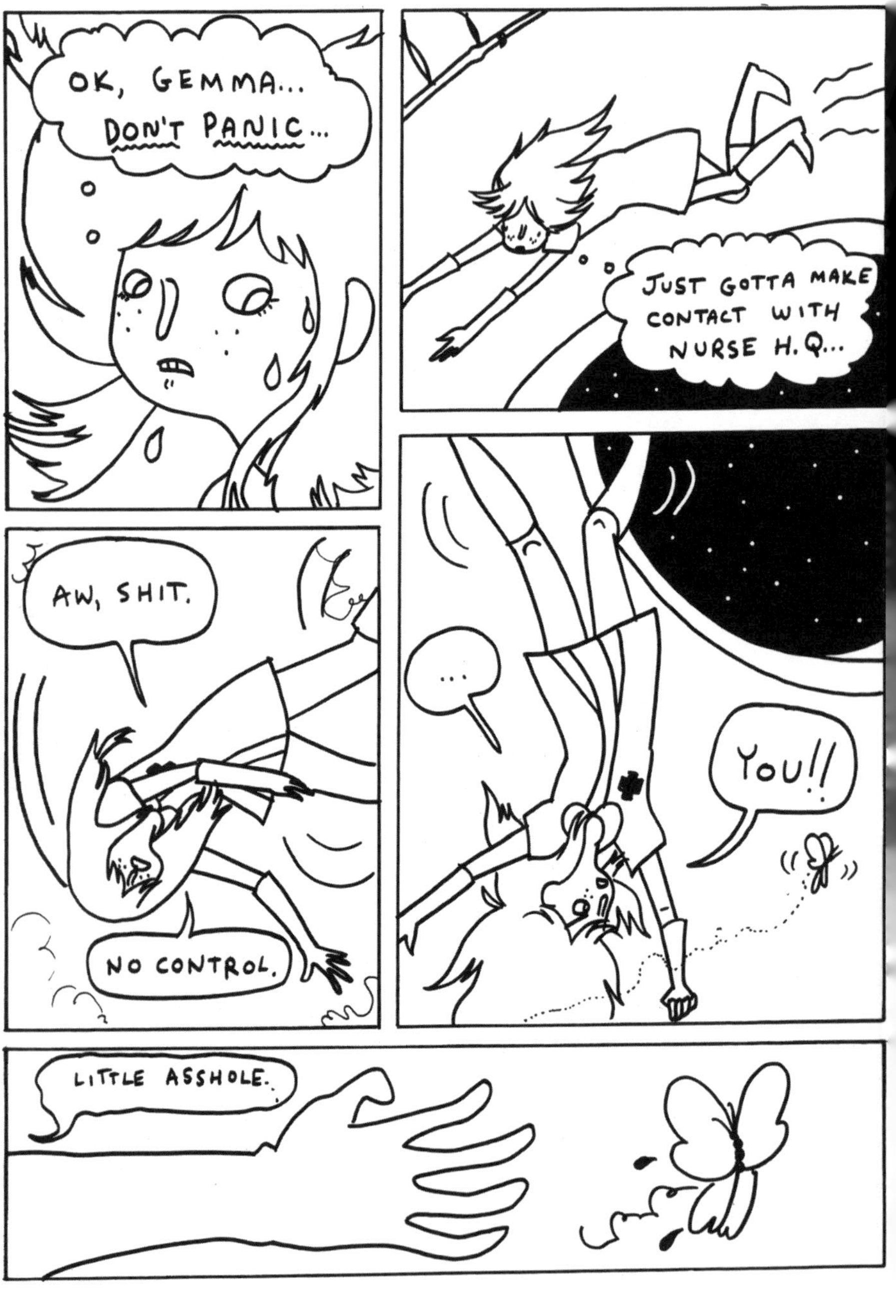
OK, GEMMA... DON'T PANIC...
JUST GOTTA MAKE CONTACT WITH NURSE H.Q...
AW, SHIT.
NO CONTROL.
...
YOU!!
LITTLE ASSHOLE.

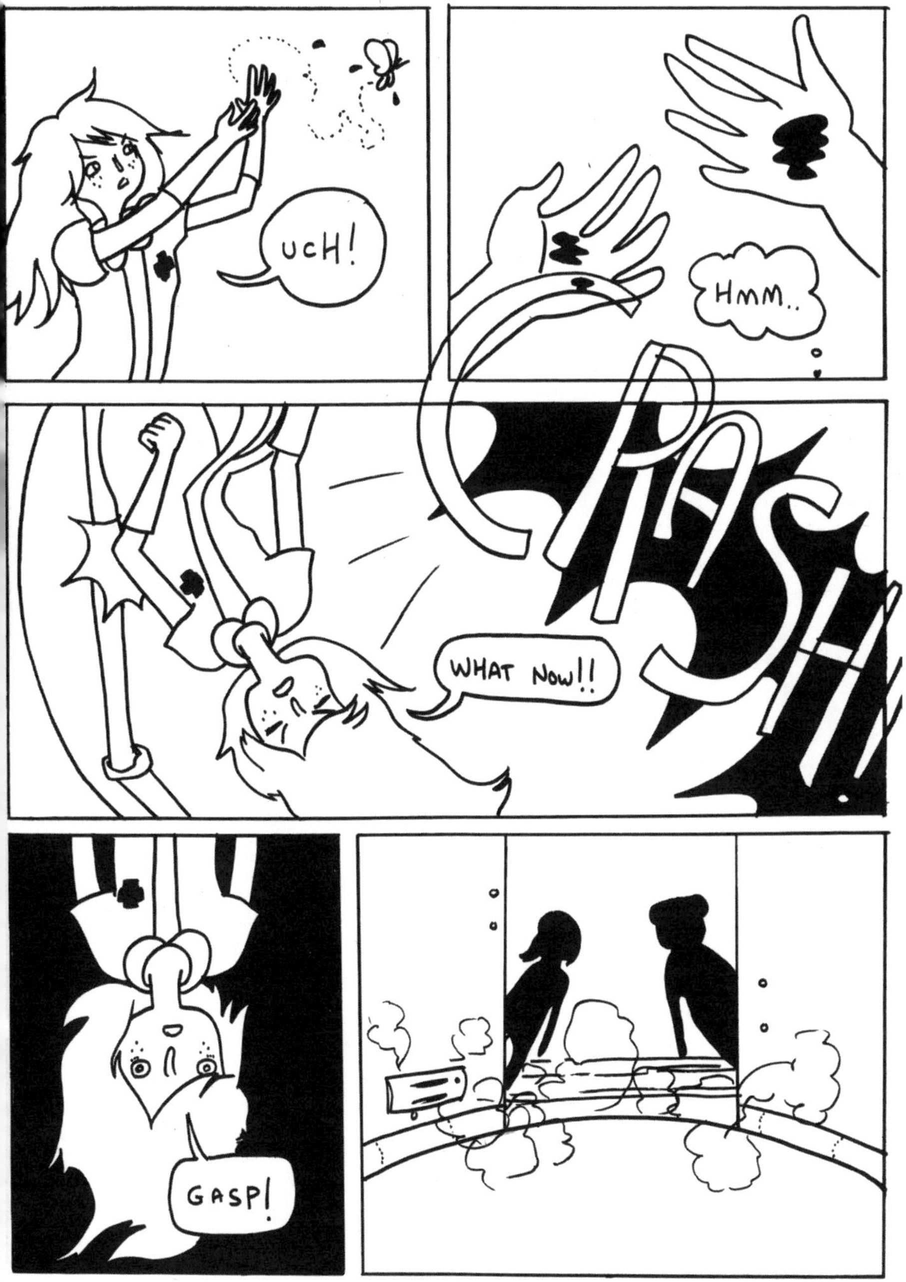

UCH!
HMM..
CRASH!
WHAT NOW!!
GASP!

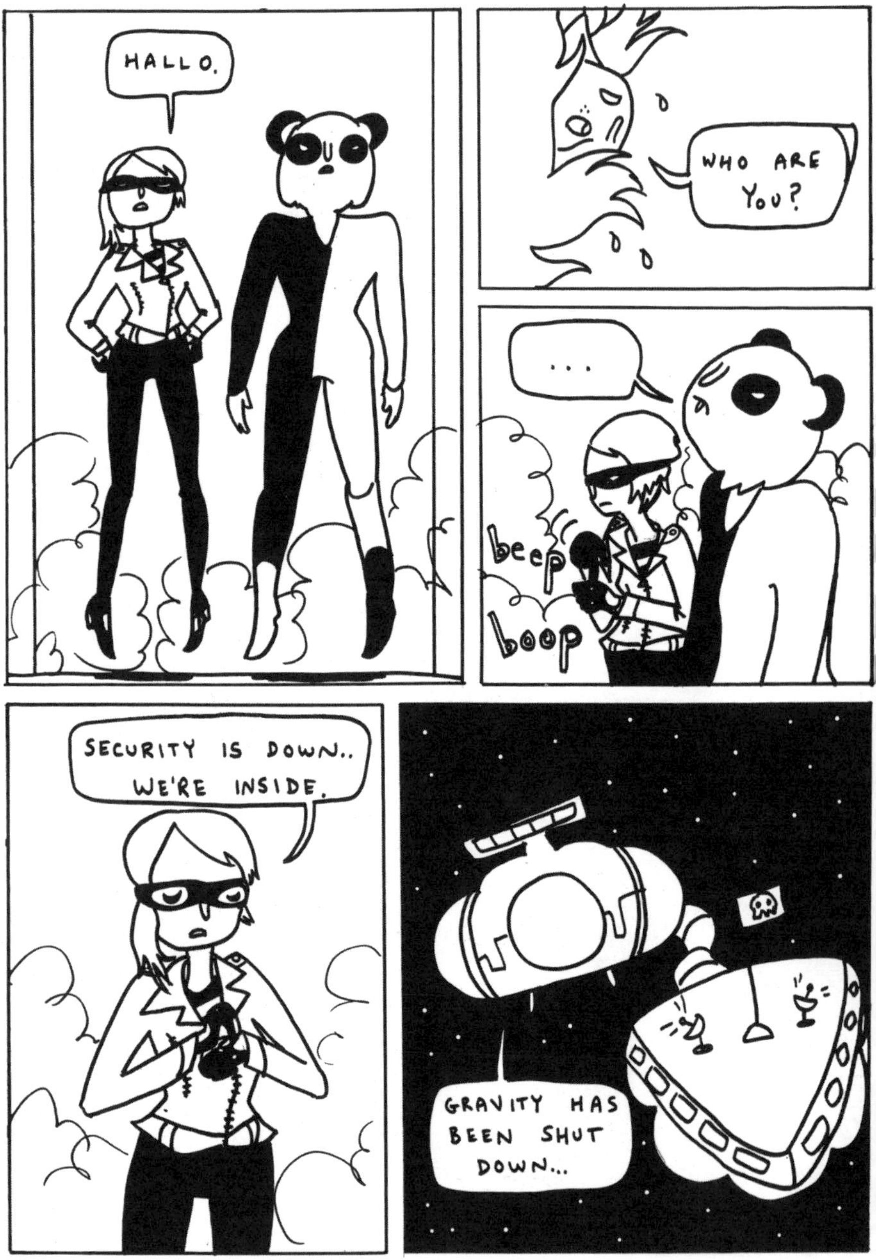
HALLO.
WHO ARE YOU?
...
beep
boop
SECURITY IS DOWN..
WE'RE INSIDE.
GRAVITY HAS BEEN SHUT DOWN...

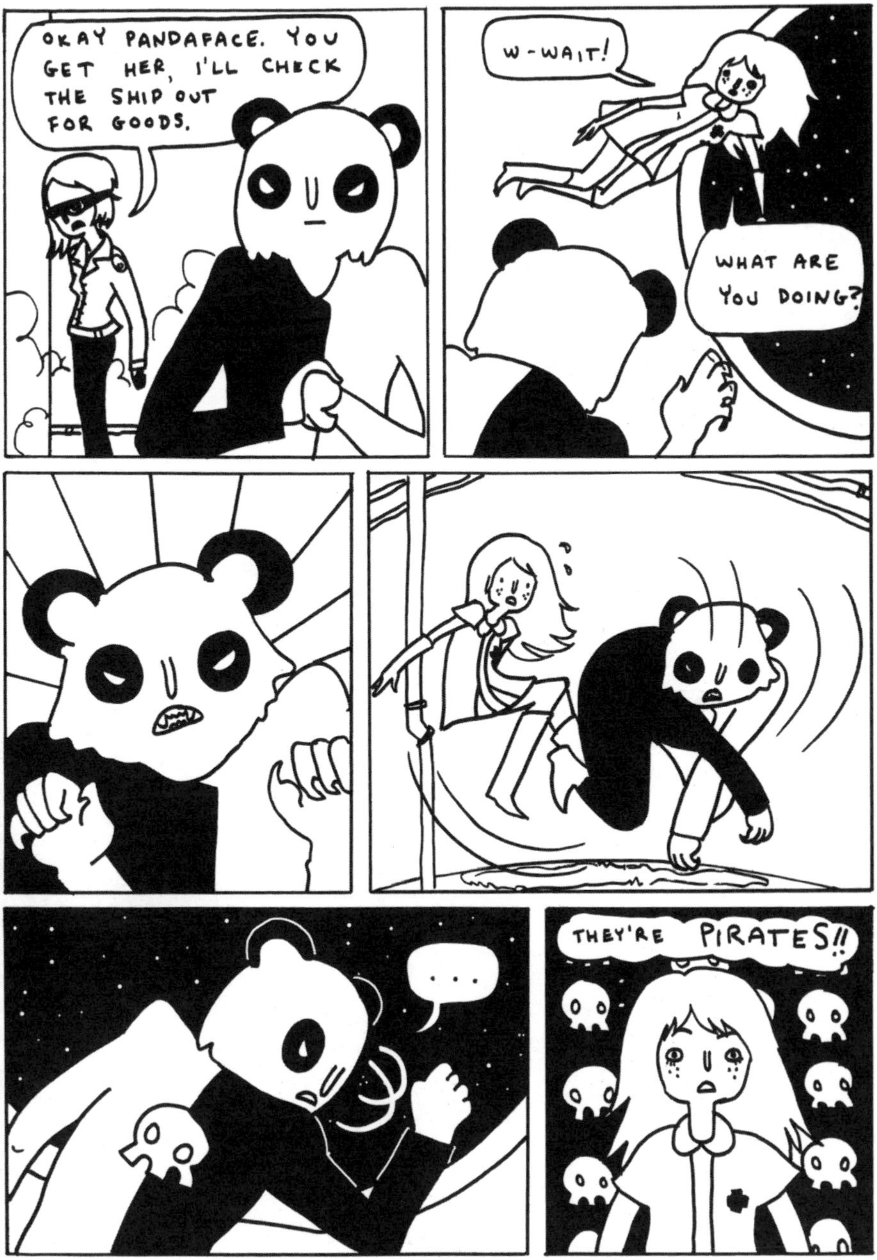
OKAY PANDAFACE. YOU GET HER, I'LL CHECK THE SHIP OUT FOR GOODS.
W-WAIT!
WHAT ARE YOU DOING?
...
THEY'RE PIRATES!!

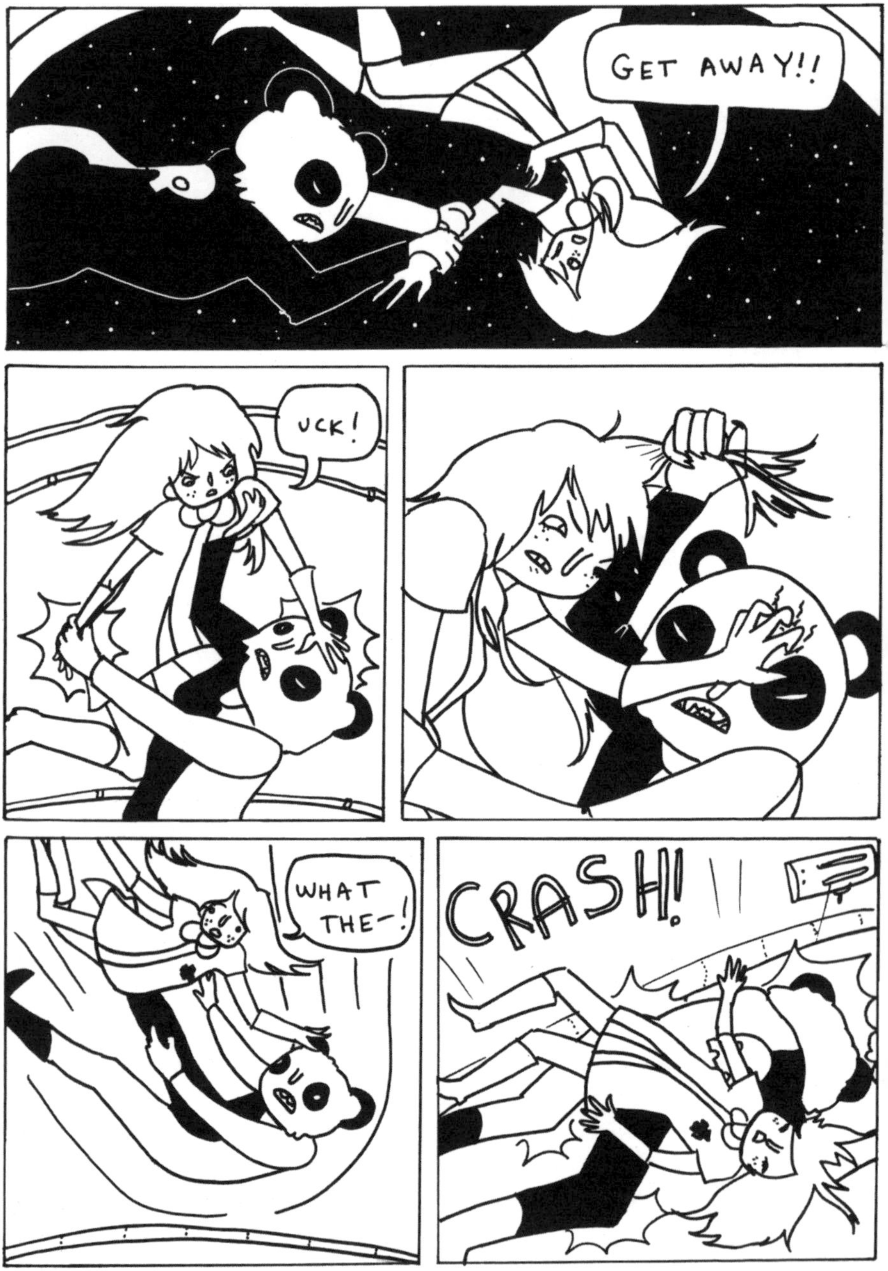
GET AWAY!!
UCK!
WHAT THE-!
CRASH!

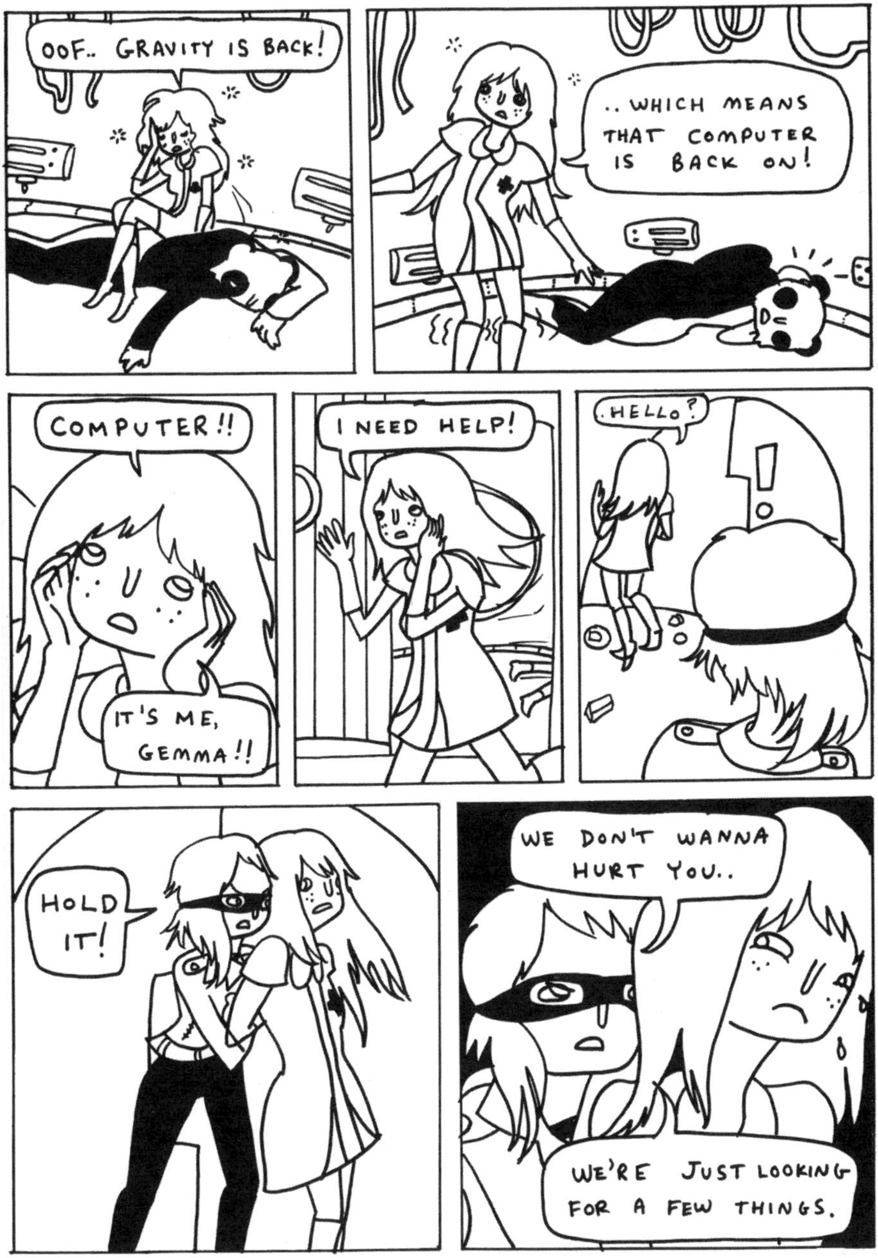
OOF.. GRAVITY IS BACK!
..WHICH MEANS THAT COMPUTER IS BACK ON!
COMPUTER!!
IT'S ME, GEMMA!!
I NEED HELP!
.HELLO?
!
HOLD IT!
WE DON'T WANNA HURT YOU..
WE'RE JUST LOOKING FOR A FEW THINGS.

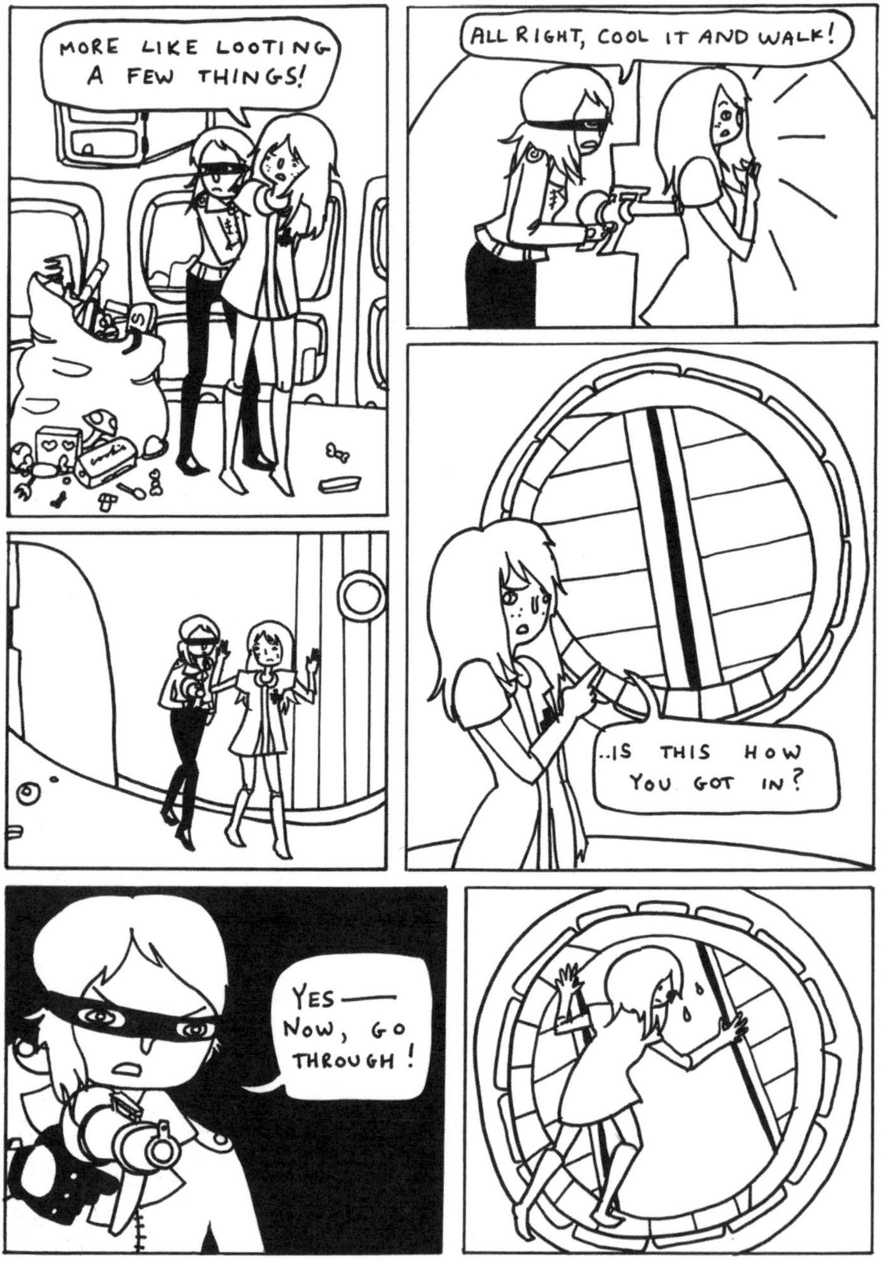
MORE LIKE LOOTING A FEW THINGS!
ALL RIGHT, COOL IT AND WALK!
..IS THIS HOW YOU GOT IN?
YES— NOW, GO THROUGH!

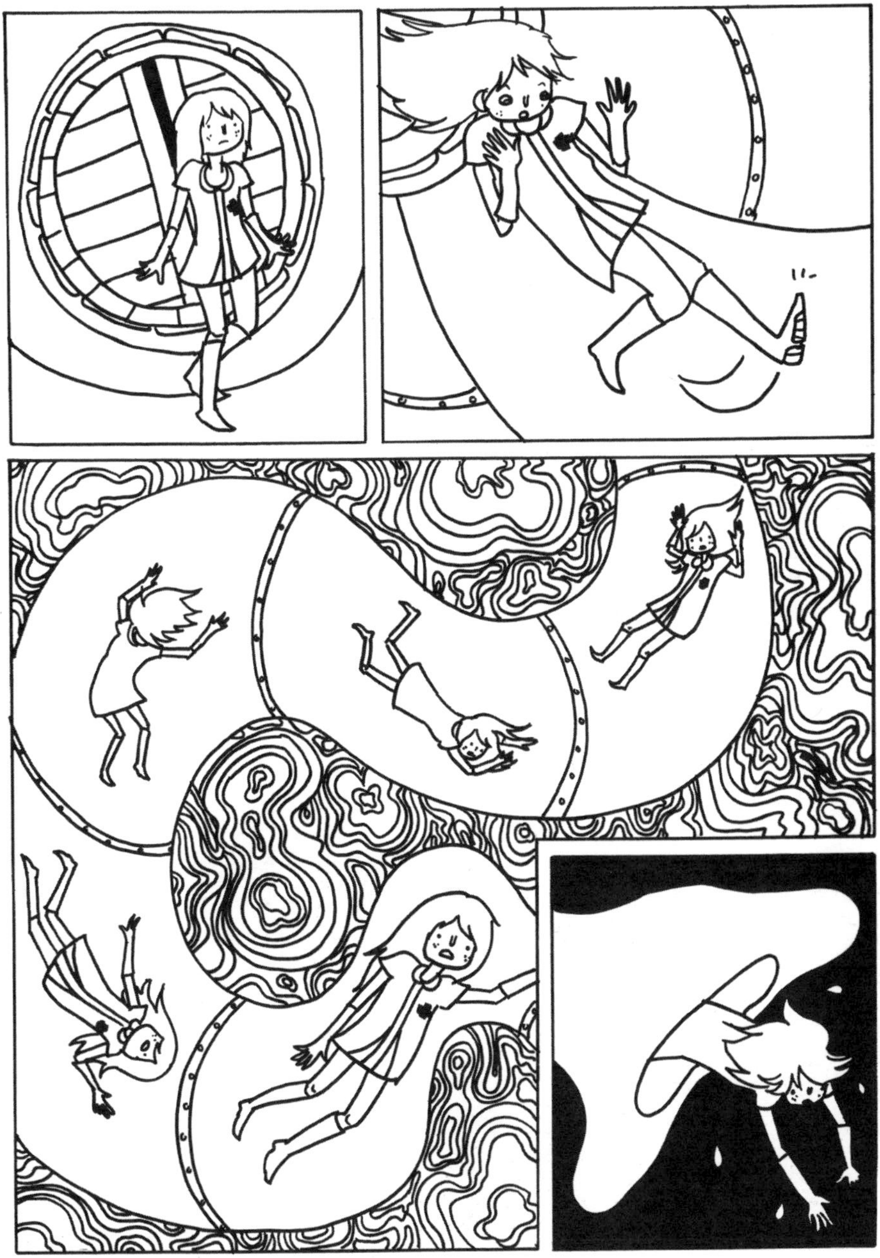

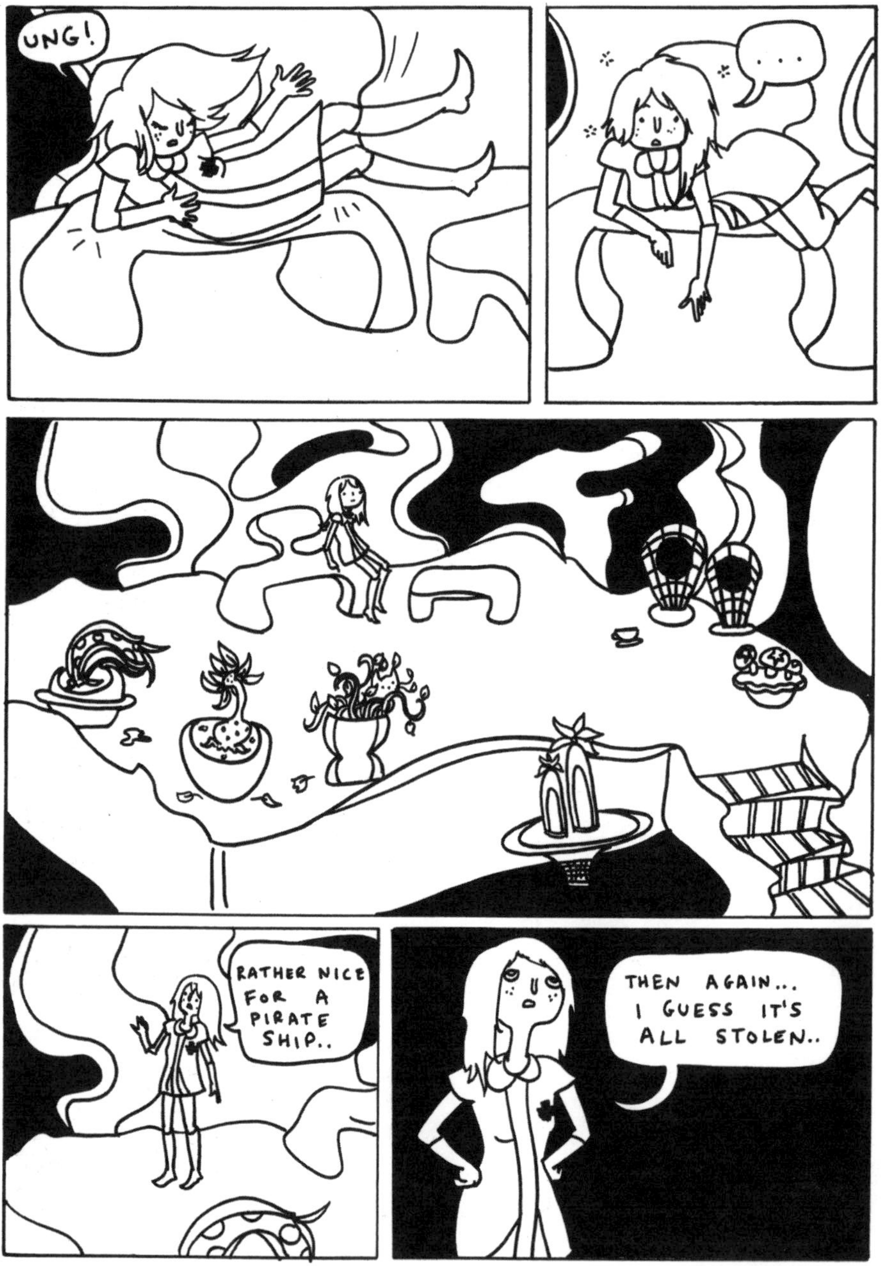
UNG!
...
RATHER NICE FOR A PIRATE SHIP..
THEN AGAIN... I GUESS IT'S ALL STOLEN..

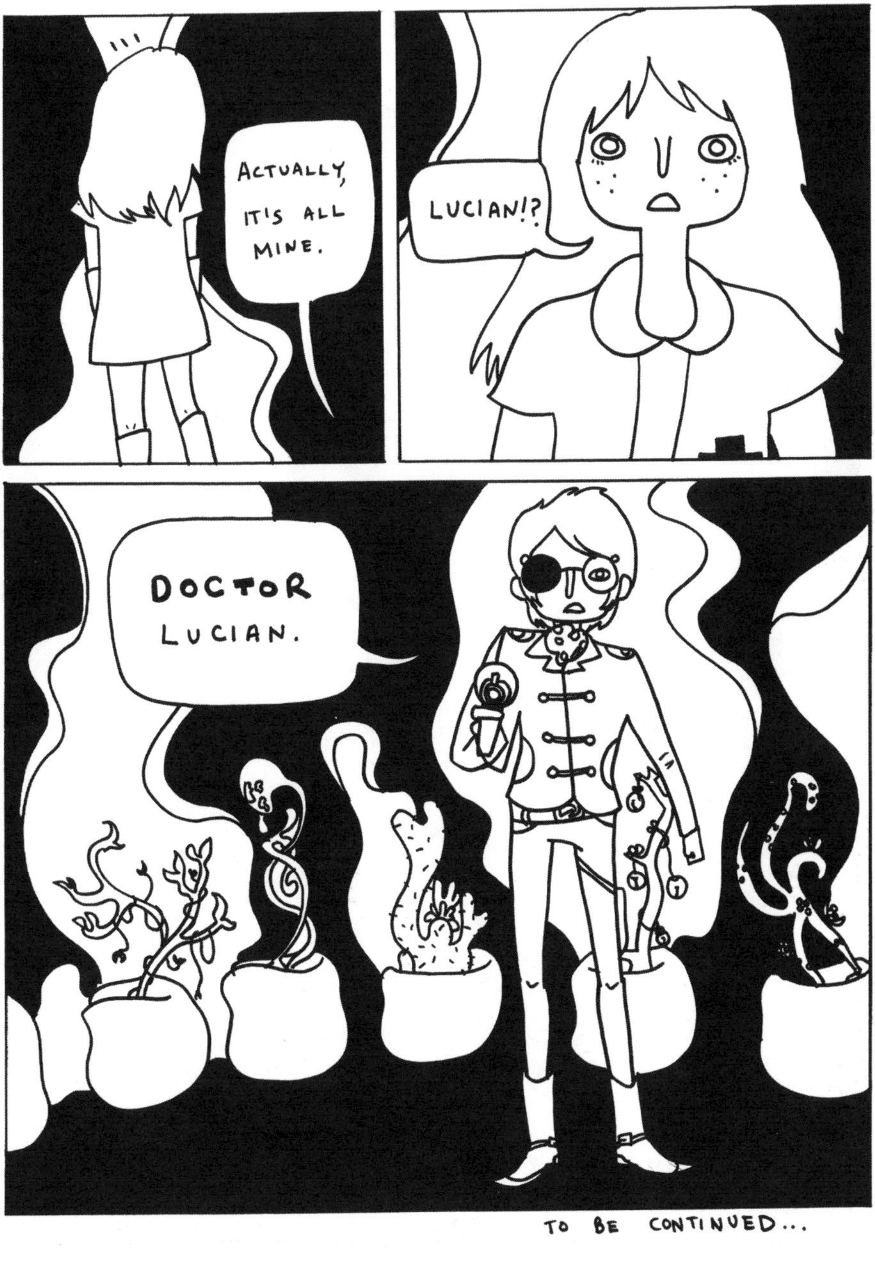
ACTUALLY, IT'S ALL MINE.
LUCIAN!?
DOCTOR LUCIAN.

TO BE CONTINUED...

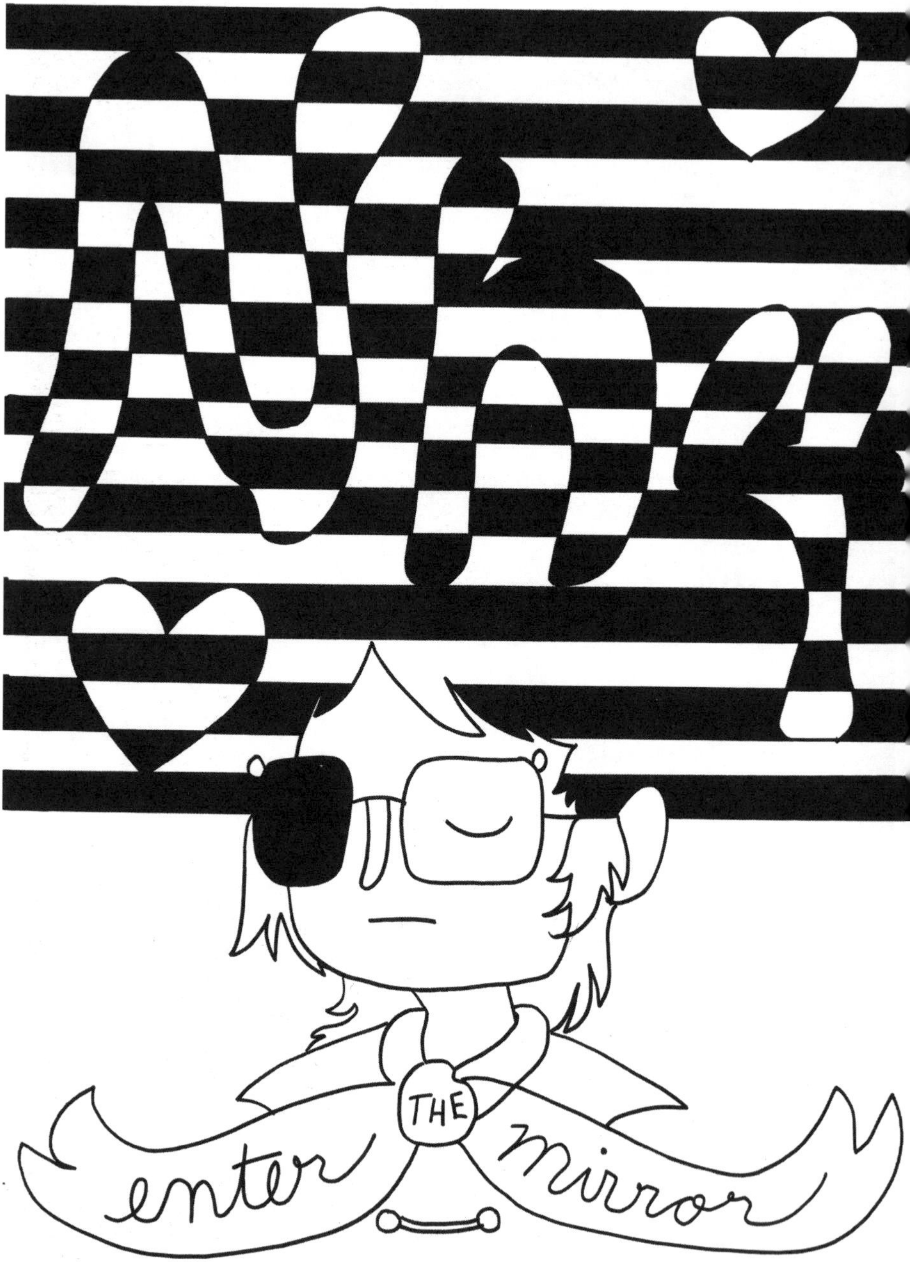
enter THE mirror

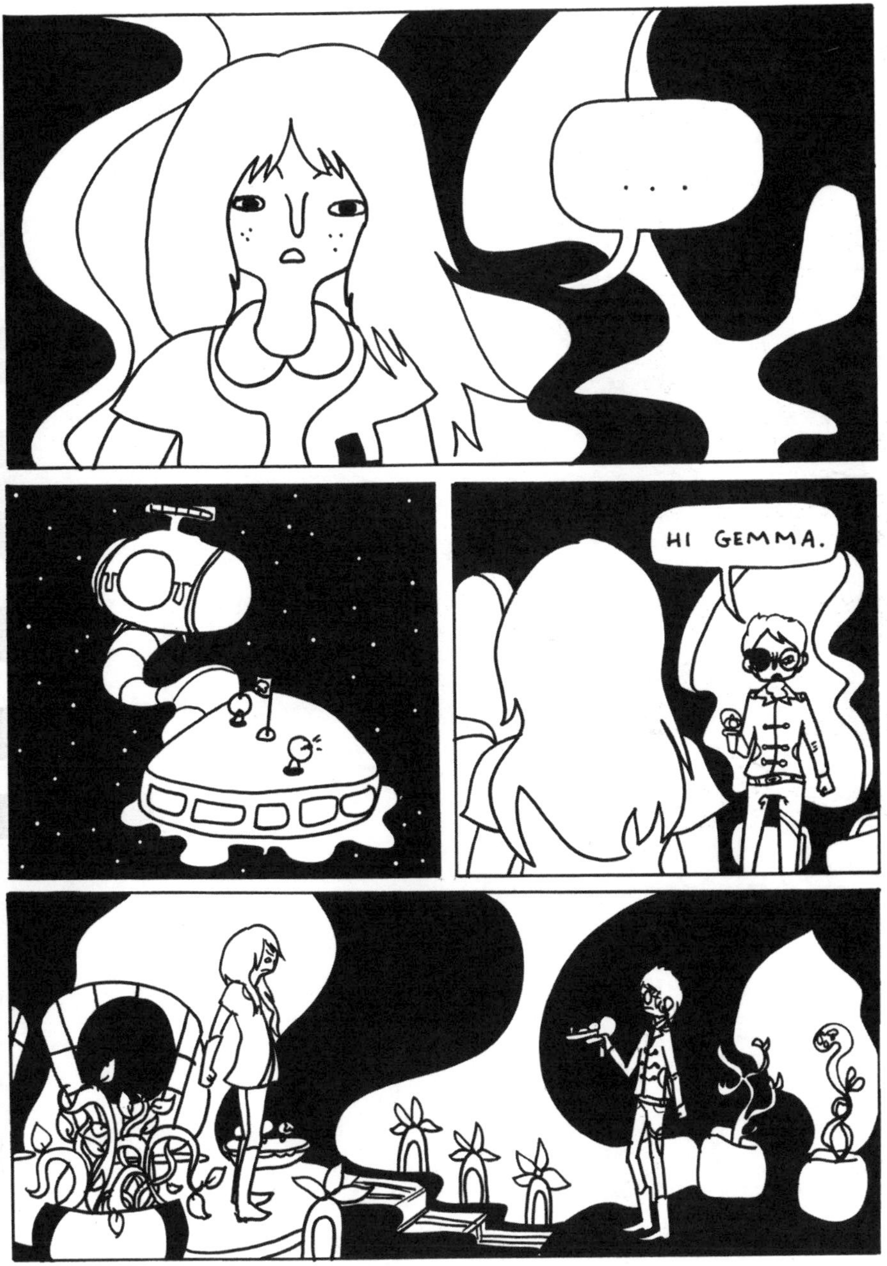
...
HI GEMMA.

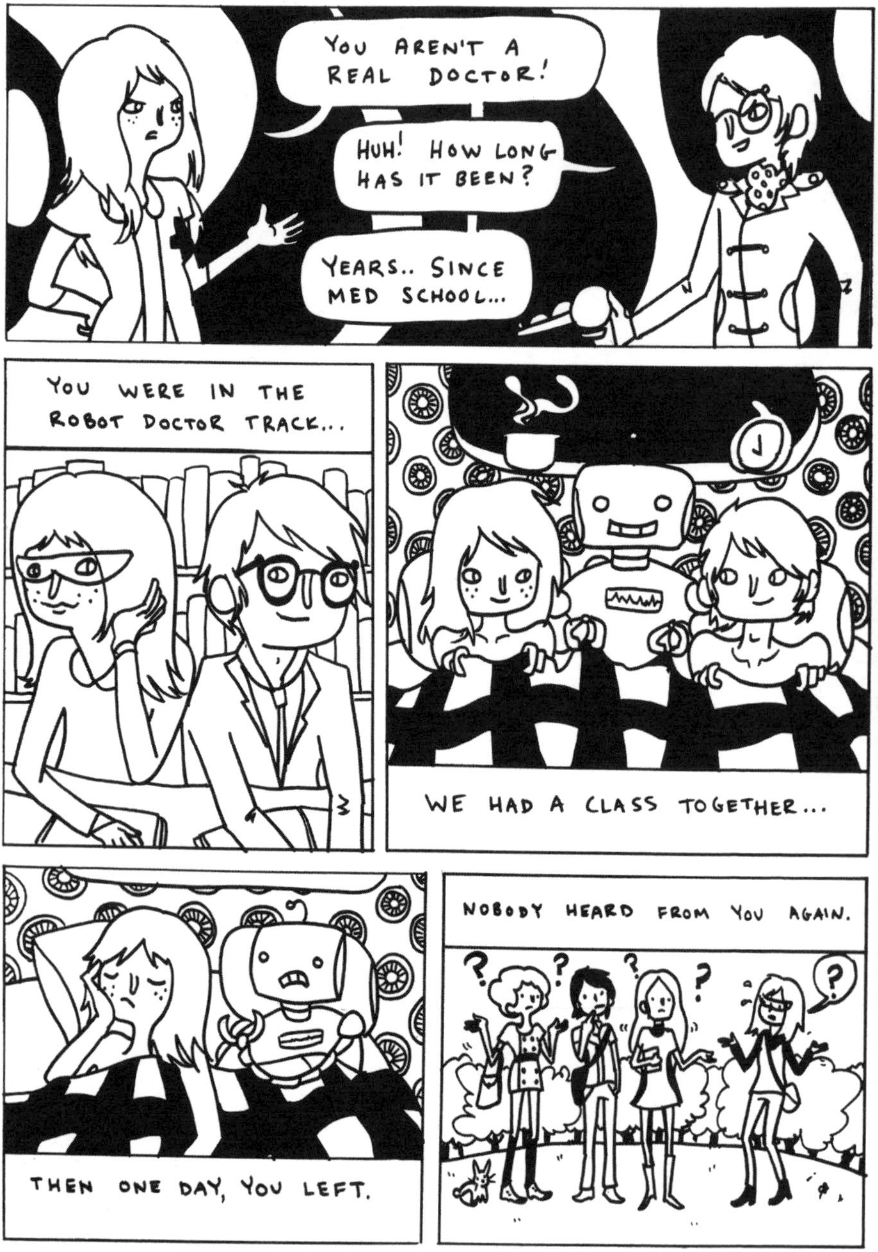
YOU AREN'T A REAL DOCTOR!
HUH! HOW LONG HAS IT BEEN?
YEARS.. SINCE MED SCHOOL...
YOU WERE IN THE ROBOT DOCTOR TRACK...
WE HAD A CLASS TOGETHER...
THEN ONE DAY, YOU LEFT.
NOBODY HEARD FROM YOU AGAIN.
?
?
?
?
?

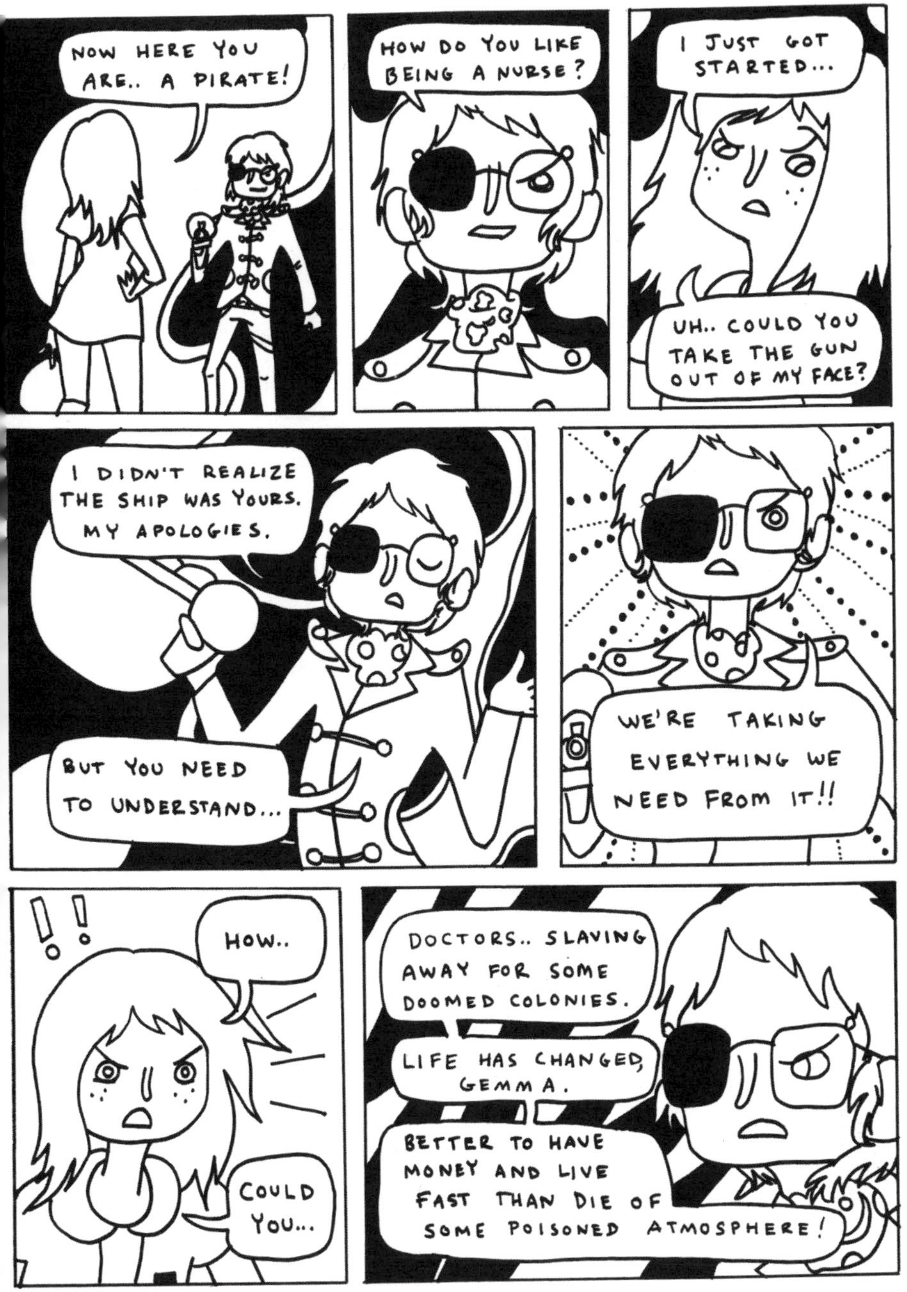
NOW HERE YOU ARE.. A PIRATE!
HOW DO YOU LIKE BEING A NURSE?
I JUST GOT STARTED...
UH.. COULD YOU TAKE THE GUN OUT OF MY FACE?
I DIDN'T REALIZE THE SHIP WAS YOURS. MY APOLOGIES.
BUT YOU NEED TO UNDERSTAND...
WE'RE TAKING EVERYTHING WE NEED FROM IT!!
!!
HOW..
COULD YOU...
DOCTORS.. SLAVING AWAY FOR SOME DOOMED COLONIES.
LIFE HAS CHANGED, GEMMA.
BETTER TO HAVE MONEY AND LIVE FAST THAN DIE OF SOME POISONED ATMOSPHERE!

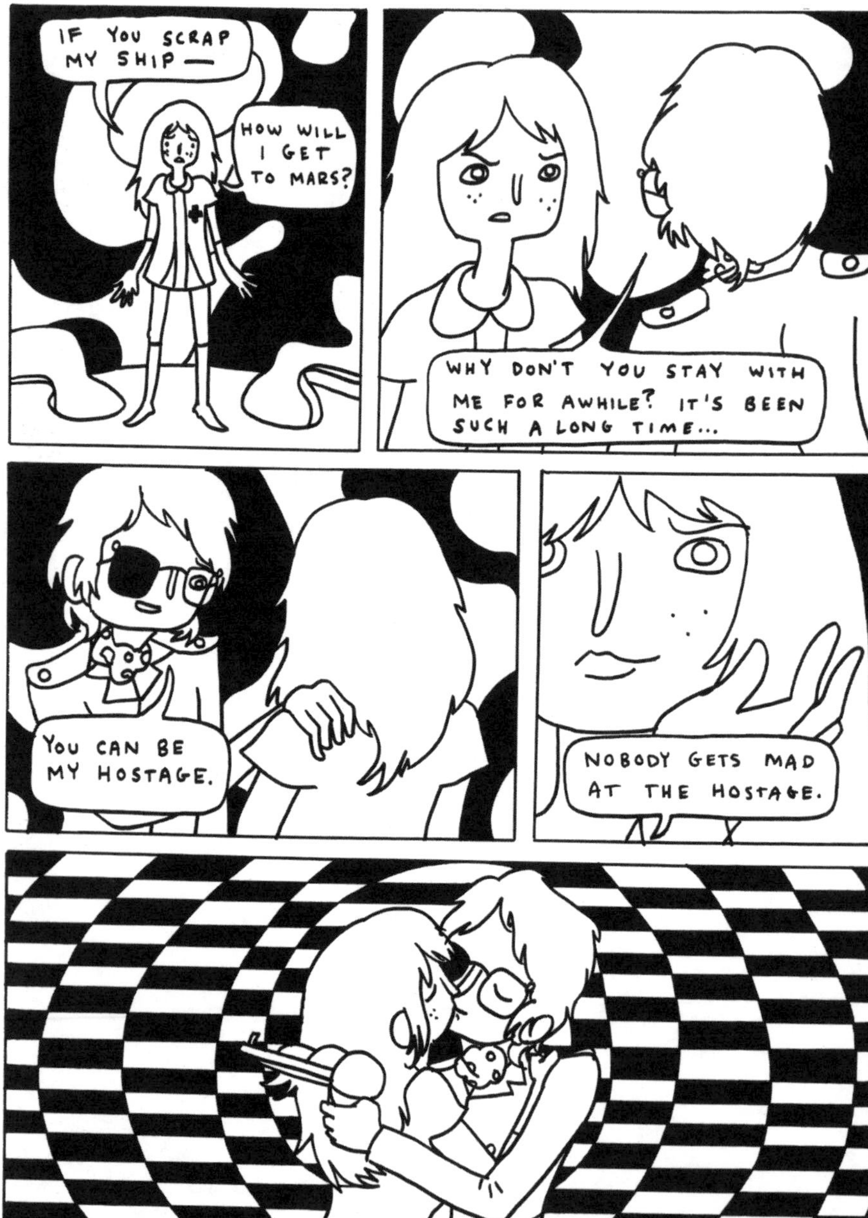
IF YOU SCRAP MY SHIP—
HOW WILL I GET TO MARS?
WHY DON'T YOU STAY WITH ME FOR AWHILE? IT'S BEEN SUCH A LONG TIME...
YOU CAN BE MY HOSTAGE.
NOBODY GETS MAD AT THE HOSTAGE.

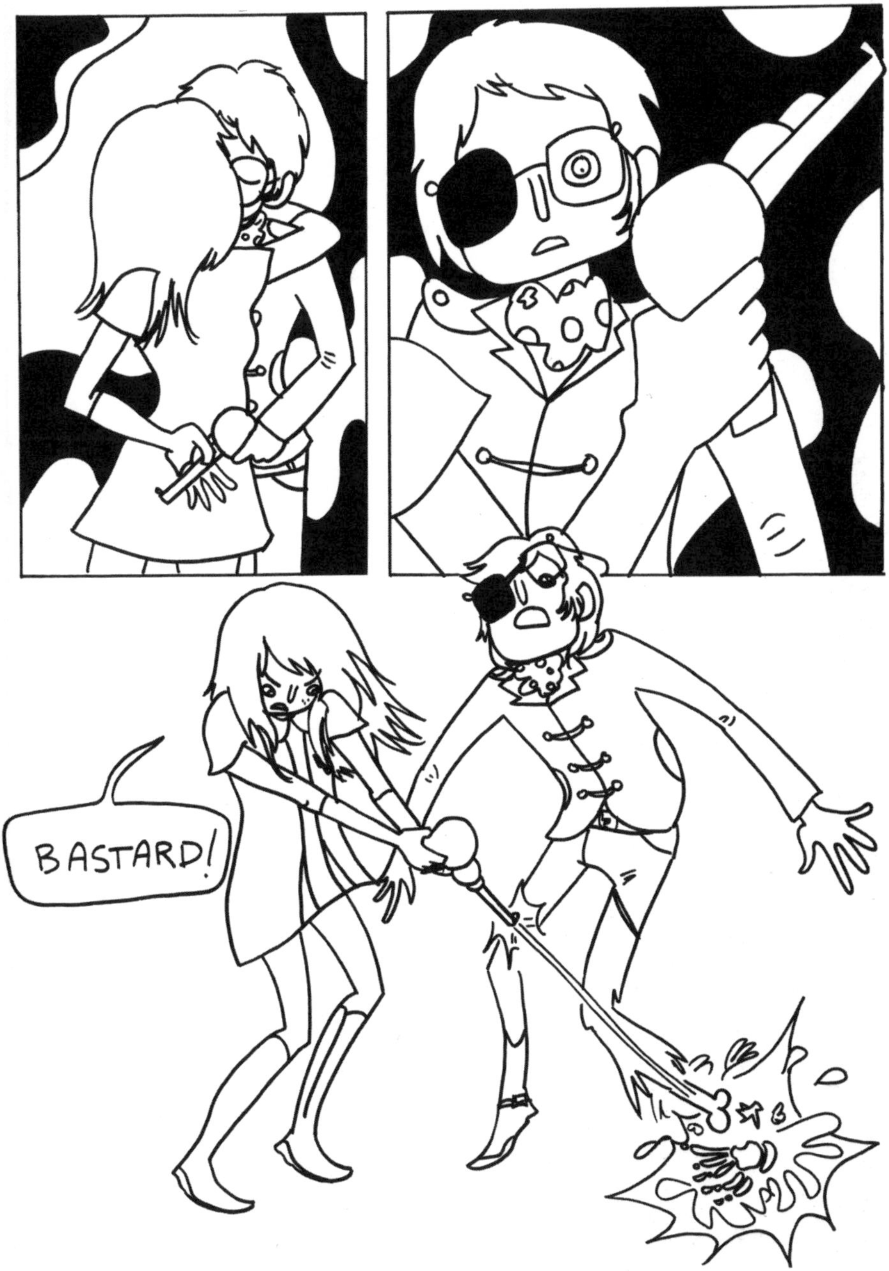
BASTARD!

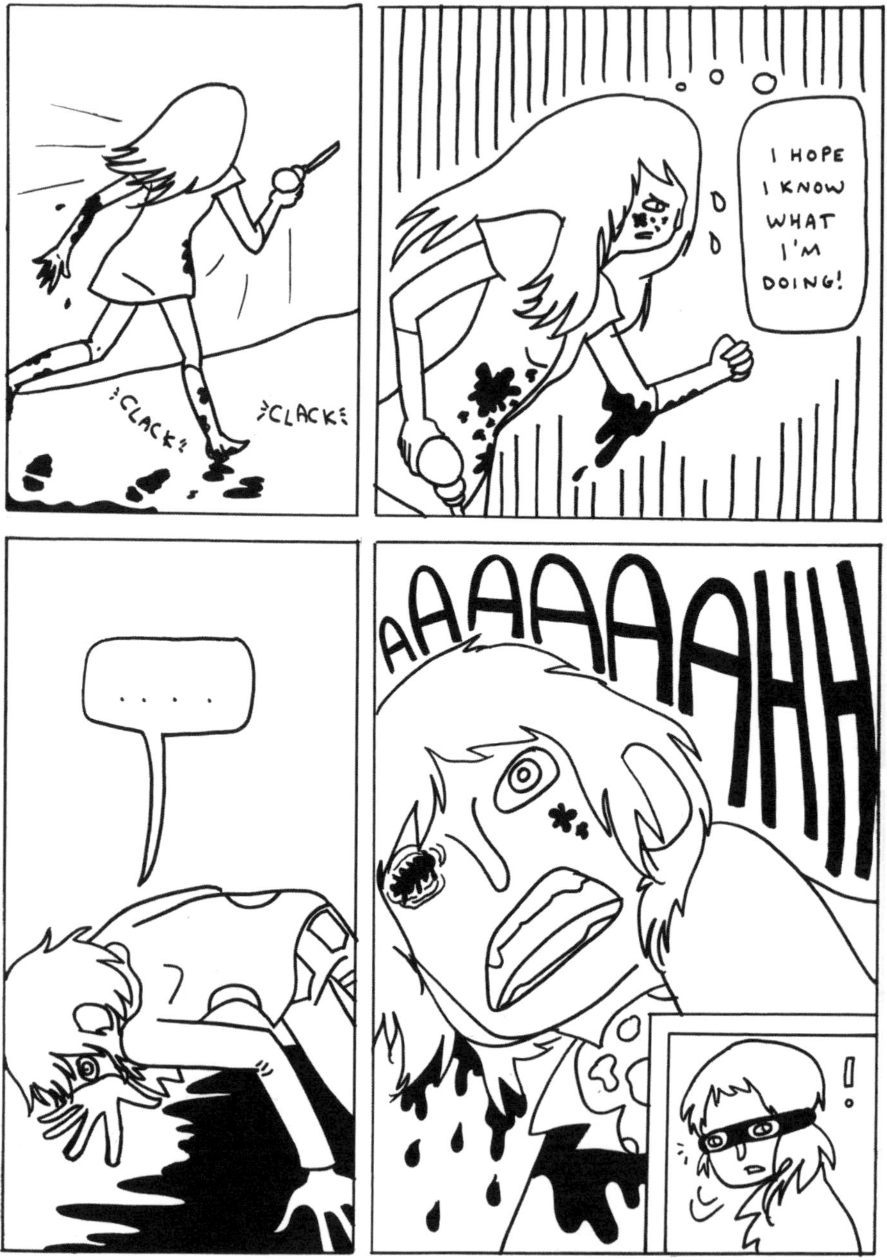
CLACK
CLACK
I HOPE I KNOW WHAT I'M DOING!
. . . .
AAAAAAHHH
!

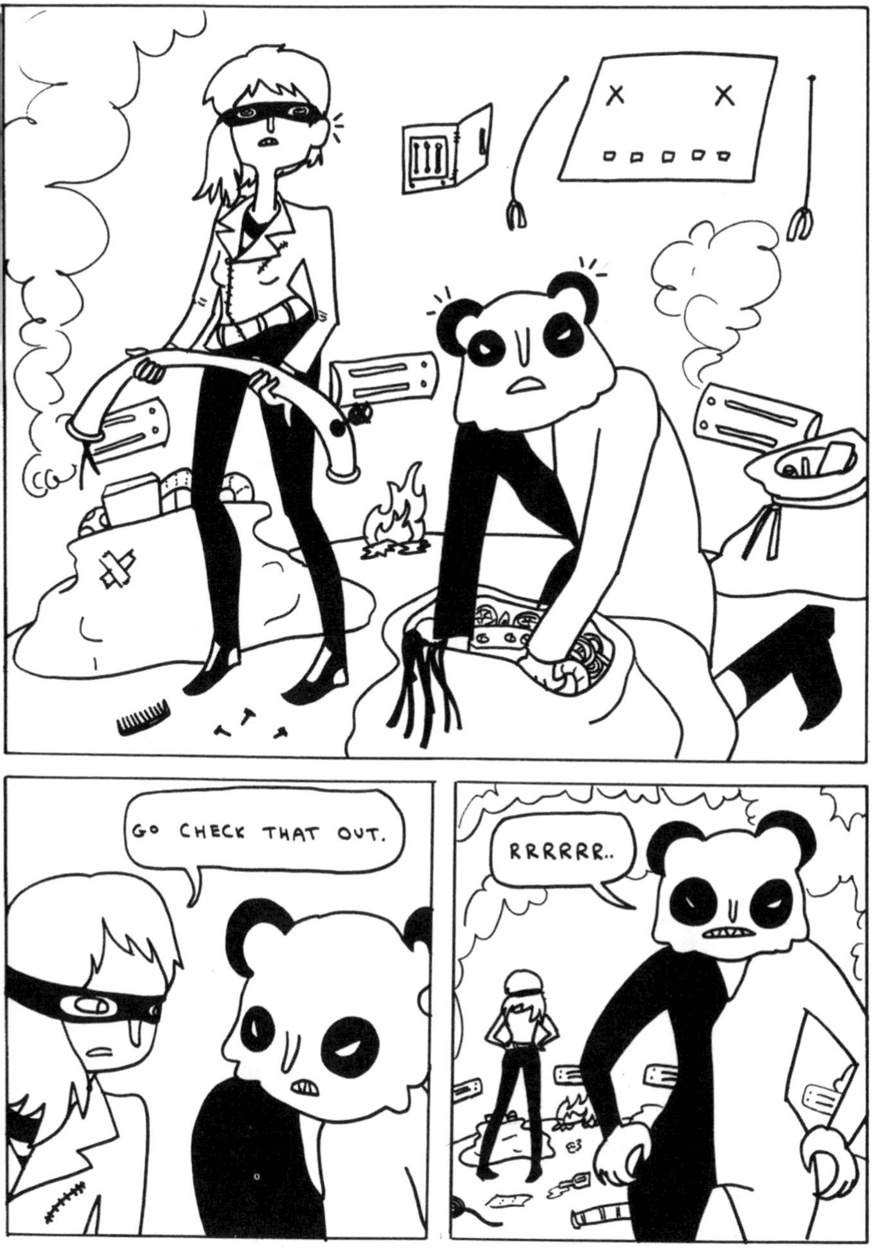
GO CHECK THAT OUT.
RRRRRR..

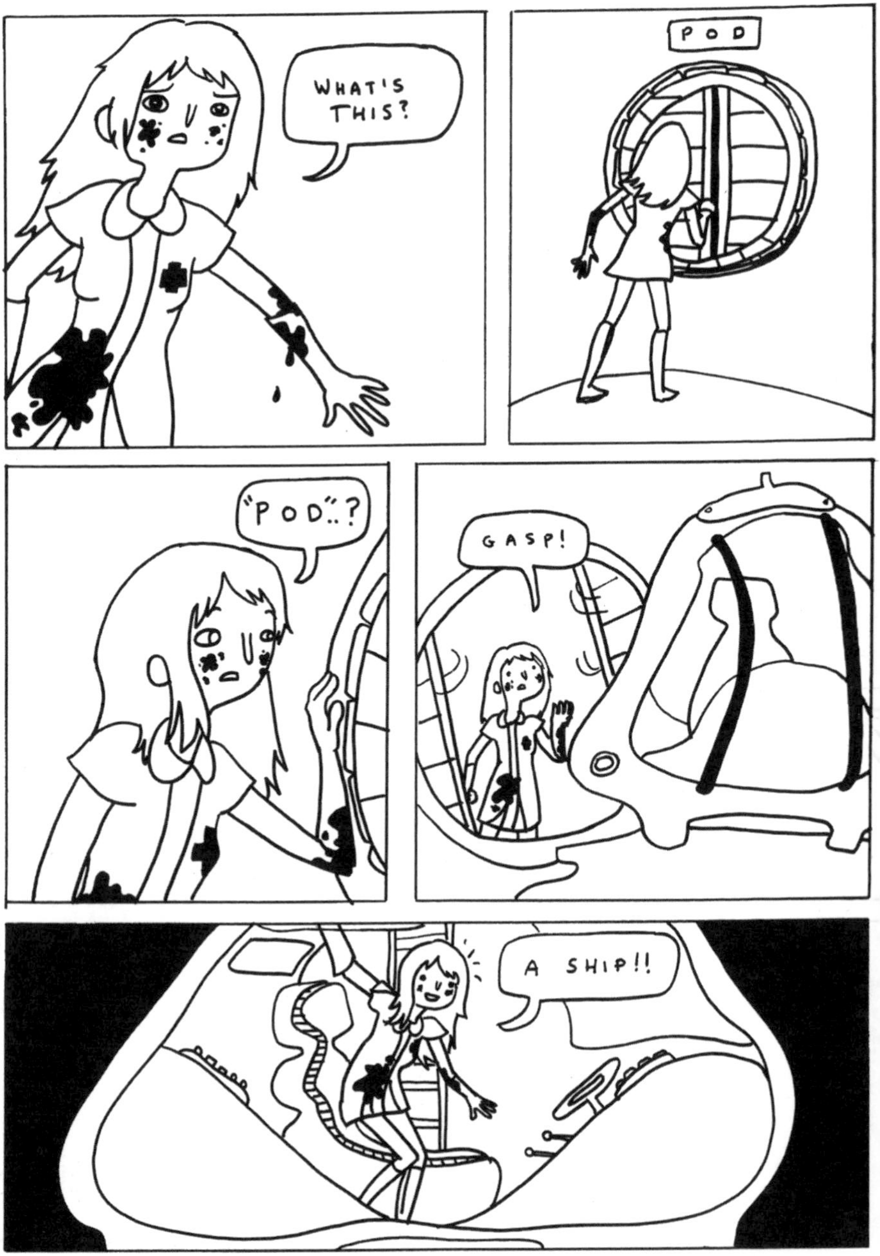
WHAT'S THIS?
POD
"POD"..?
GASP!
A SHIP!!

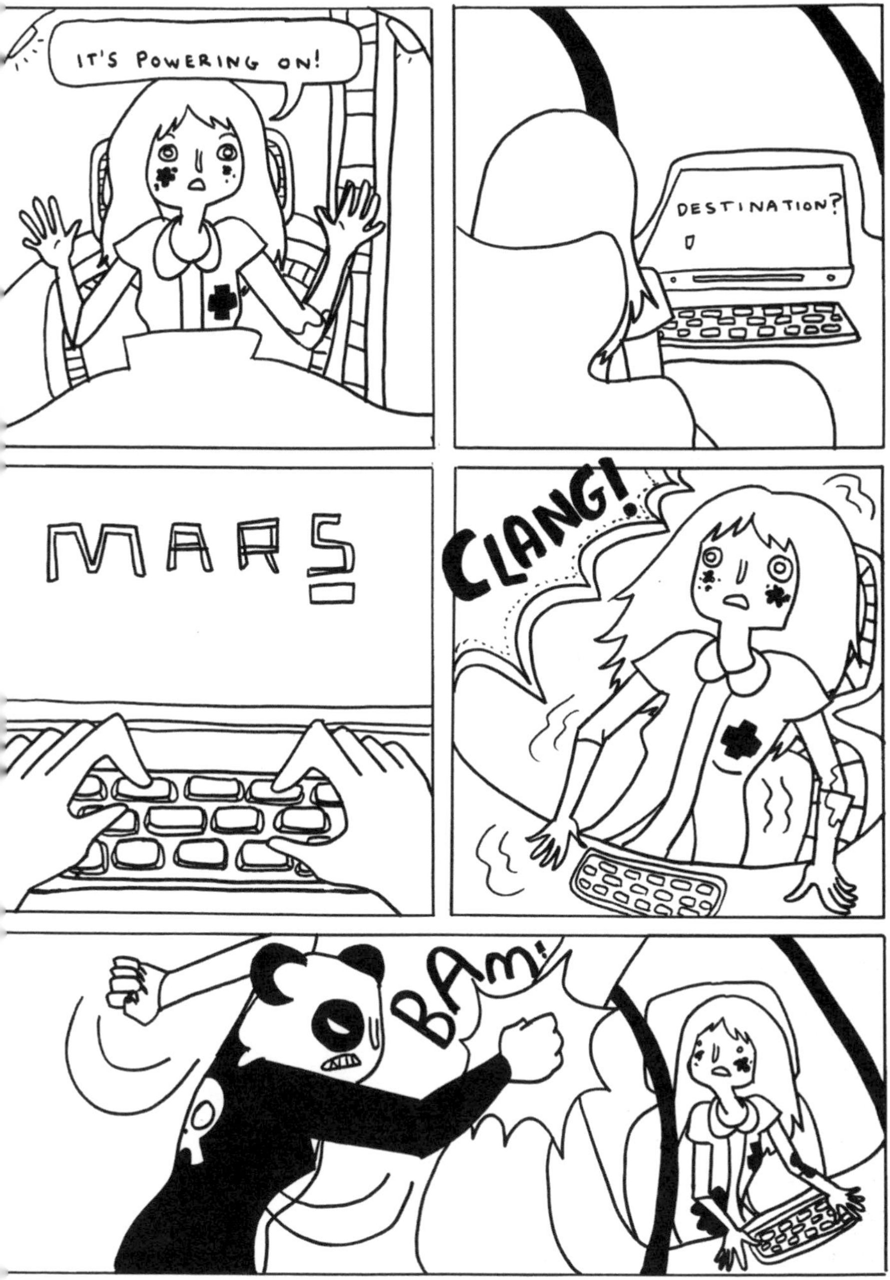
IT'S POWERING ON!
DESTINATION?
MARS
CLANG!
BAM!

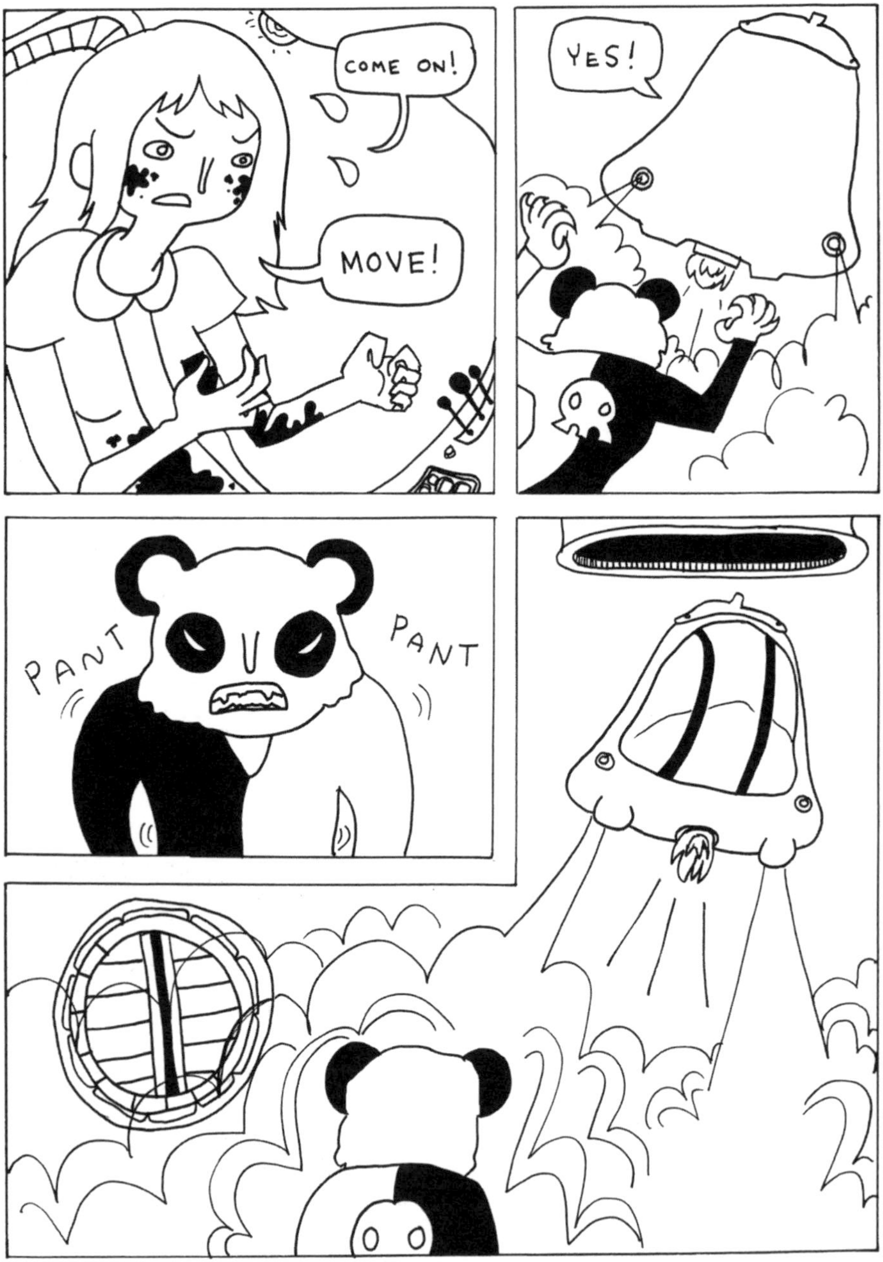
COME ON!
MOVE!
YES!
PANT
PANT

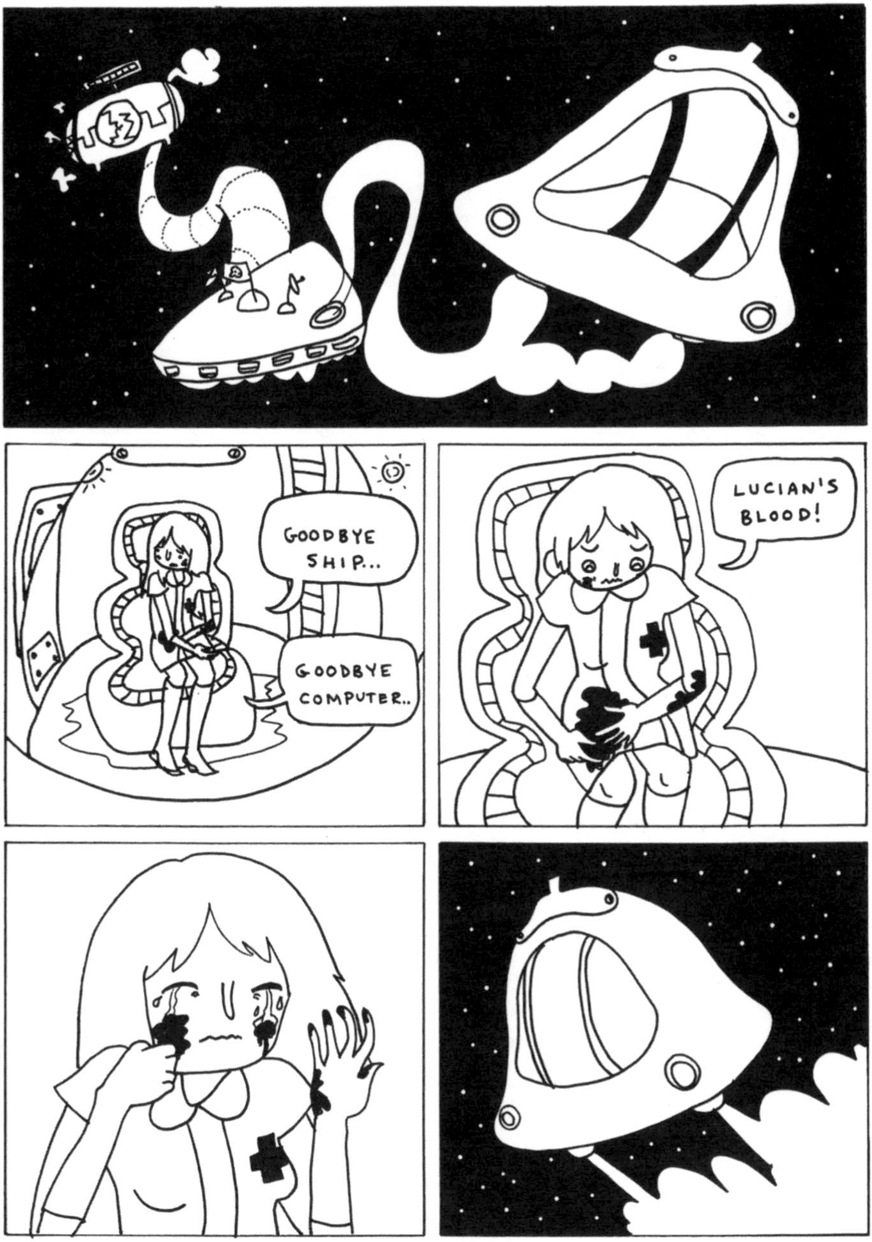
GOODBYE SHIP...
GOODBYE COMPUTER..
LUCIAN'S BLOOD!

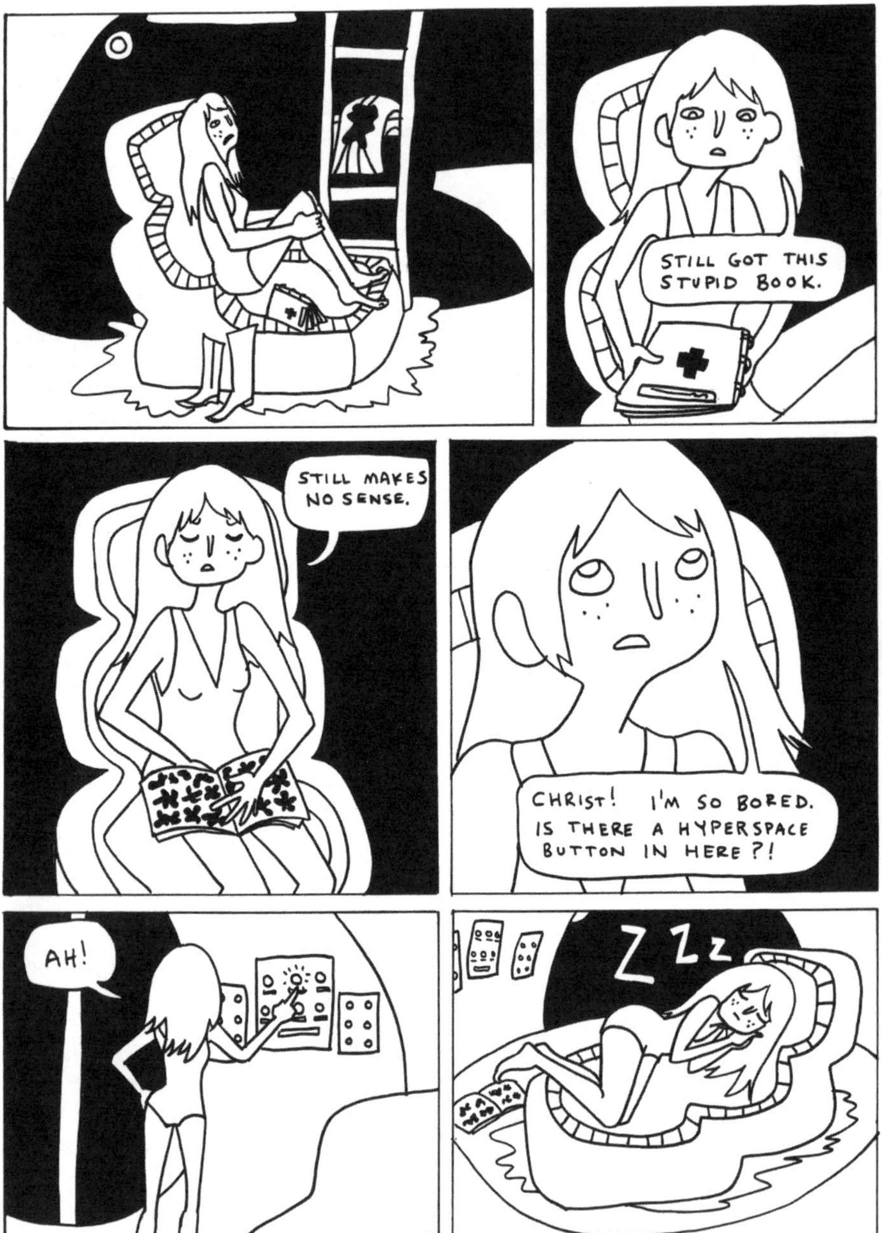
STILL GOT THIS STUPID BOOK.
STILL MAKES NO SENSE.
CHRIST! I'M SO BORED. IS THERE A HYPERSPACE BUTTON IN HERE?!
AH!
ZZz

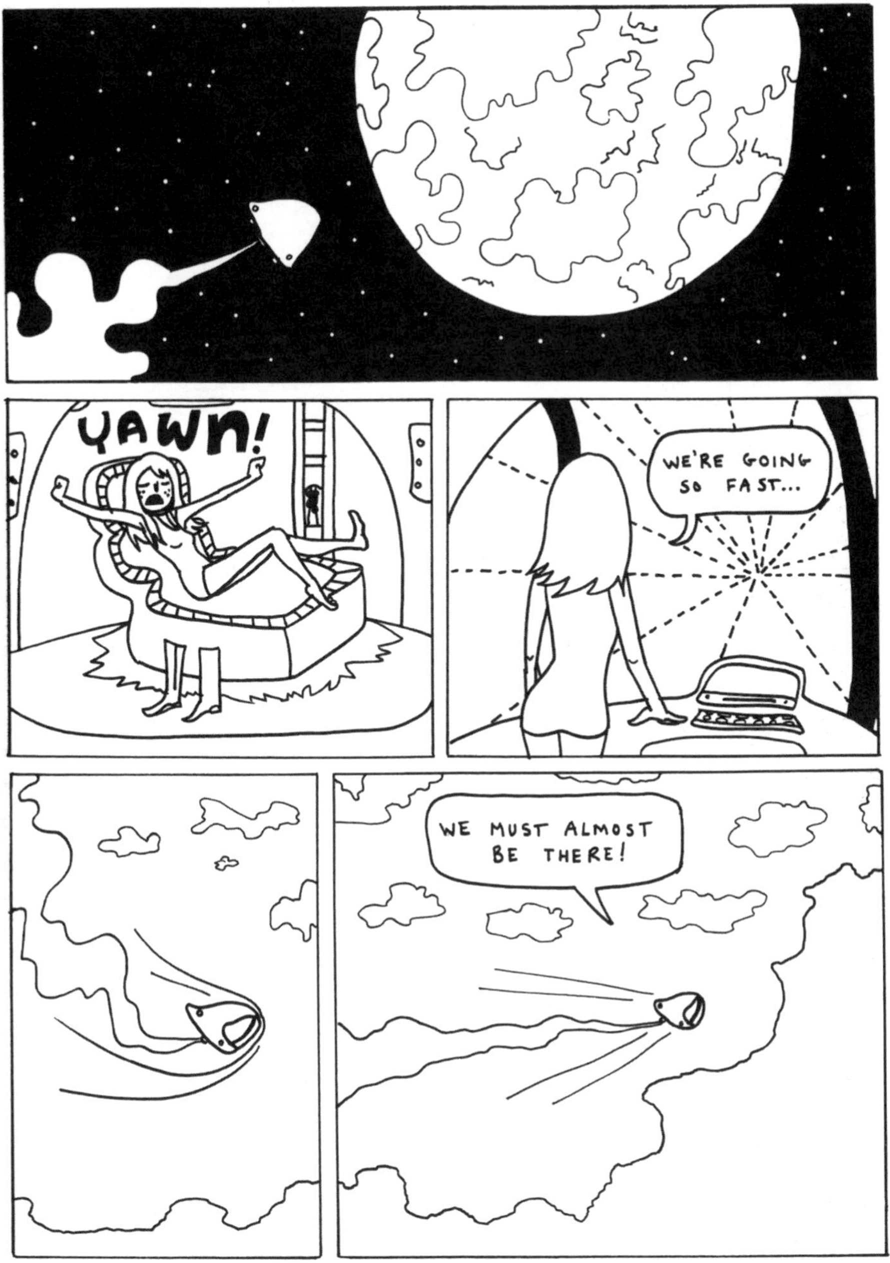
YAWN!
WE'RE GOING SO FAST...
WE MUST ALMOST BE THERE!

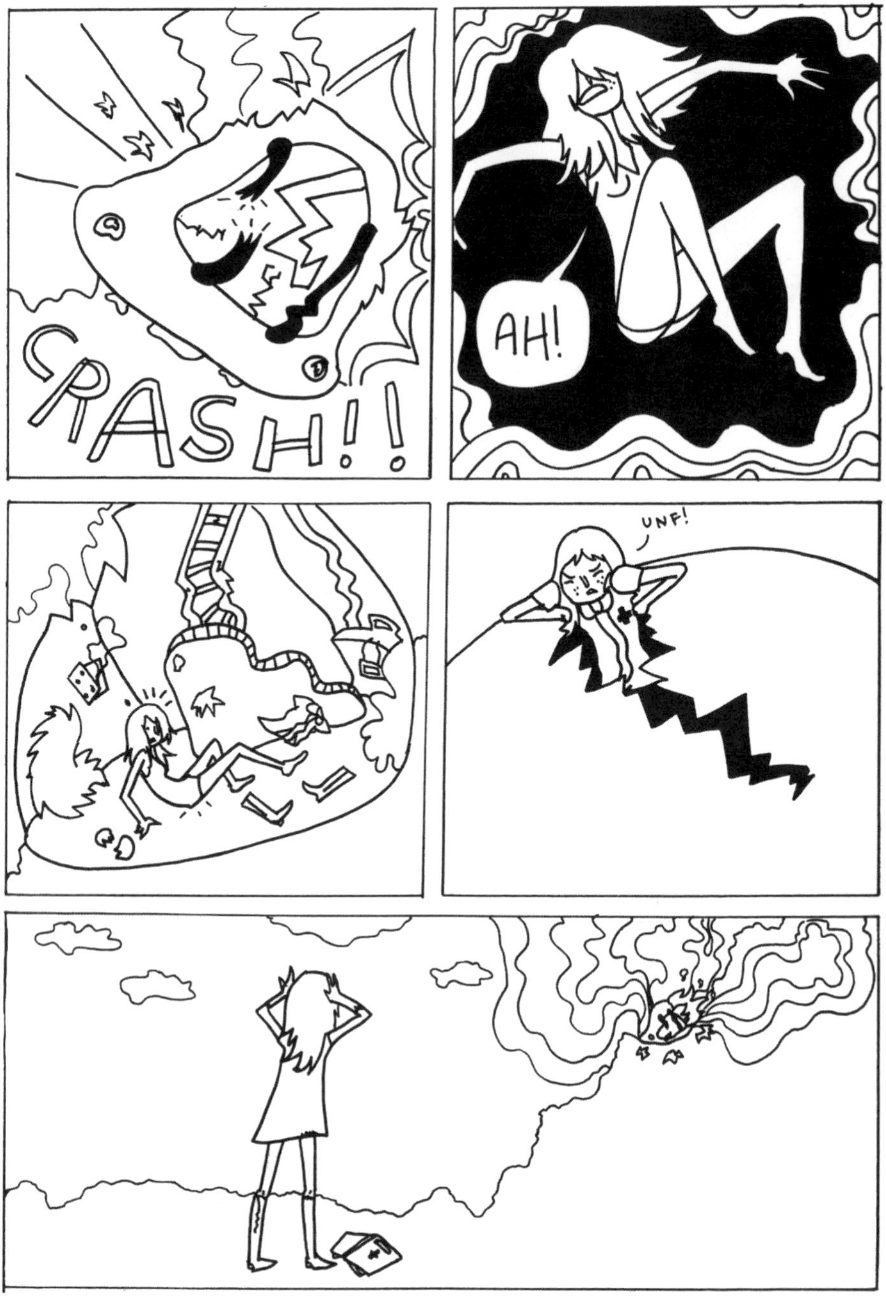
CRASH!!
AH!
UNF!

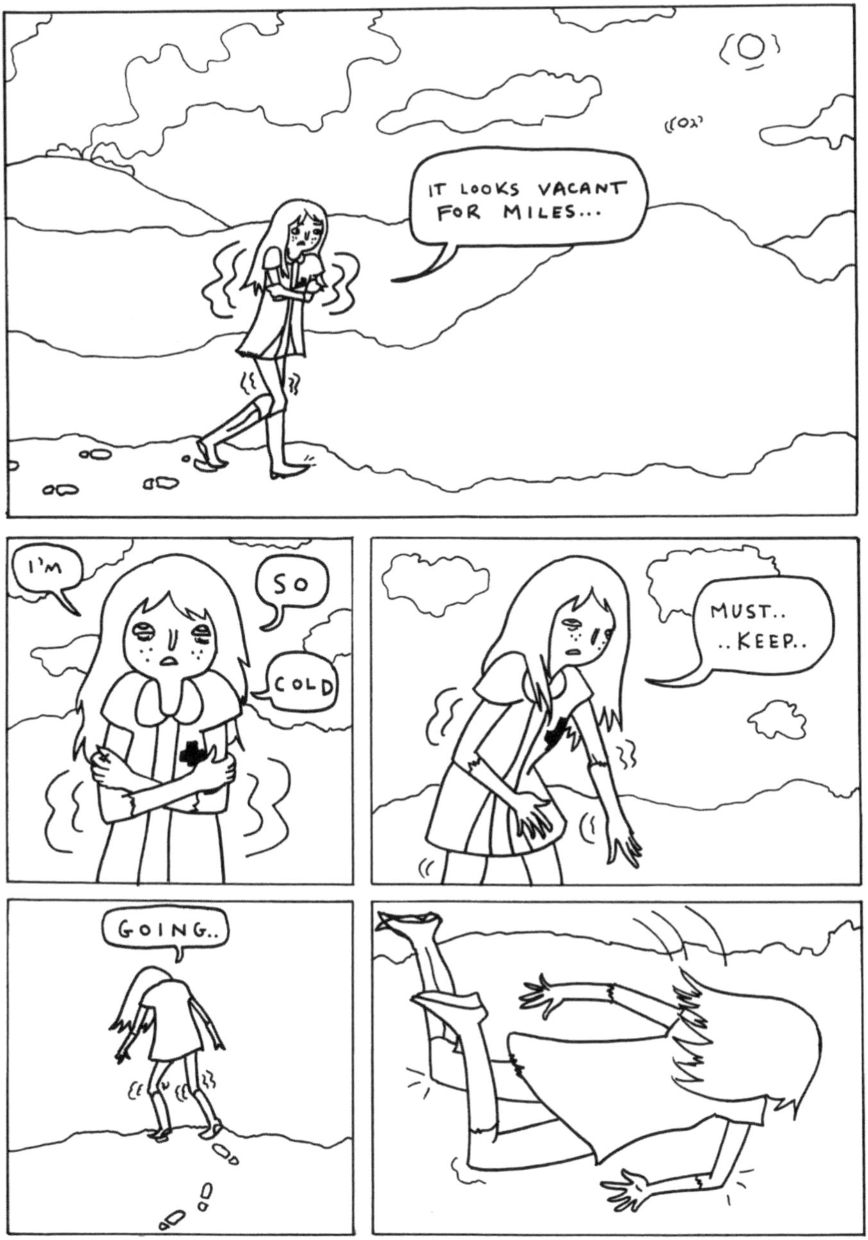
IT LOOKS VACANT FOR MILES...
I'M
SO
COLD
MUST..
..KEEP..
GOING..

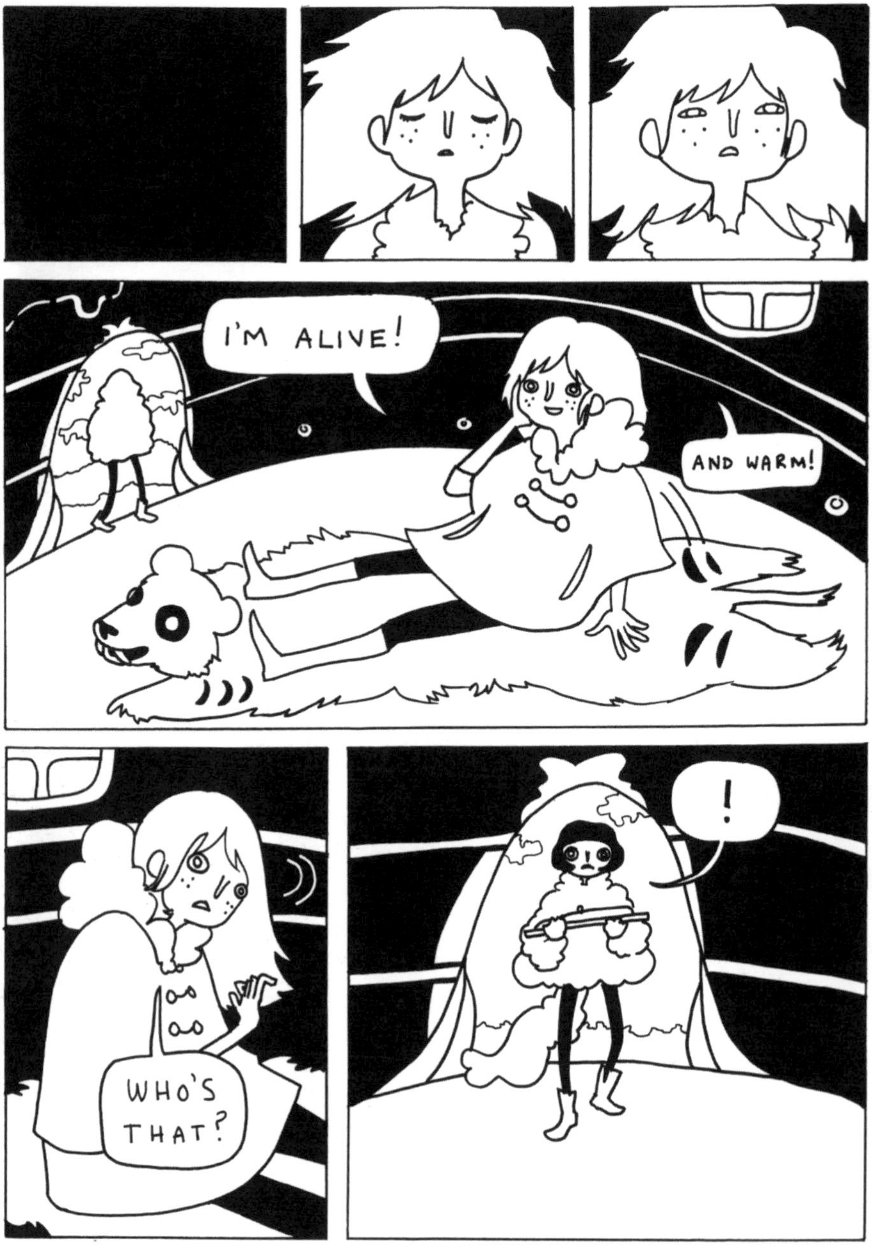
I'M ALIVE!
AND WARM!
WHO'S THAT?
!

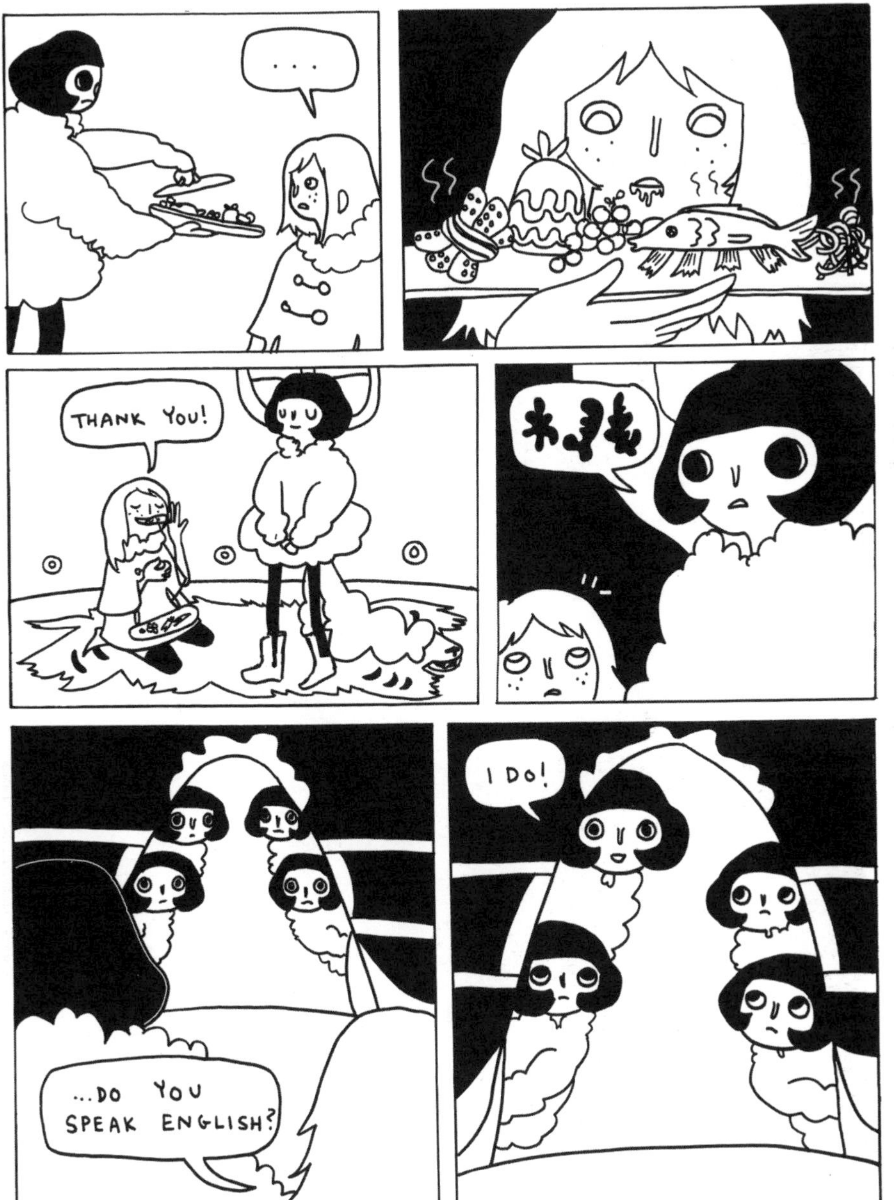
...
THANK YOU!
...DO YOU SPEAK ENGLISH?
I DO!

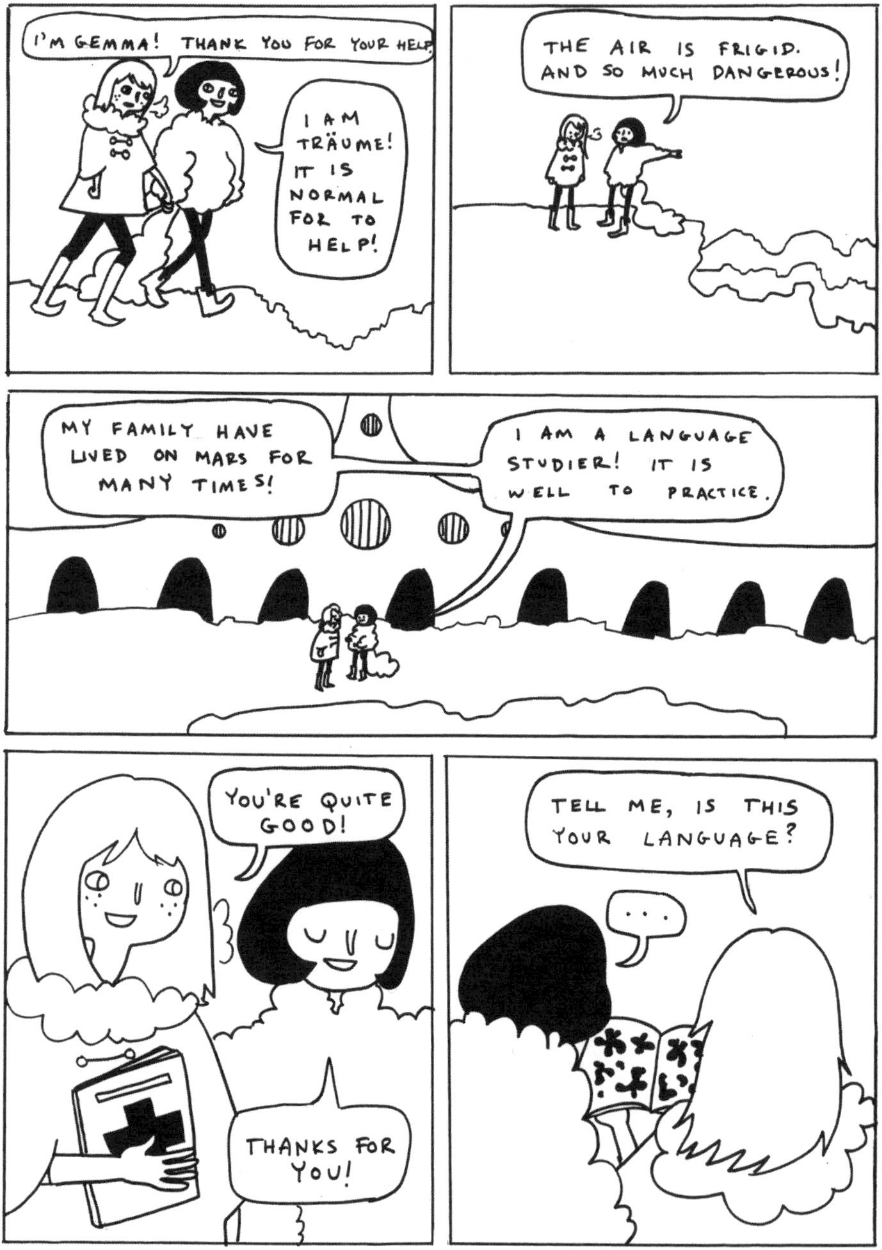
I'M GEMMA! THANK YOU FOR YOUR HELP!
I AM TRÄUME! IT IS NORMAL FOR TO HELP!
THE AIR IS FRIGID. AND SO MUCH DANGEROUS!
MY FAMILY HAVE LIVED ON MARS FOR MANY TIMES!
I AM A LANGUAGE STUDIER! IT IS WELL TO PRACTICE.
YOU'RE QUITE GOOD!
THANKS FOR YOU!
TELL ME, IS THIS YOUR LANGUAGE?
. . .

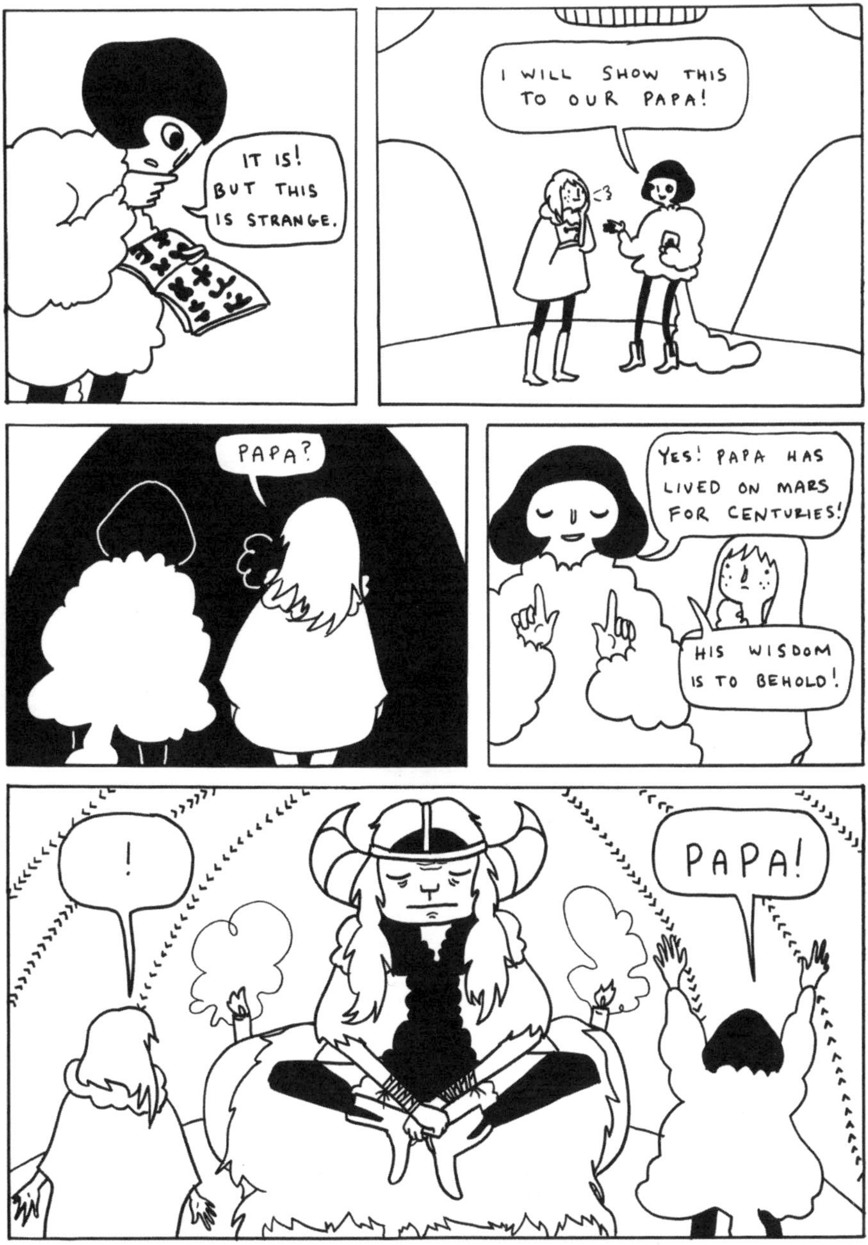
IT IS! BUT THIS IS STRANGE.
I WILL SHOW THIS TO OUR PAPA!
<3
PAPA?
YES! PAPA HAS LIVED ON MARS FOR CENTURIES!
HIS WISDOM IS TO BEHOLD!
!
PAPA!

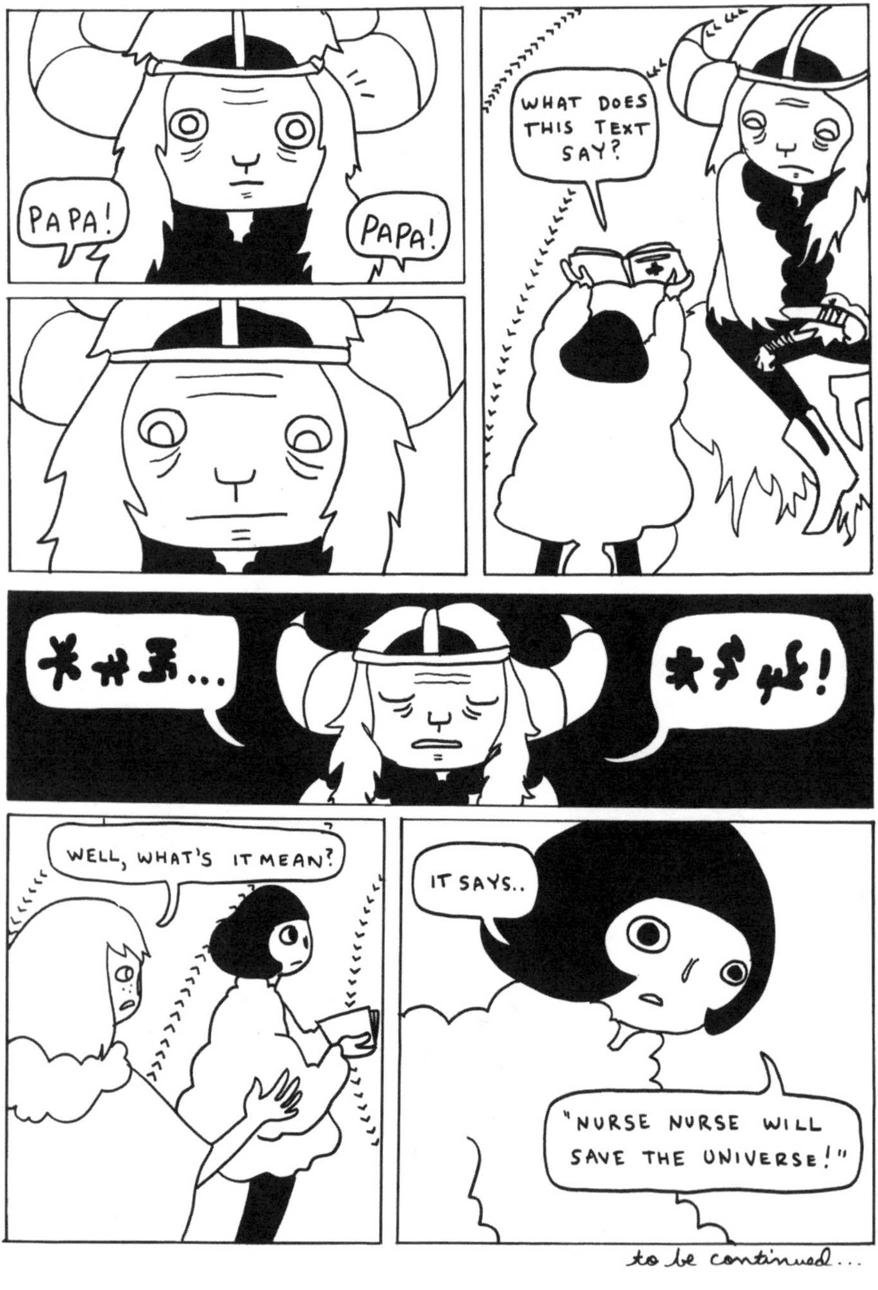
PAPA!
PAPA!
WHAT DOES THIS TEXT SAY?
WELL, WHAT'S IT MEAN?
IT SAYS..
"NURSE NURSE WILL SAVE THE UNIVERSE!"

to be continued...

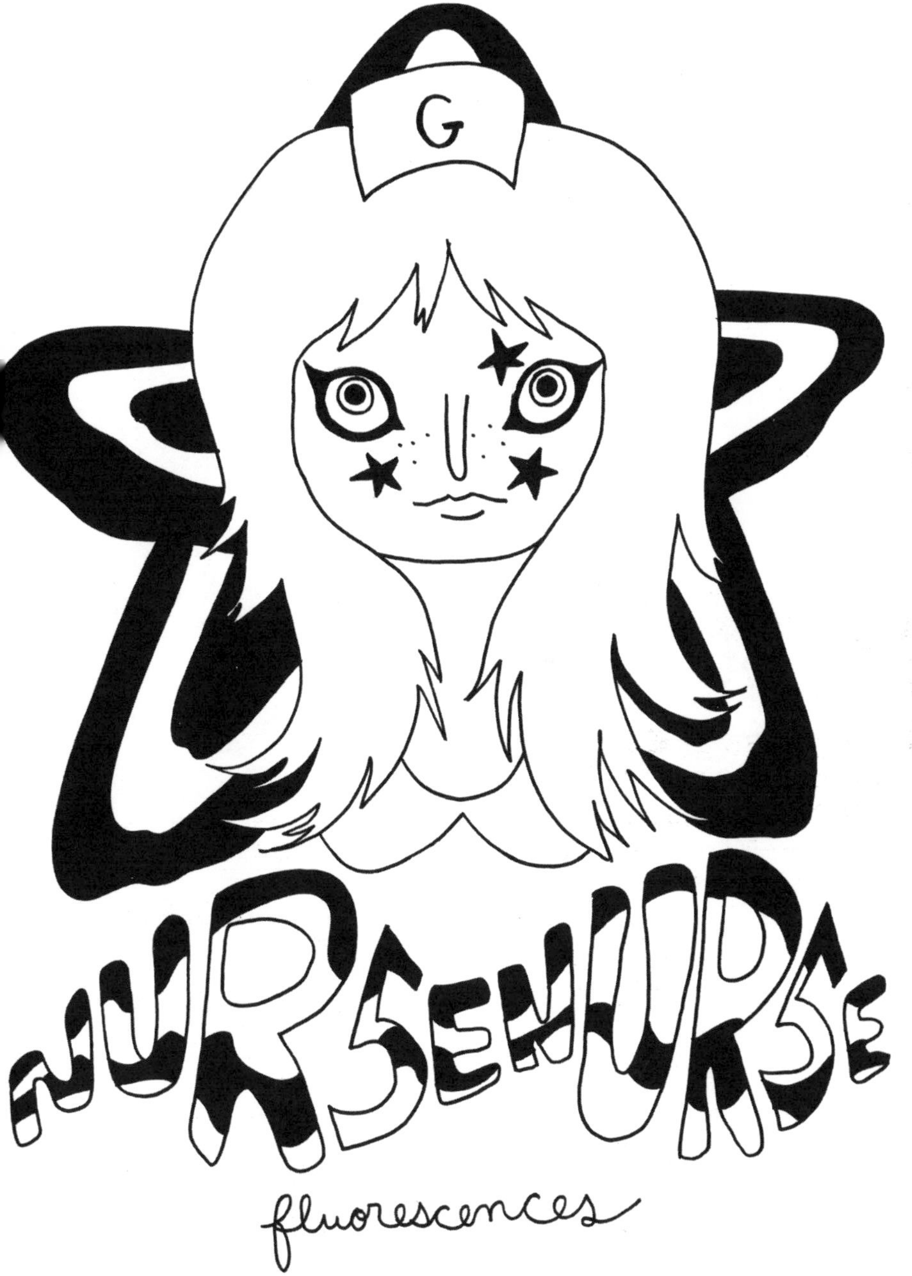
G
NURSENURSE
fluorescences

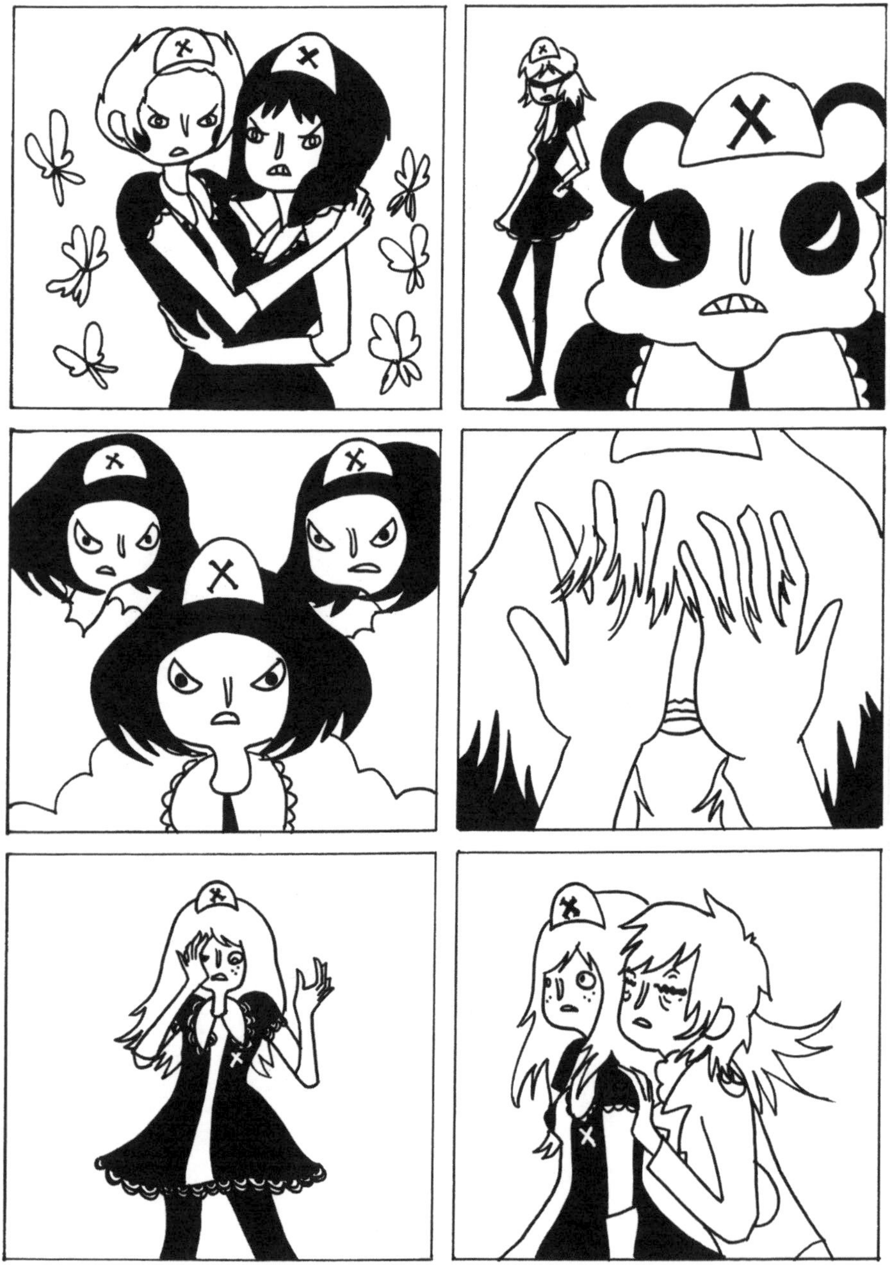

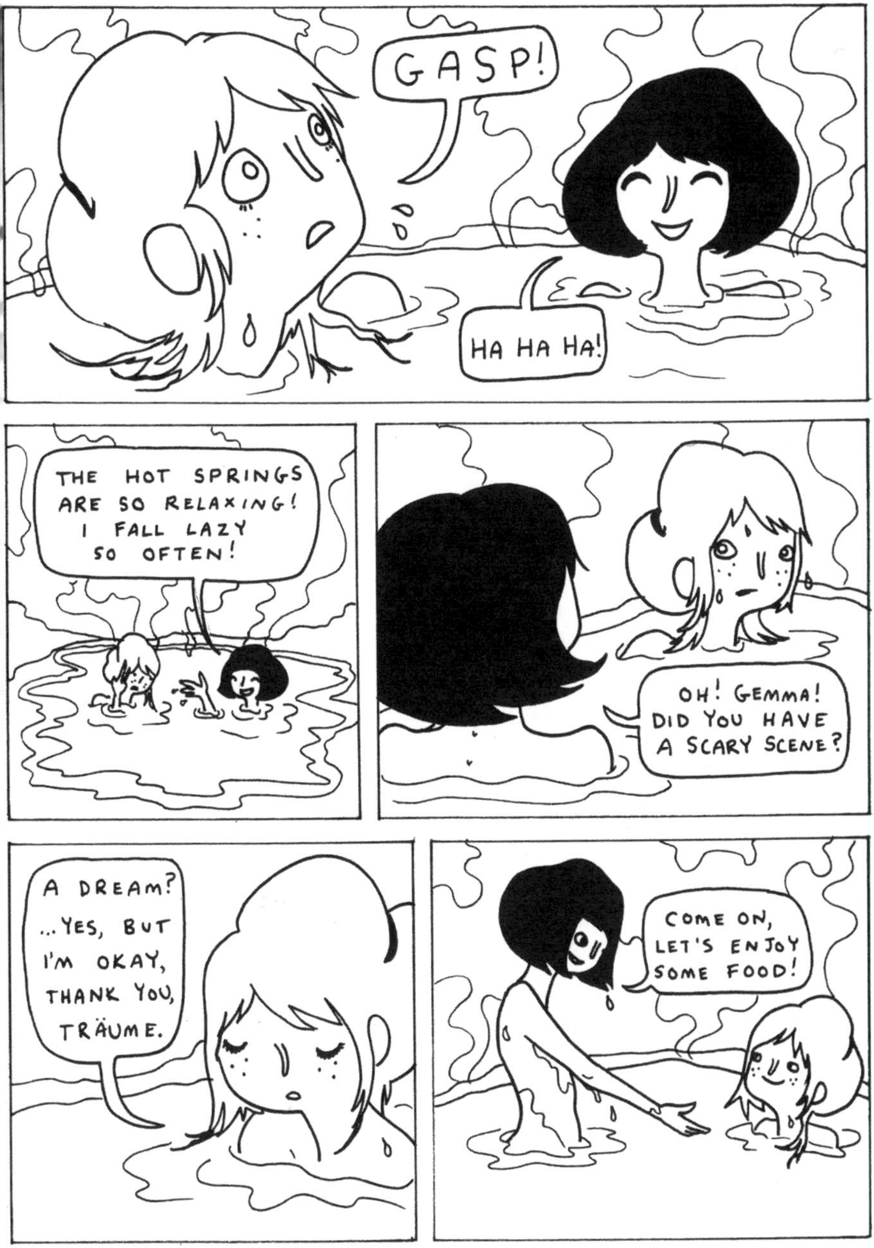
GASP!
HA HA HA!
THE HOT SPRINGS ARE SO RELAXING! I FALL LAZY SO OFTEN!
OH! GEMMA! DID YOU HAVE A SCARY SCENE?
A DREAM? ...YES, BUT I'M OKAY, THANK YOU, TRÄUME.
COME ON, LET'S ENJOY SOME FOOD!

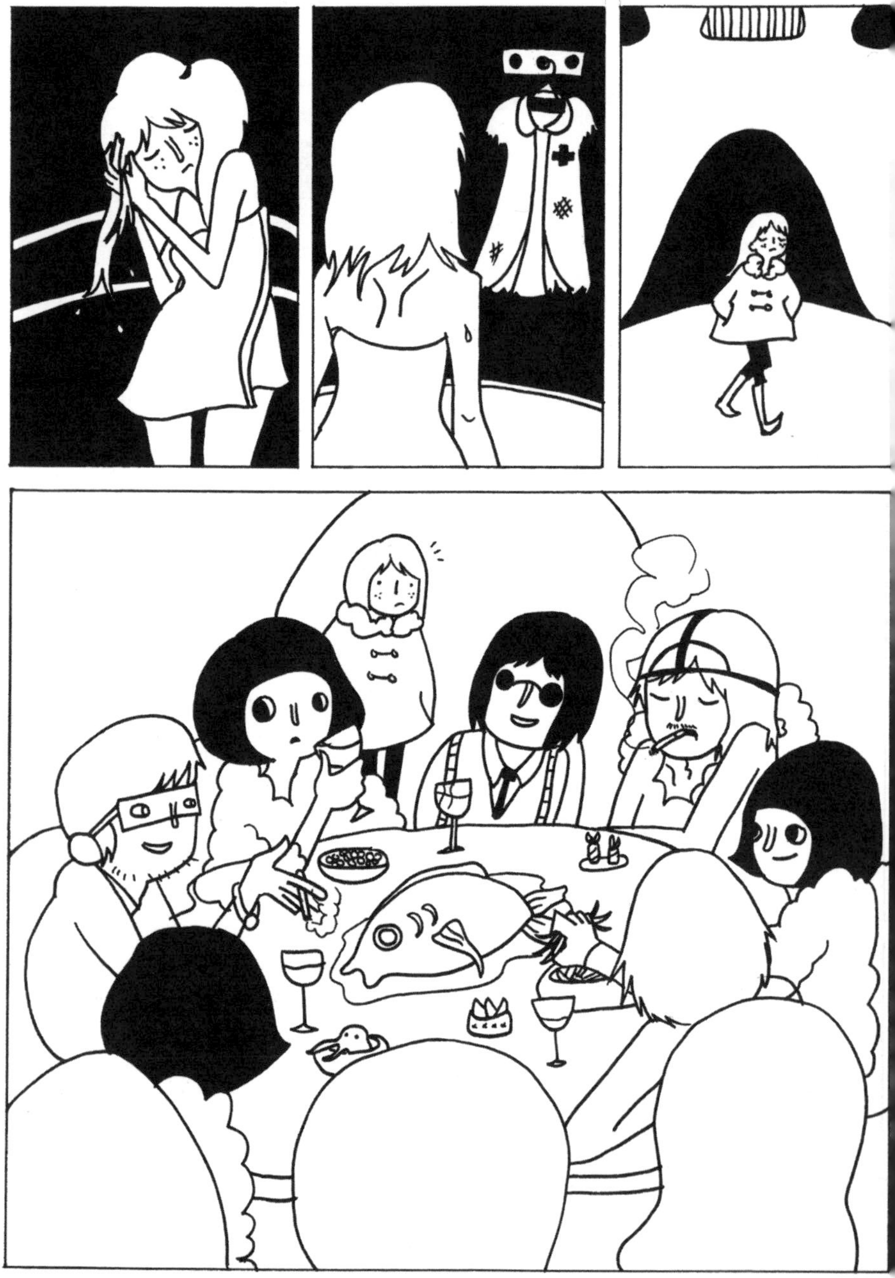

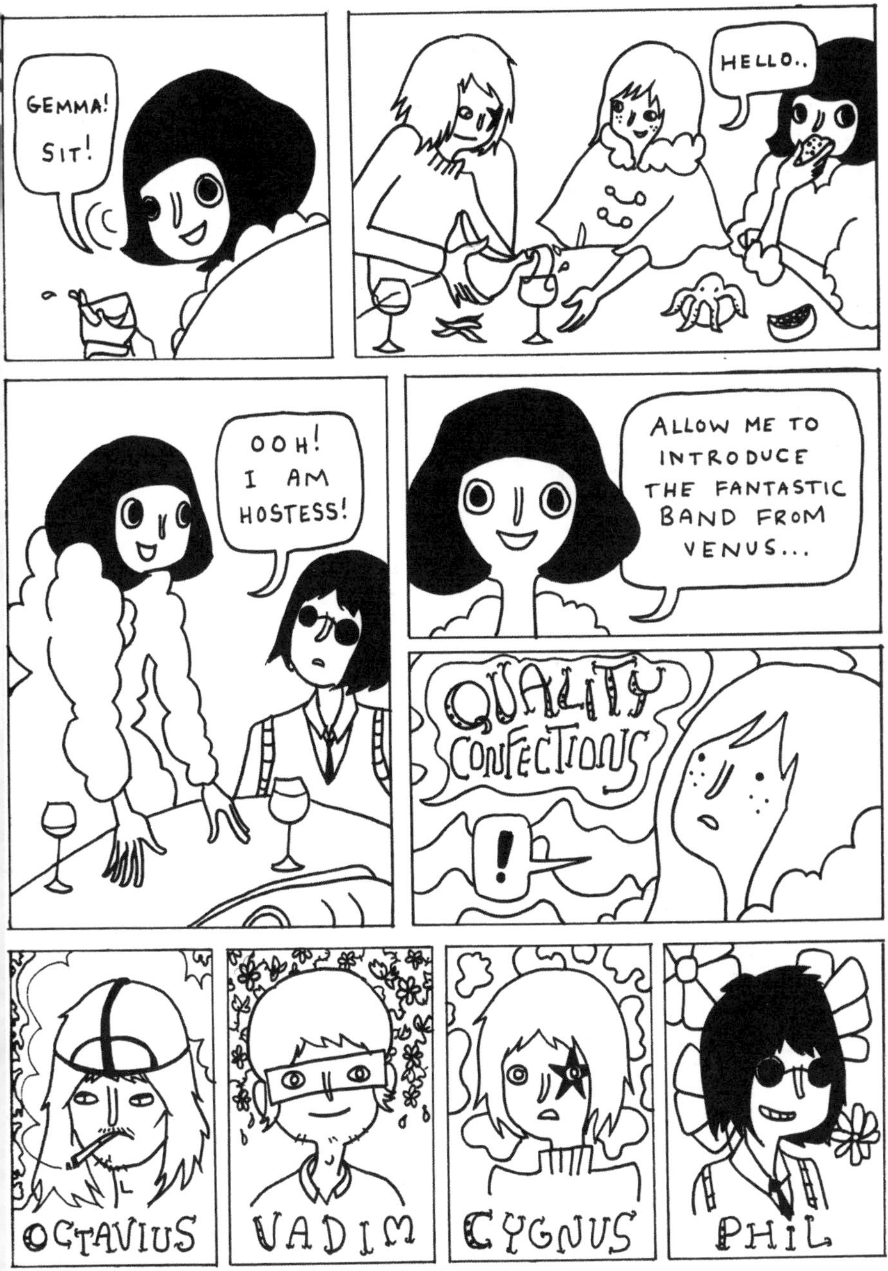
GEMMA! SIT!
HELLO..
OOH! I AM HOSTESS!
ALLOW ME TO INTRODUCE THE FANTASTIC BAND FROM VENUS...
QUALITY CONFECTIONS
!
OCTAVIUS
VADIM
CYGNUS
PHIL

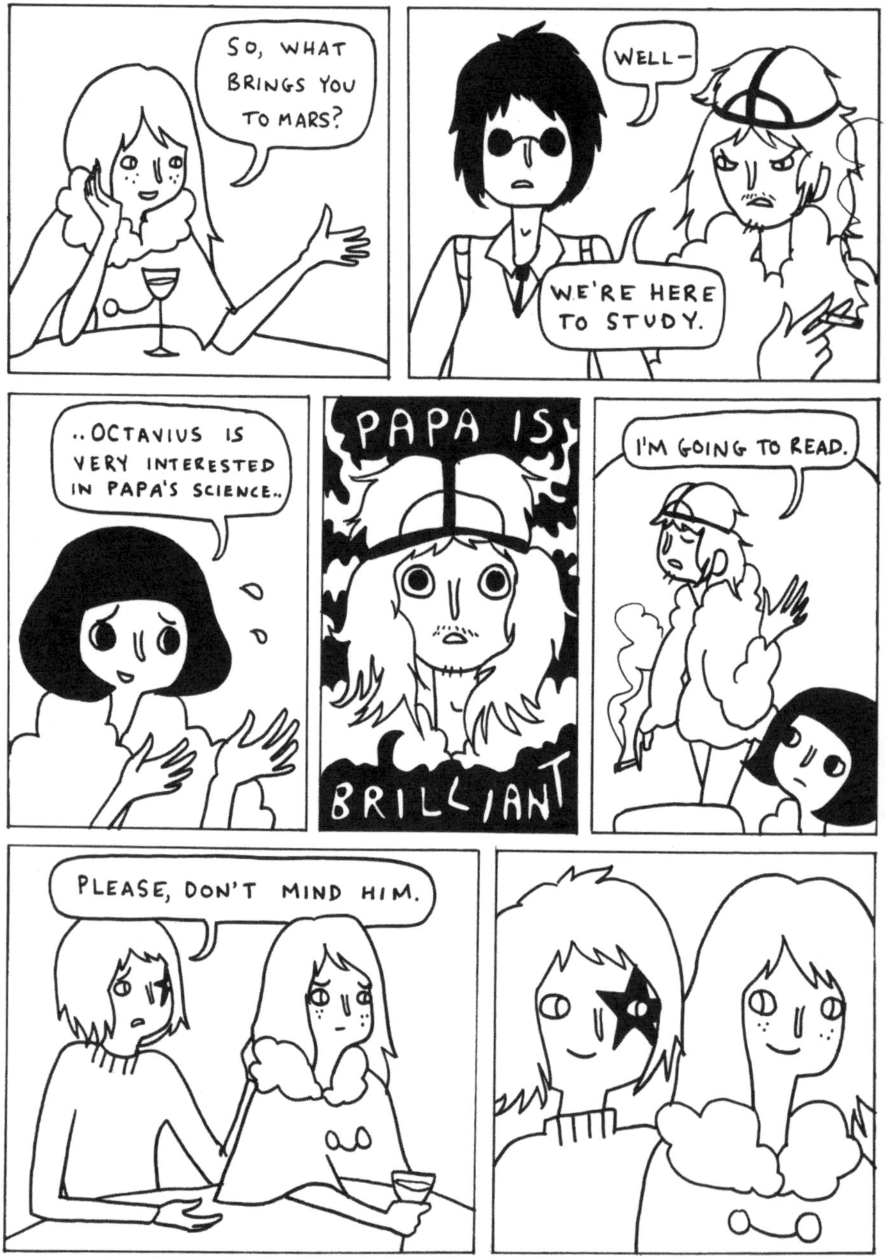
SO, WHAT BRINGS YOU TO MARS?
WELL-
WE'RE HERE TO STUDY.
..OCTAVIUS IS VERY INTERESTED IN PAPA'S SCIENCE..
PAPA IS
BRILLIANT
I'M GOING TO READ.
PLEASE, DON'T MIND HIM.

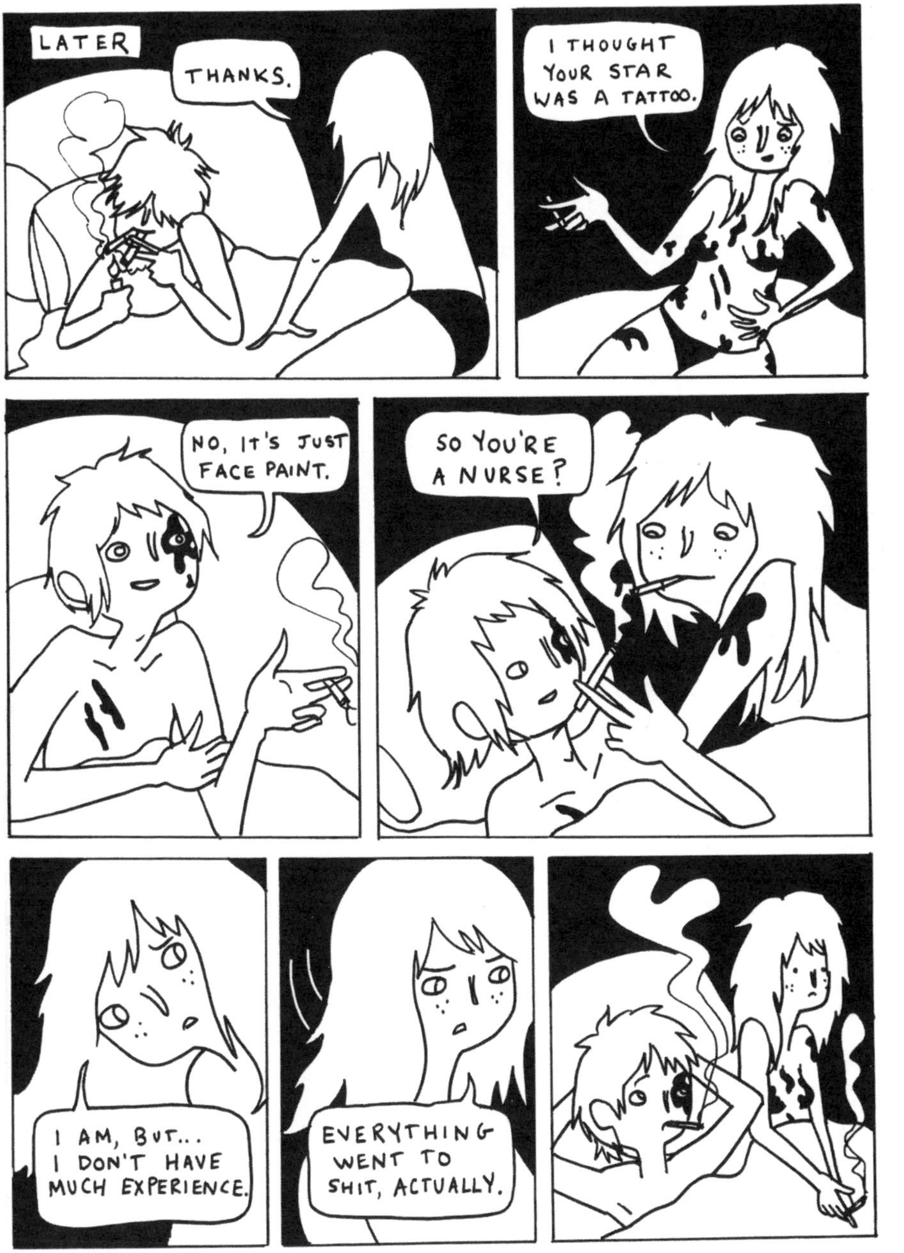

LATER
THANKS.
I THOUGHT YOUR STAR WAS A TATTOO.
NO, IT'S JUST FACE PAINT.
SO YOU'RE A NURSE?
I AM, BUT... I DON'T HAVE MUCH EXPERIENCE.
EVERYTHING WENT TO SHIT, ACTUALLY.

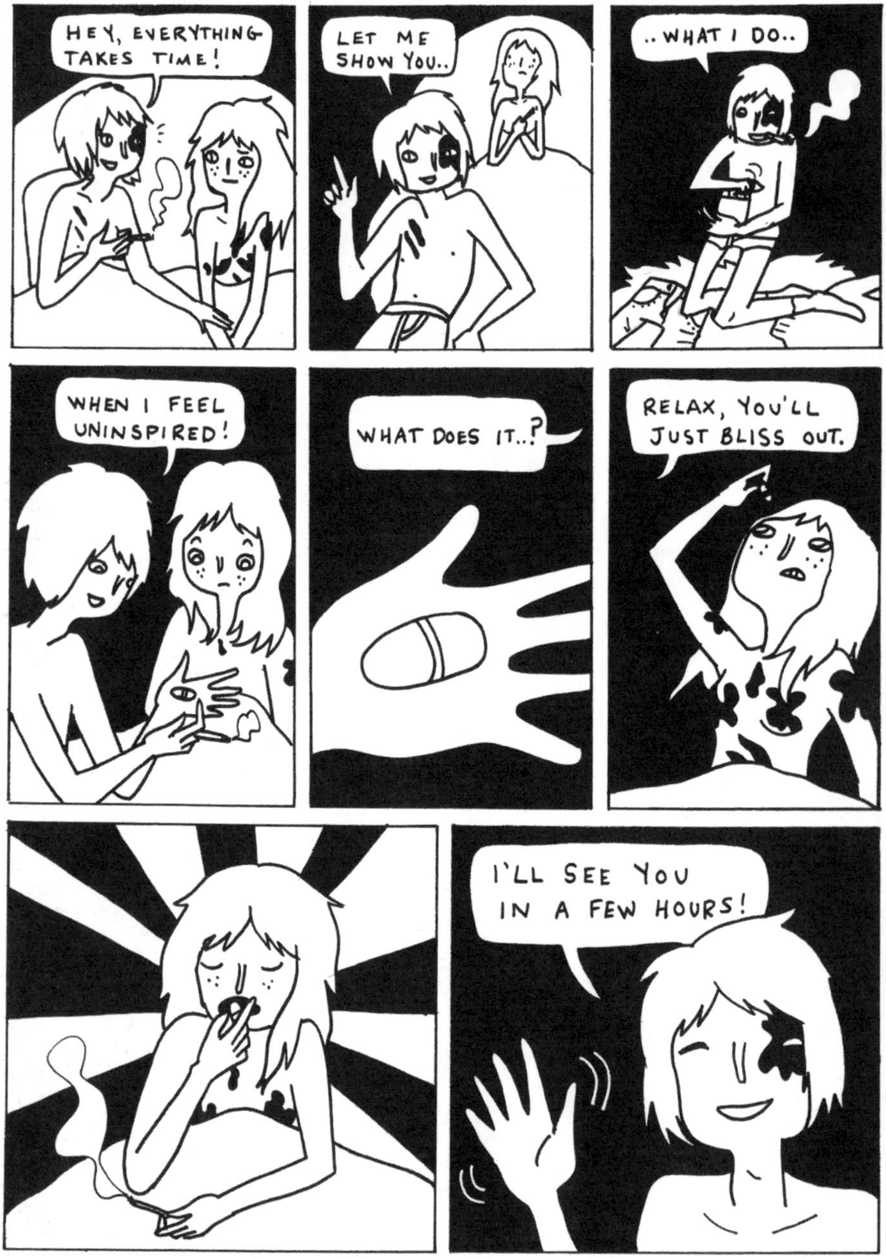
HEY, EVERYTHING TAKES TIME!
LET ME SHOW YOU..
..WHAT I DO..
WHEN I FEEL UNINSPIRED!
WHAT DOES IT..?
RELAX, YOU'LL JUST BLISS OUT.
I'LL SEE YOU IN A FEW HOURS!

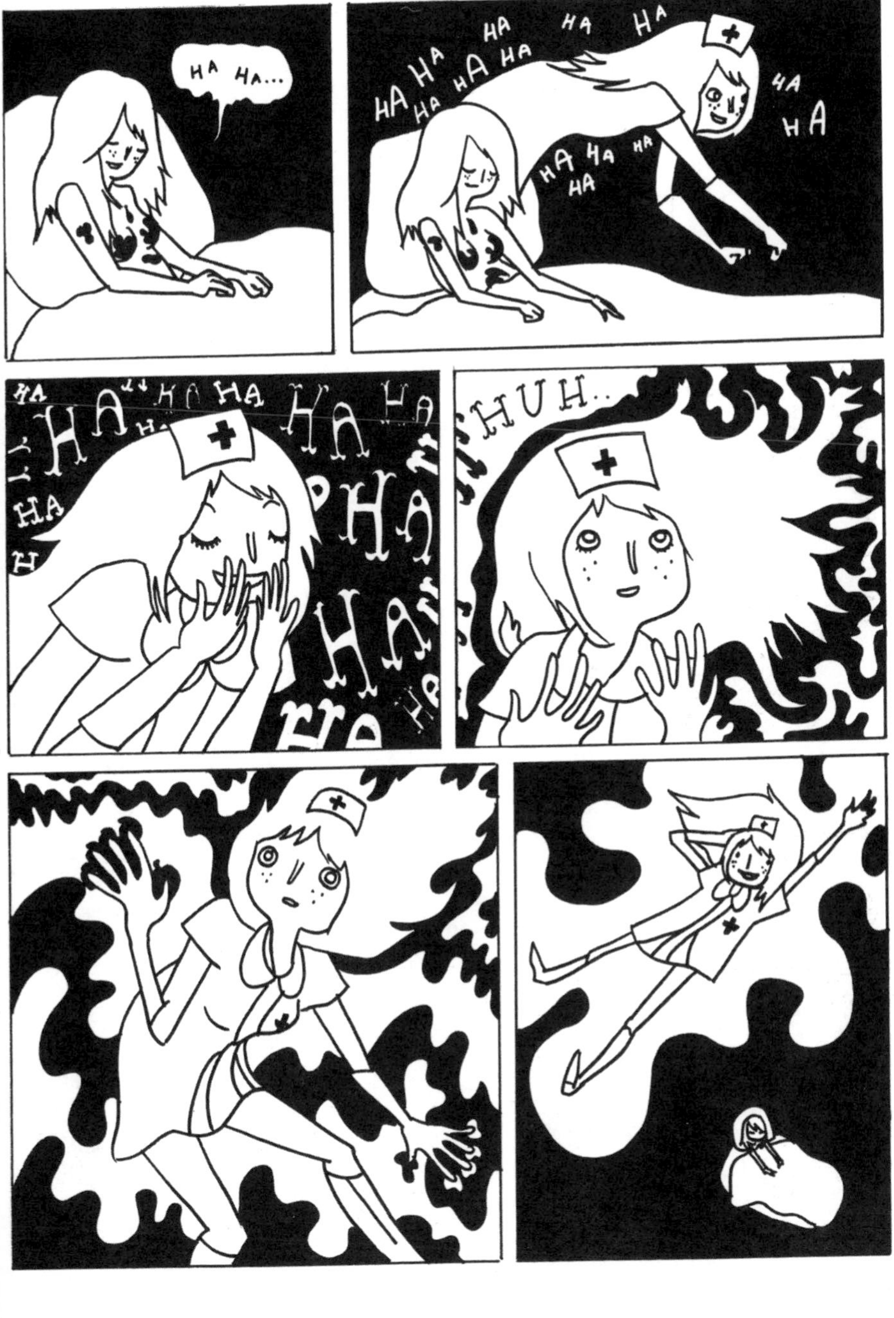

HA HA...
HA HA HA HA HA HA HA HA HA HA HA HA HA HA HA
HA HA HA HA HA HA HA HA HA HA HA
SHUH..

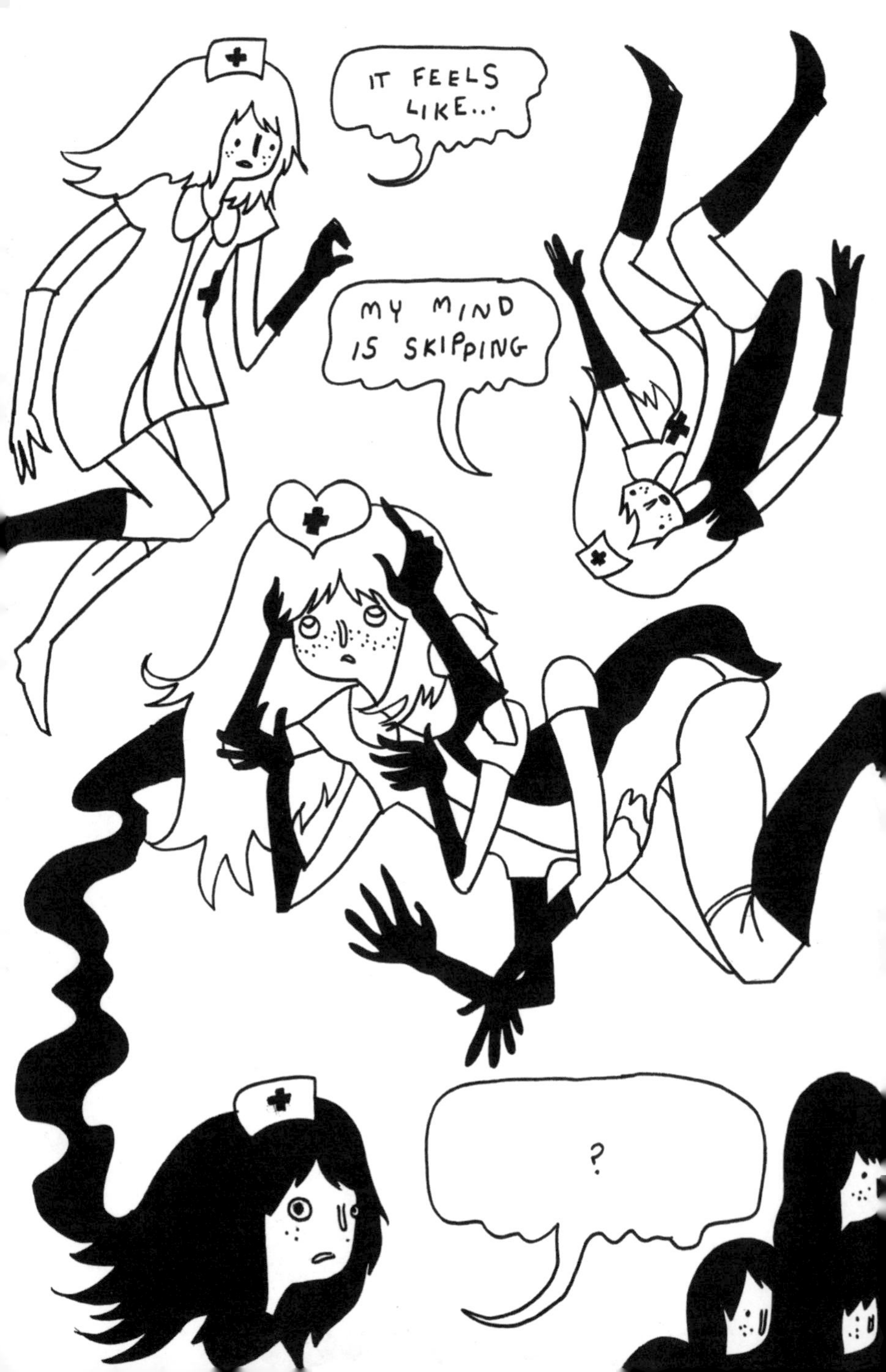
IT FEELS LIKE...
MY MIND IS SKIPPING
?

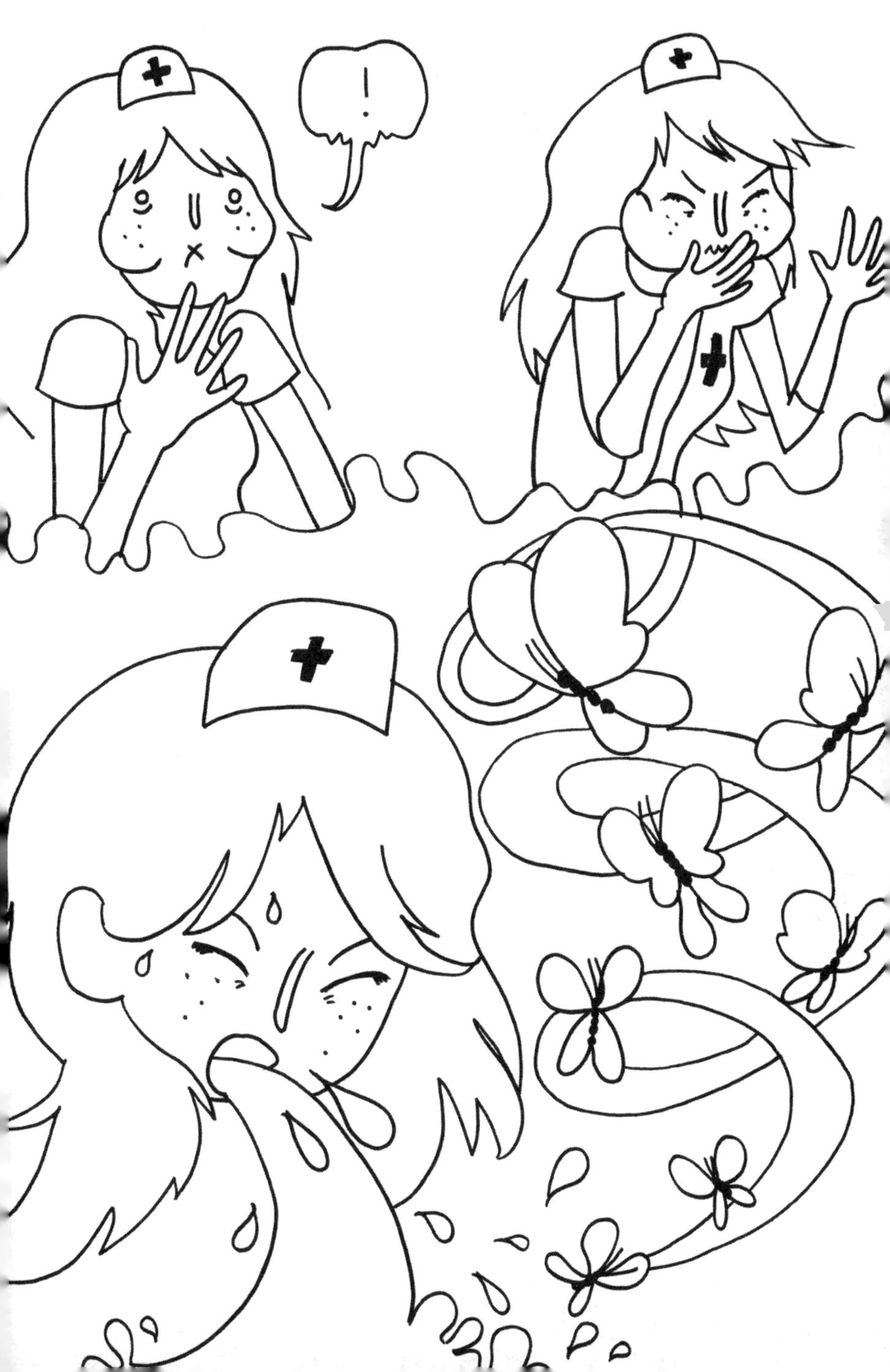
!

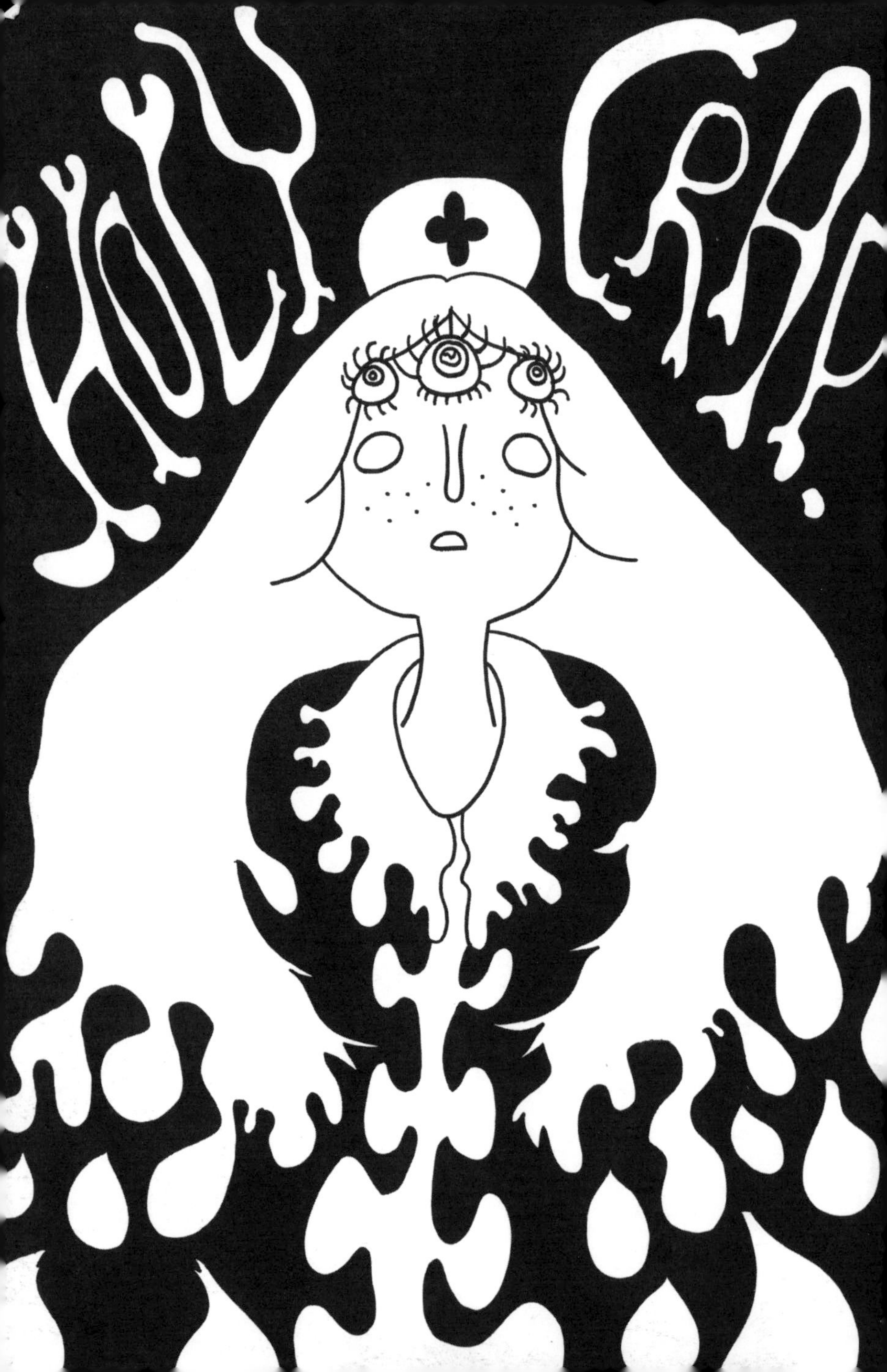
HOLY CRAP.

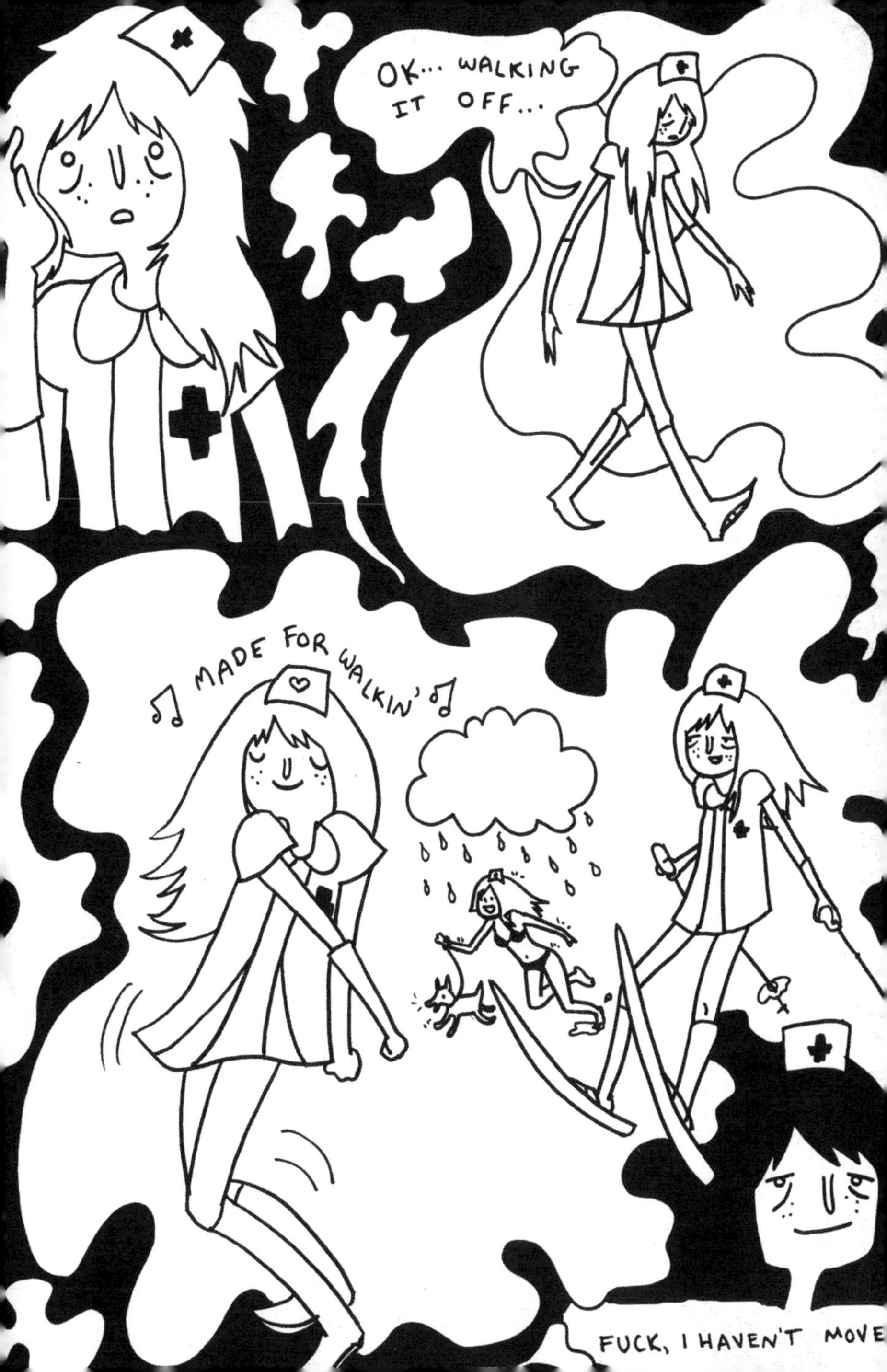
OK... WALKING IT OFF...
♫ MADE FOR WALKIN' ♫
FUCK, I HAVEN'T MOVE

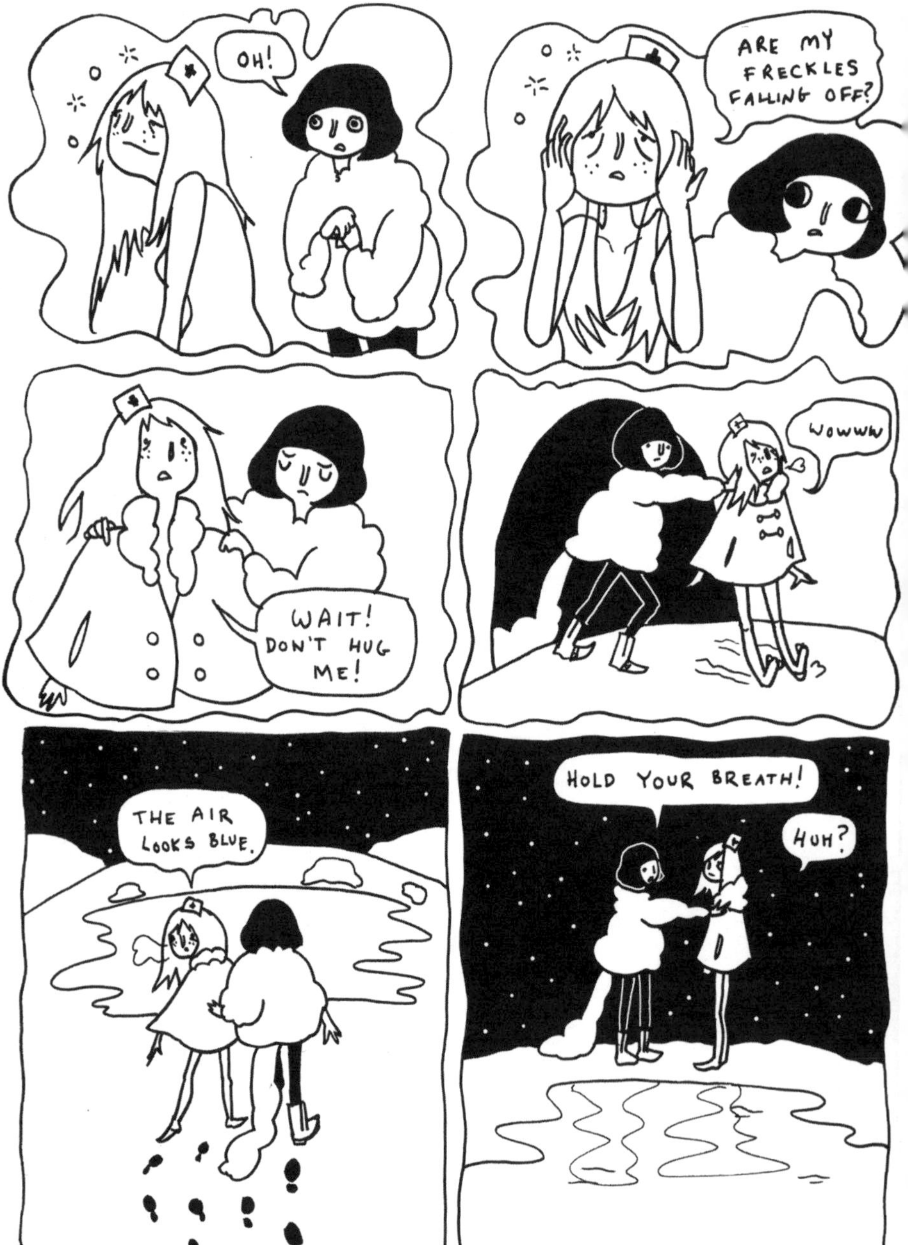
OH!
ARE MY FRECKLES FALLING OFF?
WAIT! DON'T HUG ME!
WOWWW
THE AIR LOOKS BLUE.
HOLD YOUR BREATH!
HUH?

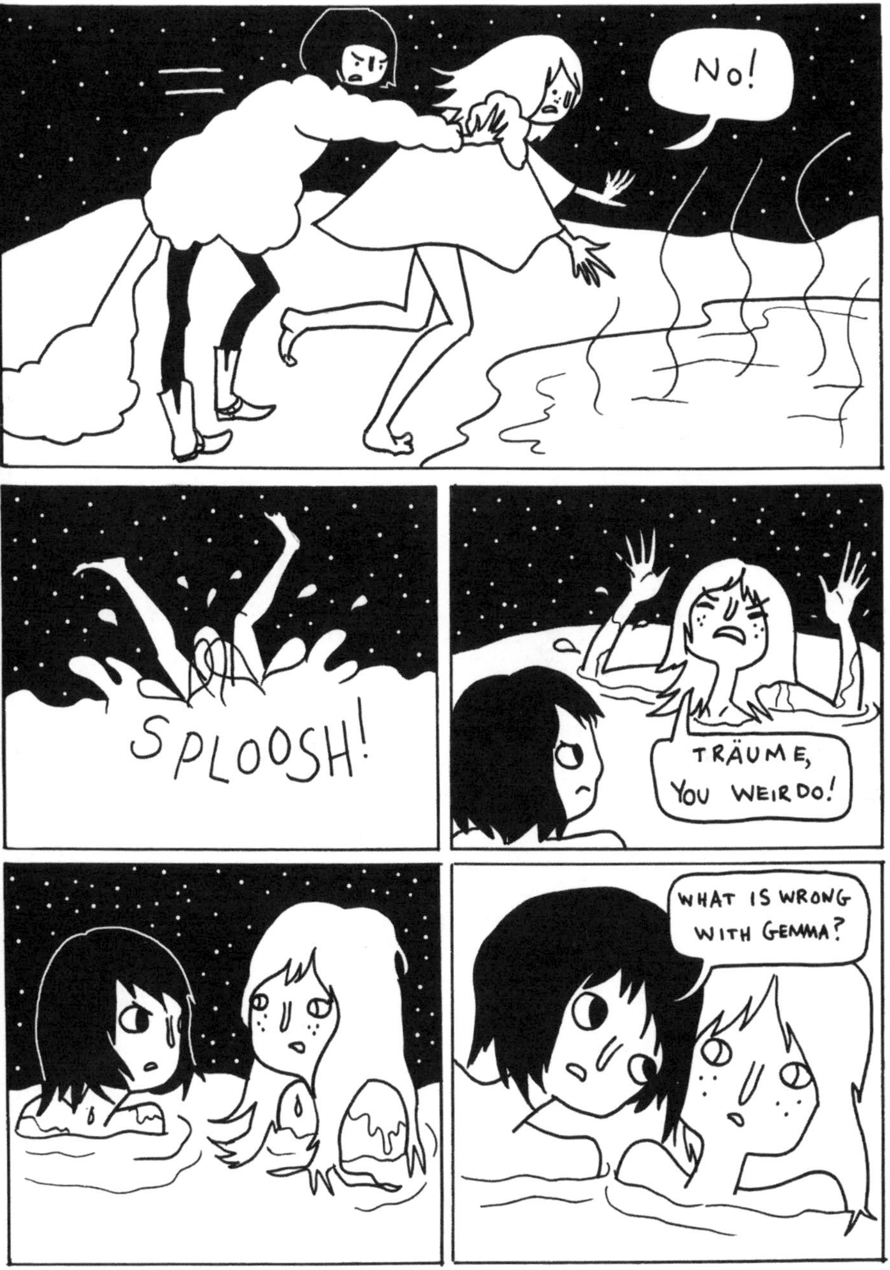
No!
SPLOOSH!
TRÄUME, YOU WEIRDO!
WHAT IS WRONG WITH GEMMA?

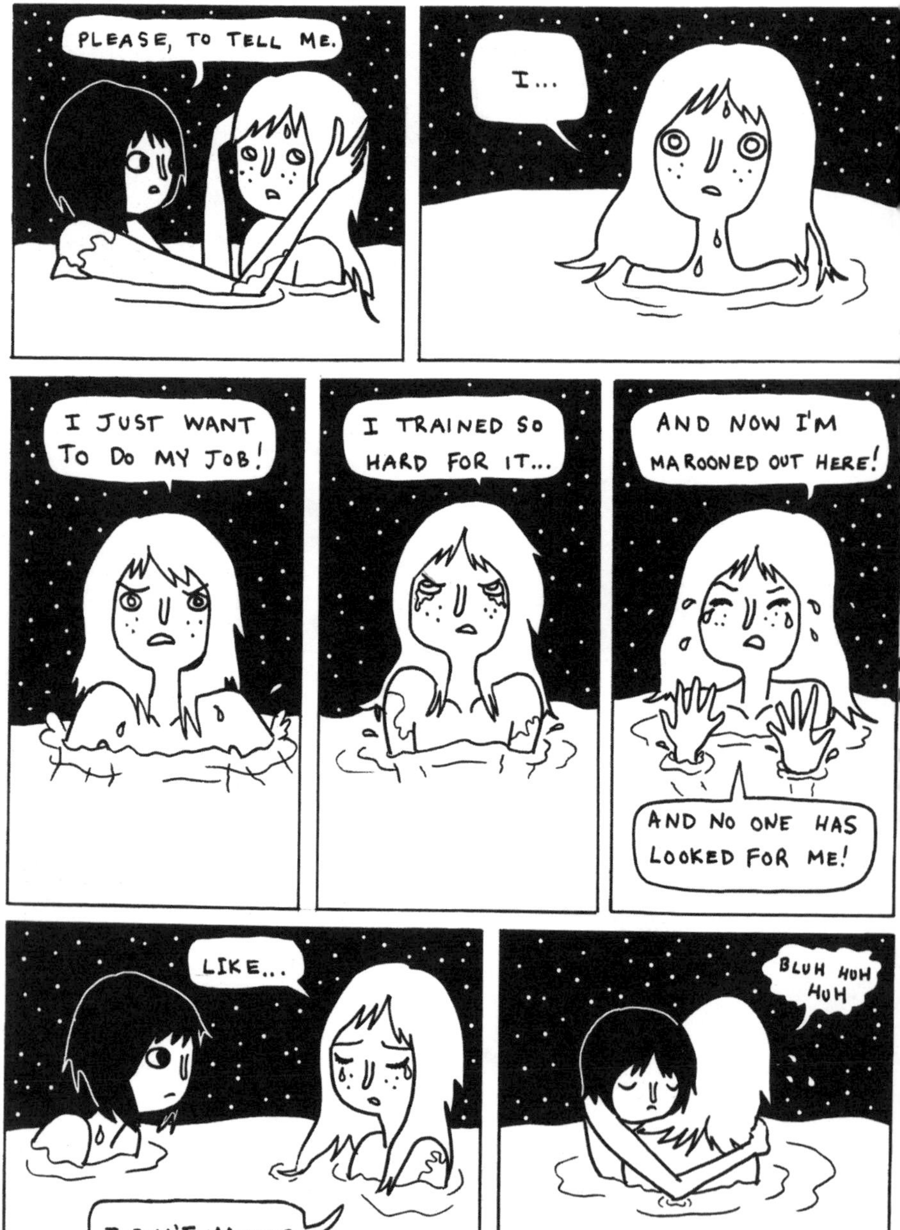
PLEASE, TO TELL ME.
I...
I JUST WANT TO DO MY JOB!
I TRAINED SO HARD FOR IT...
AND NOW I'M MAROONED OUT HERE!
AND NO ONE HAS LOOKED FOR ME!
LIKE...
I DON'T MATTER.
BLUH HUH HUH

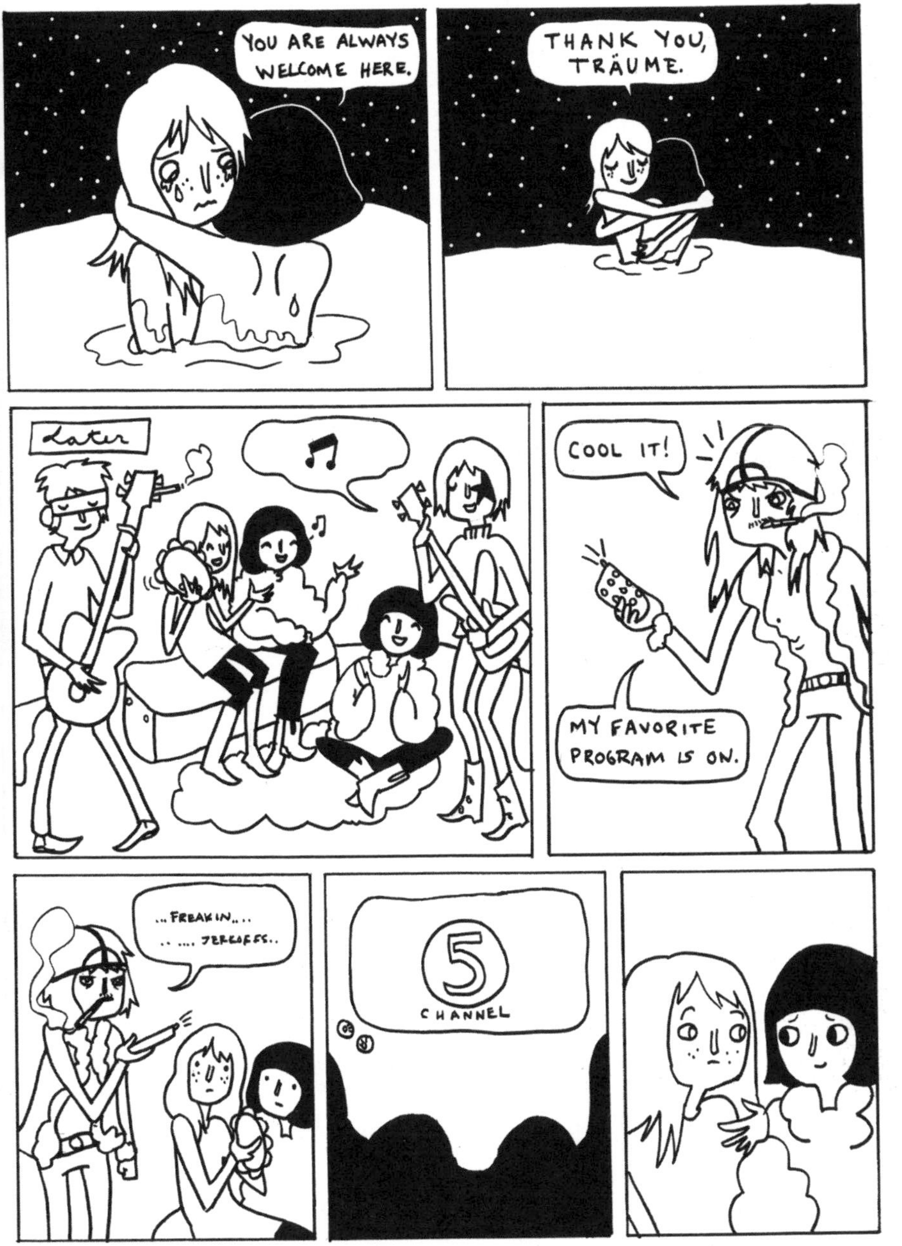
YOU ARE ALWAYS WELCOME HERE.
THANK YOU, TRÄUME.
Later
COOL IT!
MY FAVORITE PROGRAM IS ON.
...FREAKIN...
.. .... JERKOFFS..
5
CHANNEL

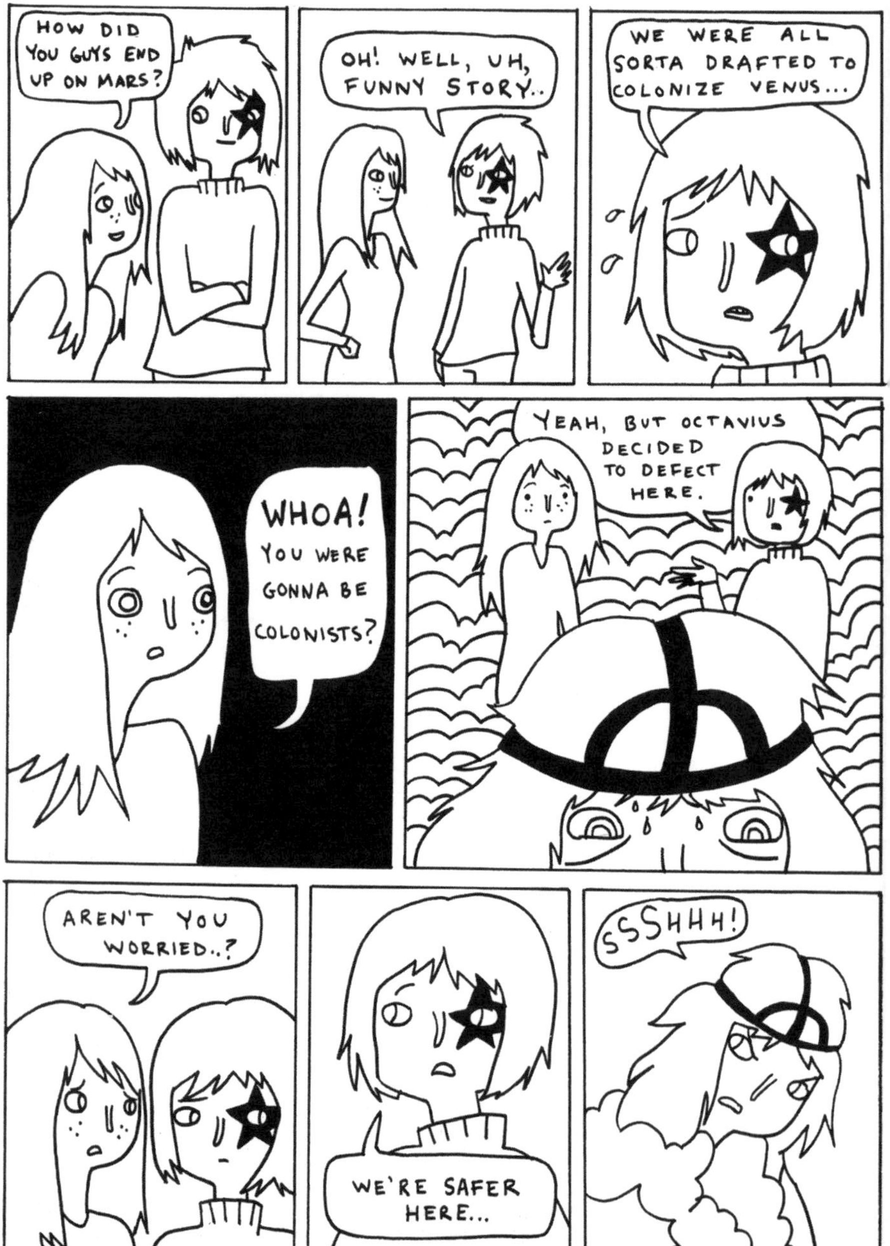
HOW DID YOU GUYS END UP ON MARS?
OH! WELL, UH, FUNNY STORY..
WE WERE ALL SORTA DRAFTED TO COLONIZE VENUS...
WHOA! YOU WERE GONNA BE COLONISTS?
YEAH, BUT OCTAVIUS DECIDED TO DEFECT HERE.
AREN'T YOU WORRIED..?
WE'RE SAFER HERE...
sSSHHH!

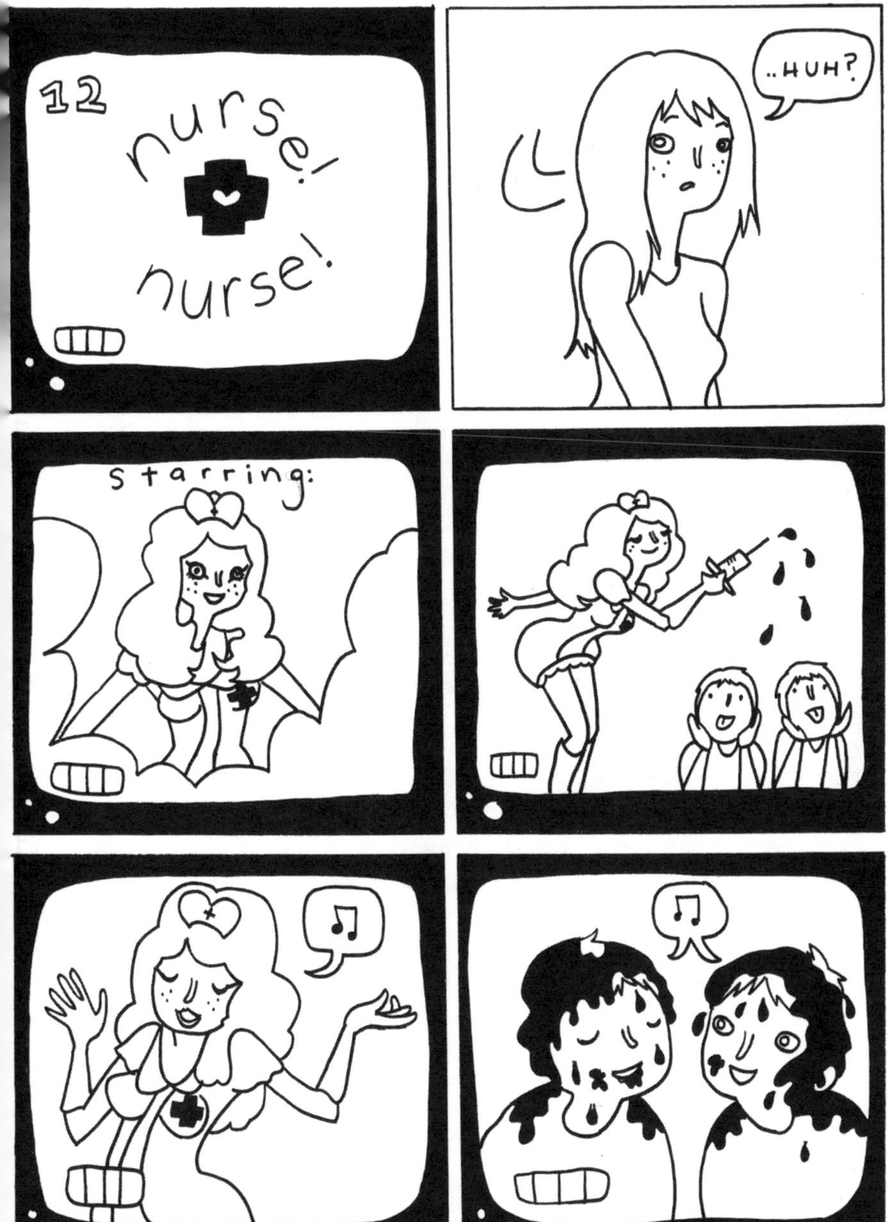
12
nurse!
nurse!
..HUH?
starring:
♫
♫

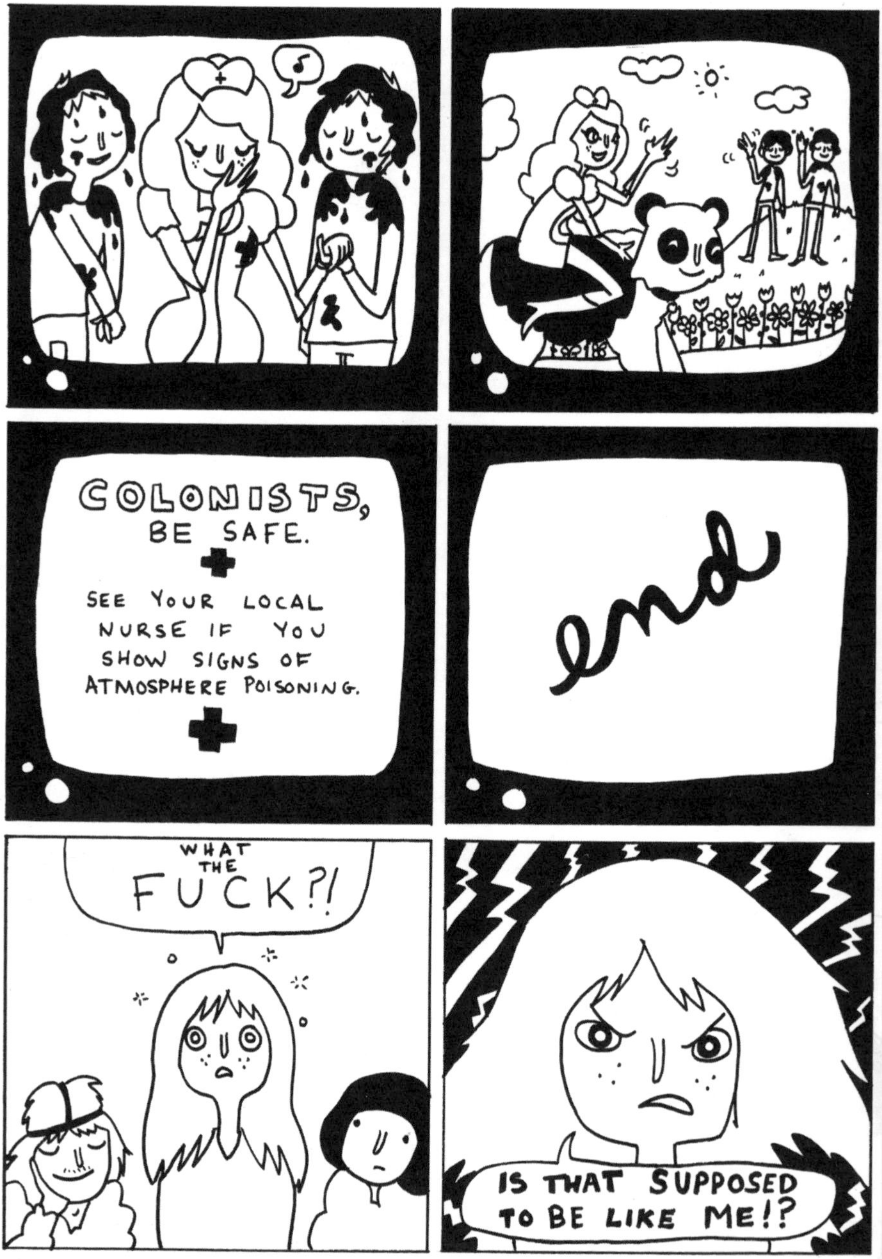
COLONISTS, BE SAFE.
SEE YOUR LOCAL NURSE IF YOU SHOW SIGNS OF ATMOSPHERE POISONING.
end
WHAT THE FUCK?!
IS THAT SUPPOSED TO BE LIKE ME!?

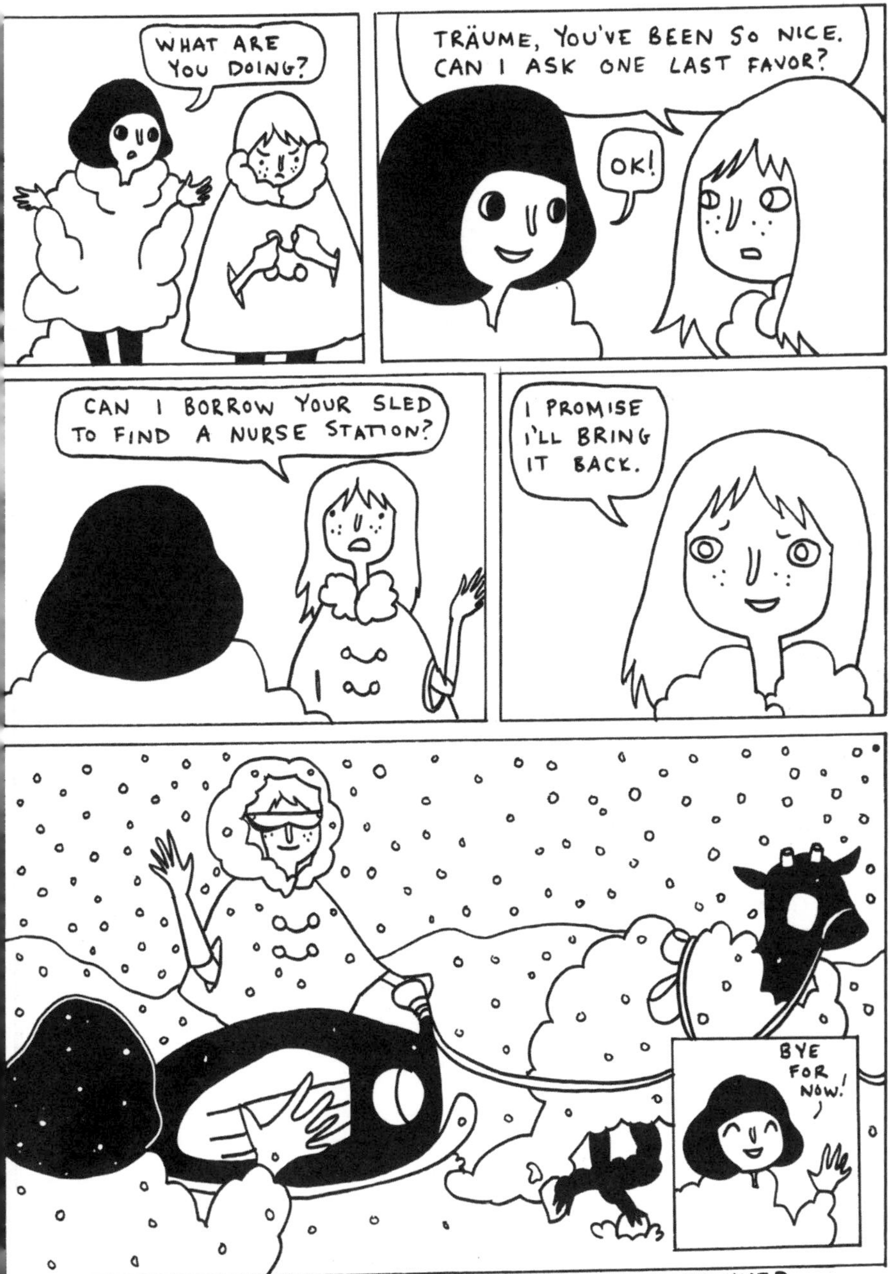
WHAT ARE YOU DOING?
TRÄUME, YOU'VE BEEN SO NICE. CAN I ASK ONE LAST FAVOR?
OK!
CAN I BORROW YOUR SLED TO FIND A NURSE STATION?
I PROMISE I'LL BRING IT BACK.
BYE FOR NOW!

TO BE CONTINUED...

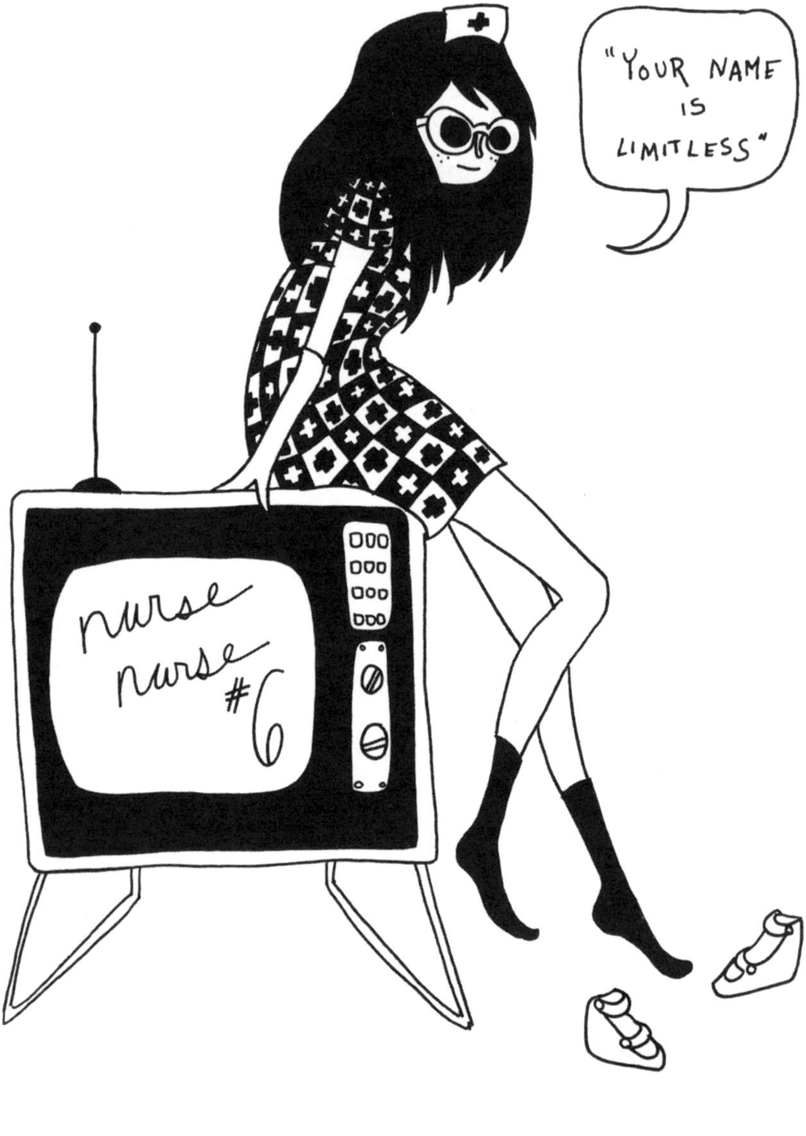
"YOUR NAME IS LIMITLESS"
nurse nurse #6

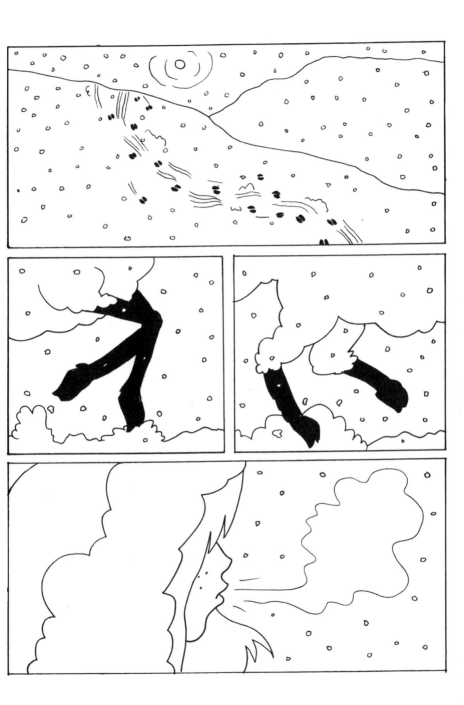

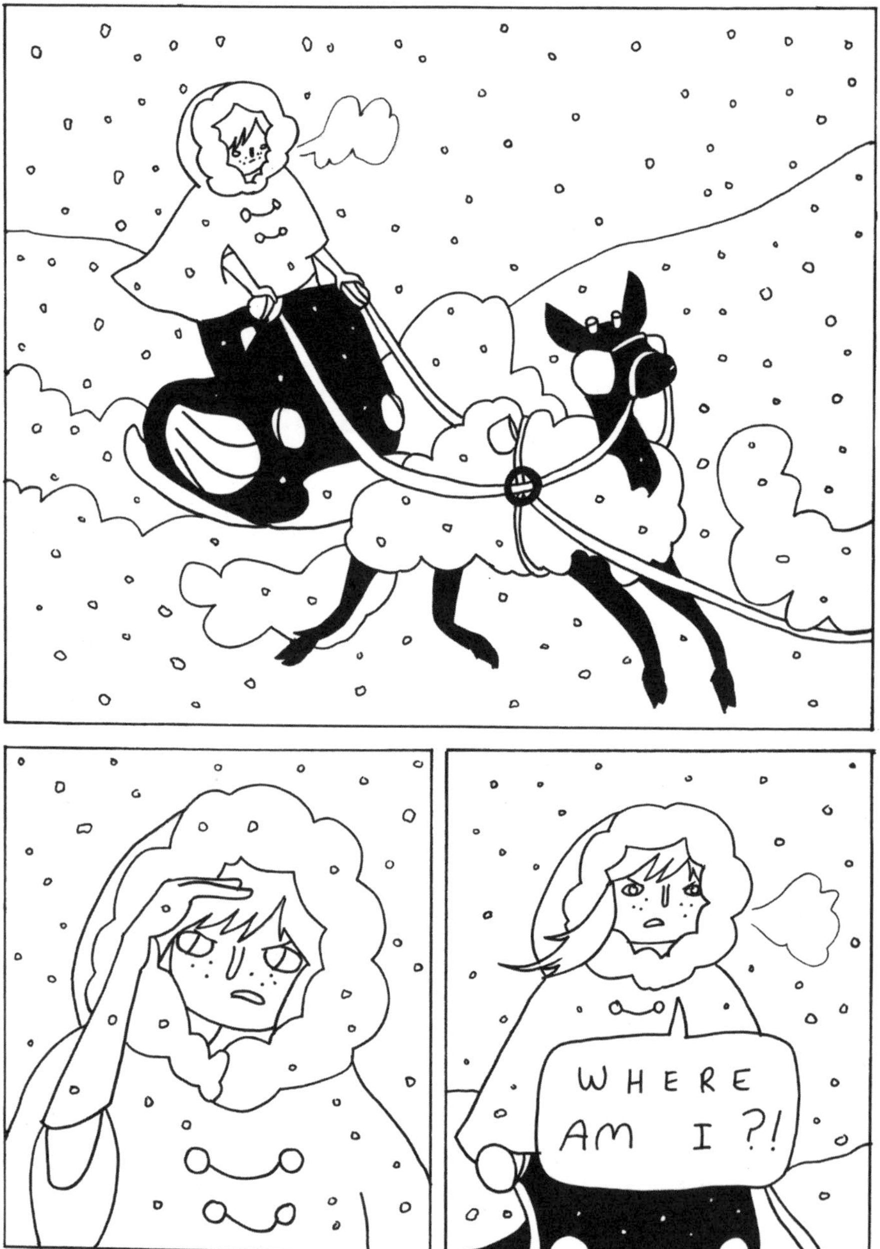
WHERE AM I ?!

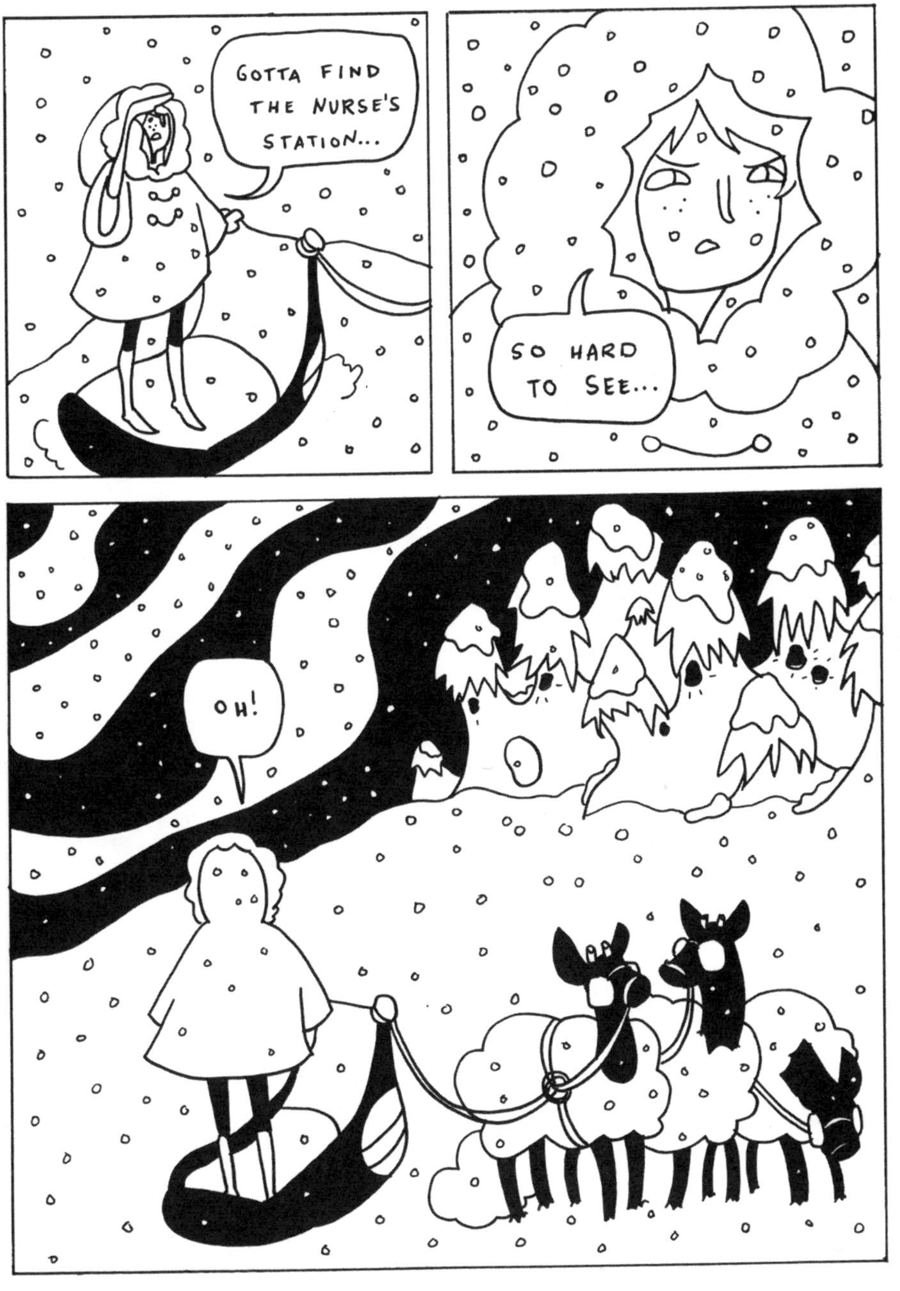
GOTTA FIND THE NURSE'S STATION...
SO HARD TO SEE...
OH!

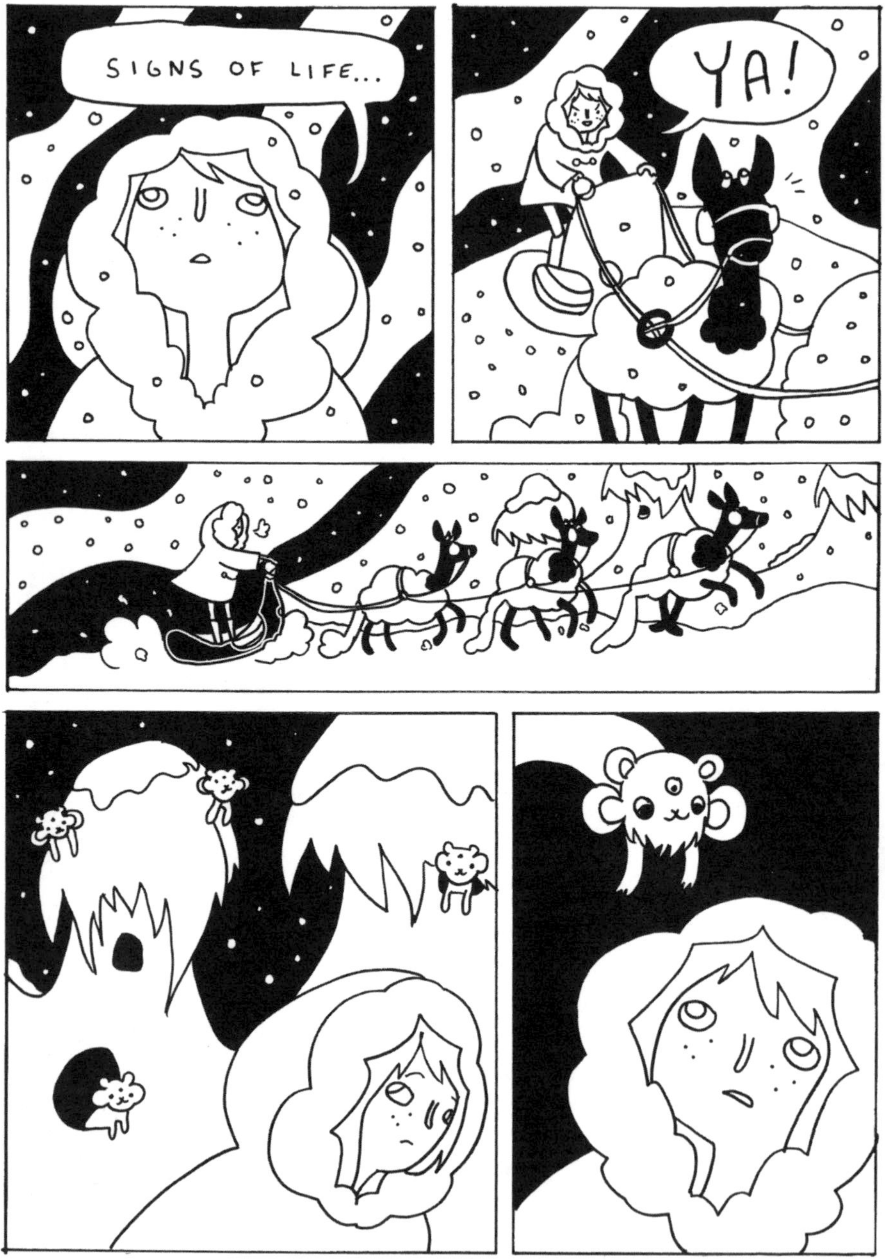
SIGNS OF LIFE...
YA!

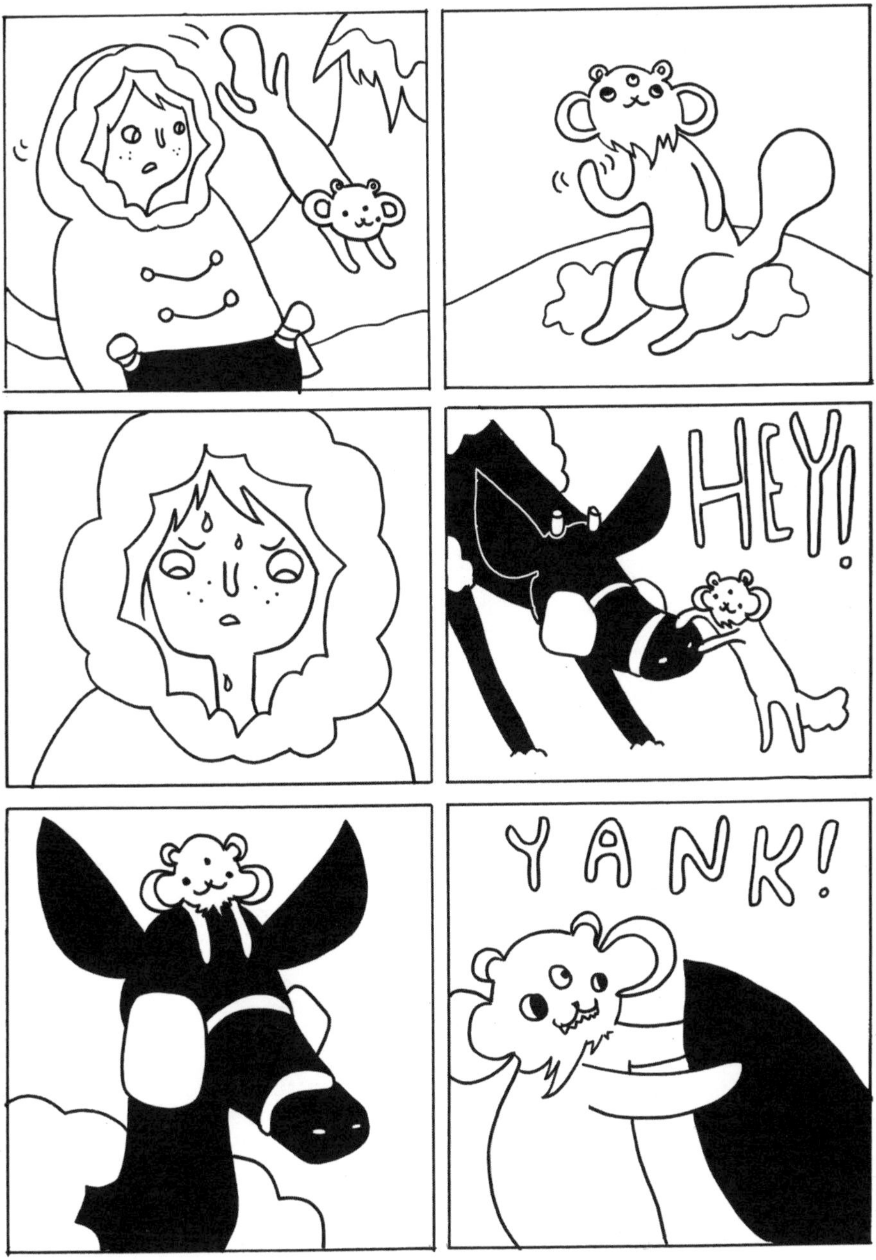
HEY!
YANK!

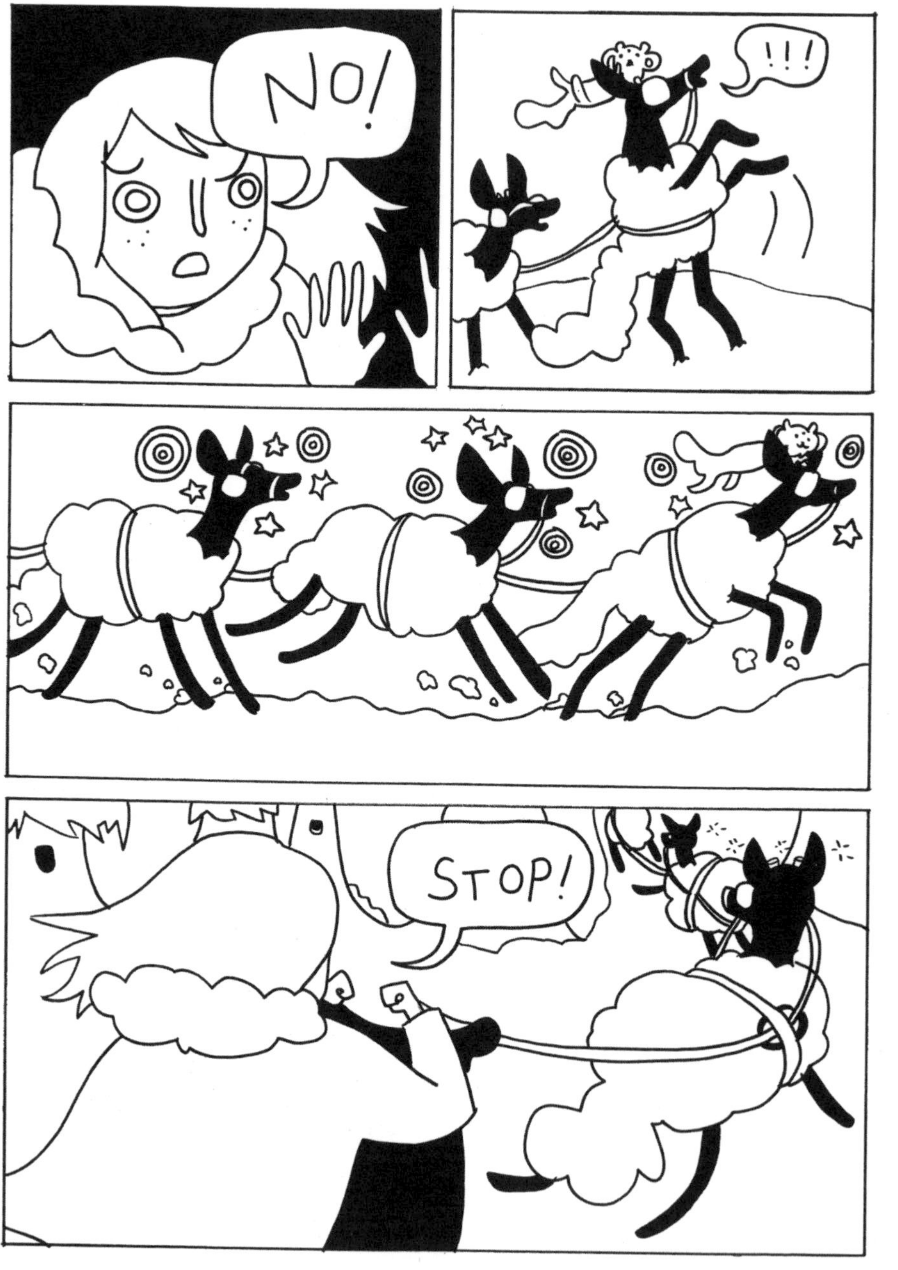
NO!
!!!
STOP!

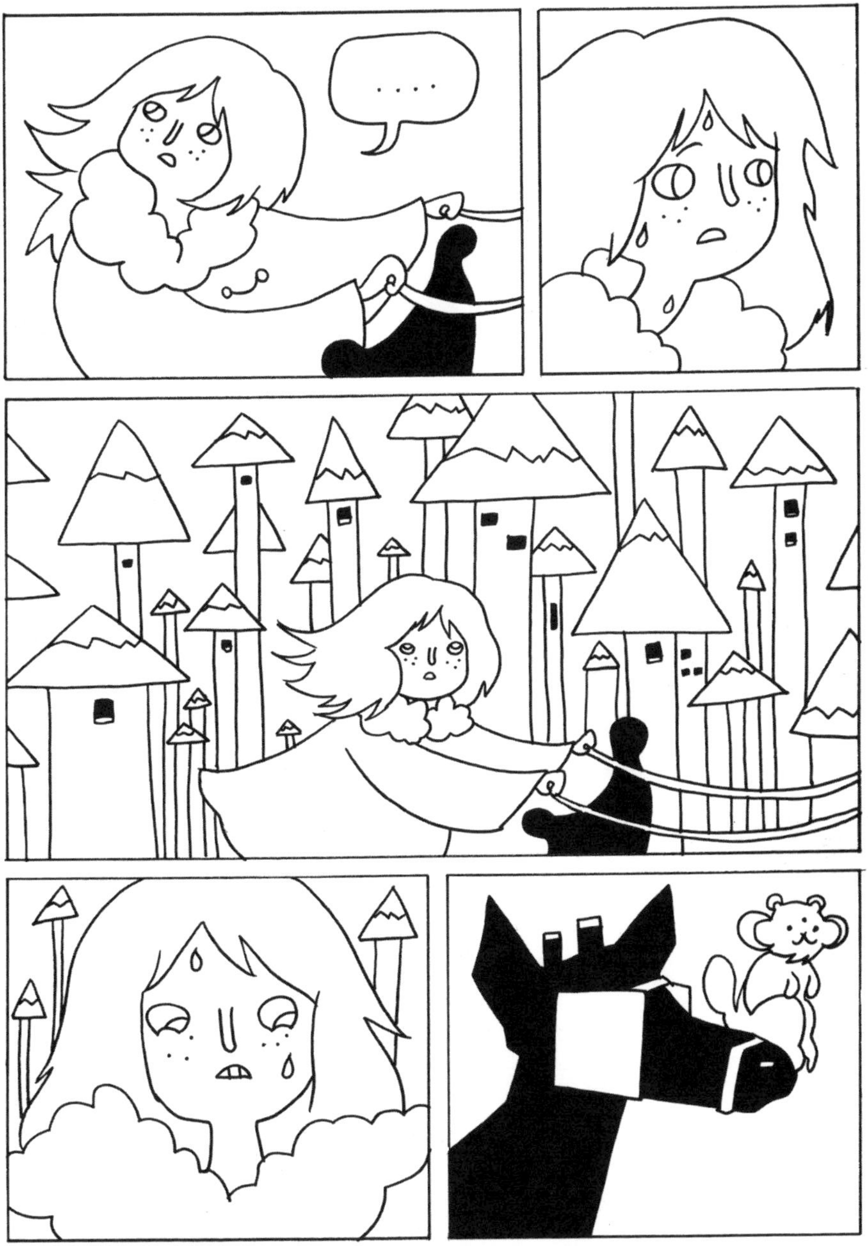
.....

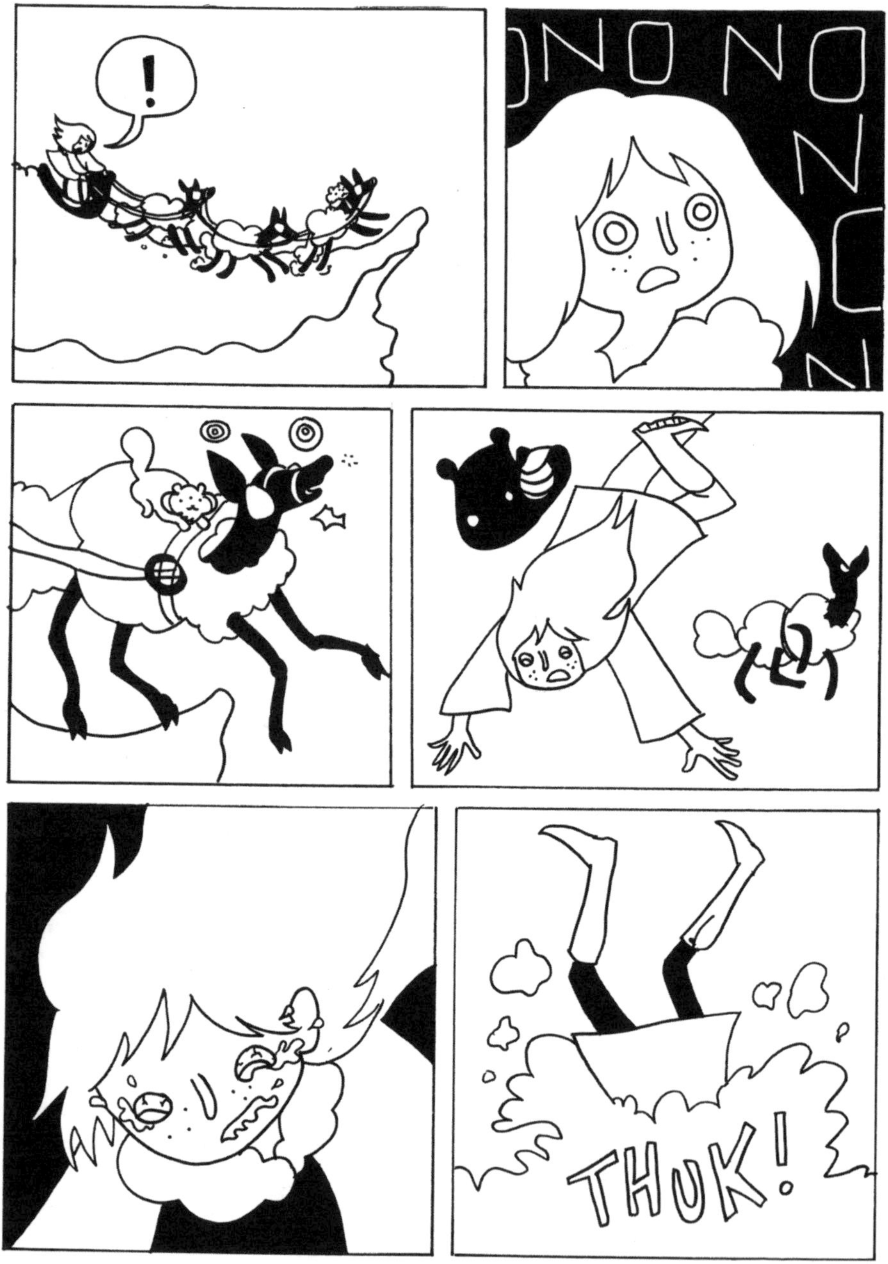
!
ONONONON
THUK!

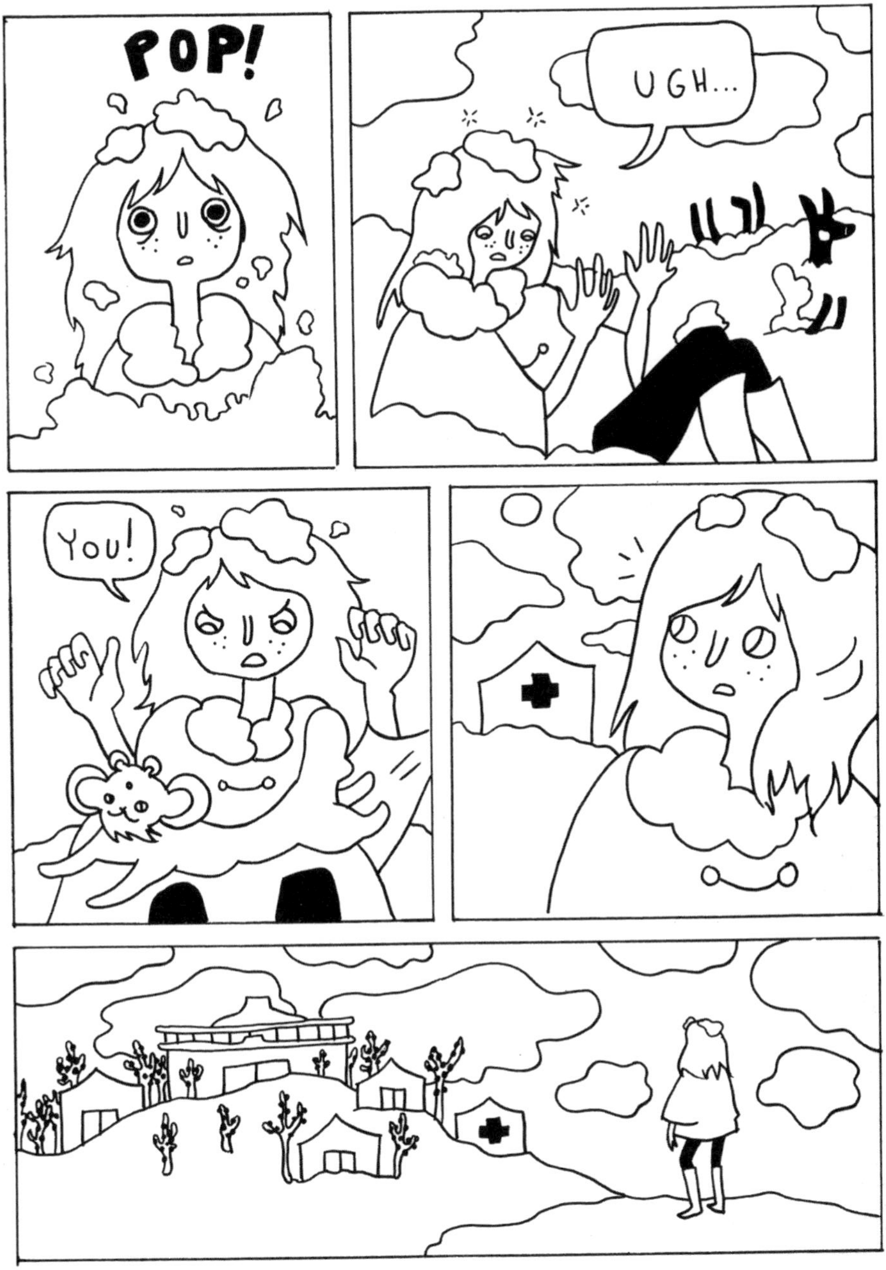
POP!
UGH...
YOU!

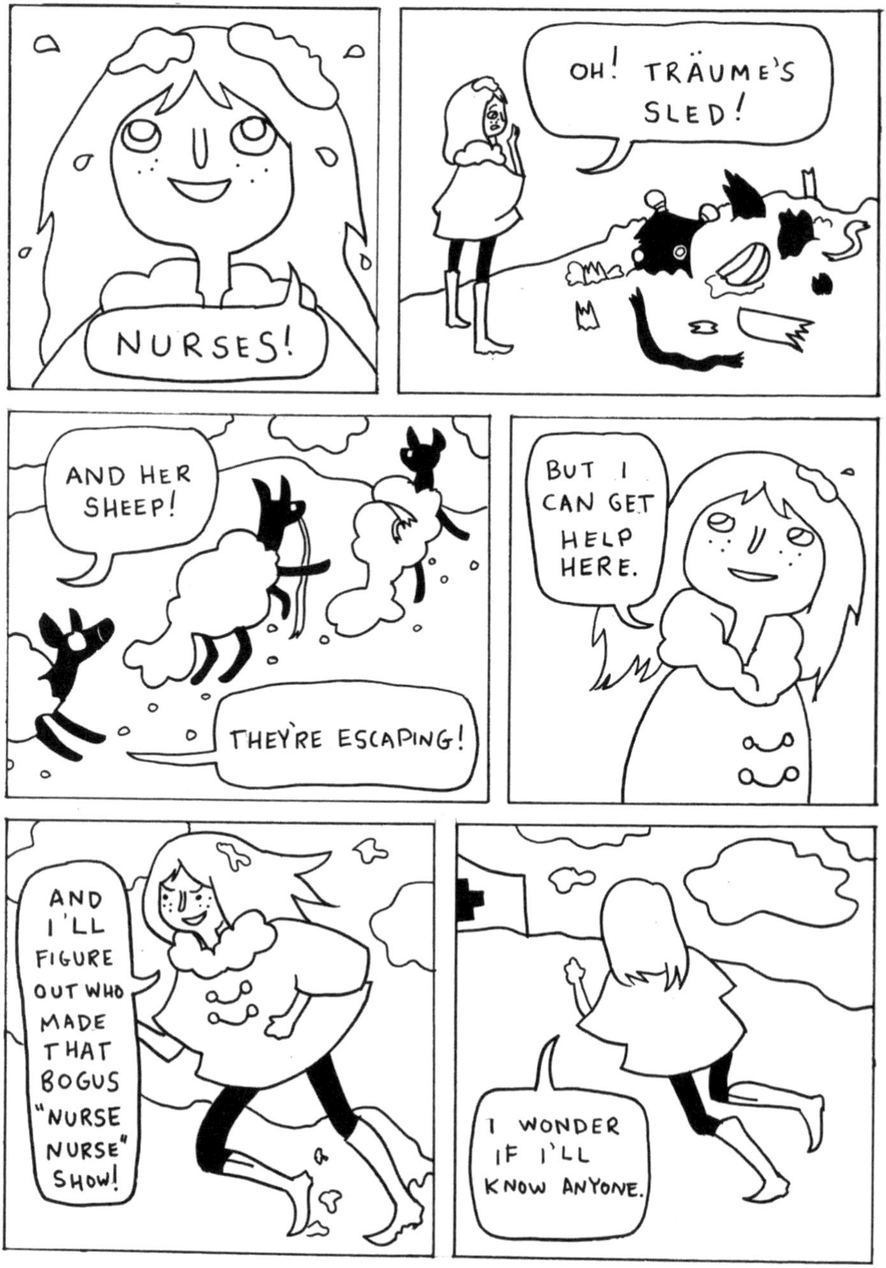
NURSES!
OH! TRÄUME'S SLED!
AND HER SHEEP!
THEY'RE ESCAPING!
BUT I CAN GET HELP HERE.
AND I'LL FIGURE OUT WHO MADE THAT BOGUS "NURSE NURSE" SHOW!
I WONDER IF I'LL KNOW ANYONE.

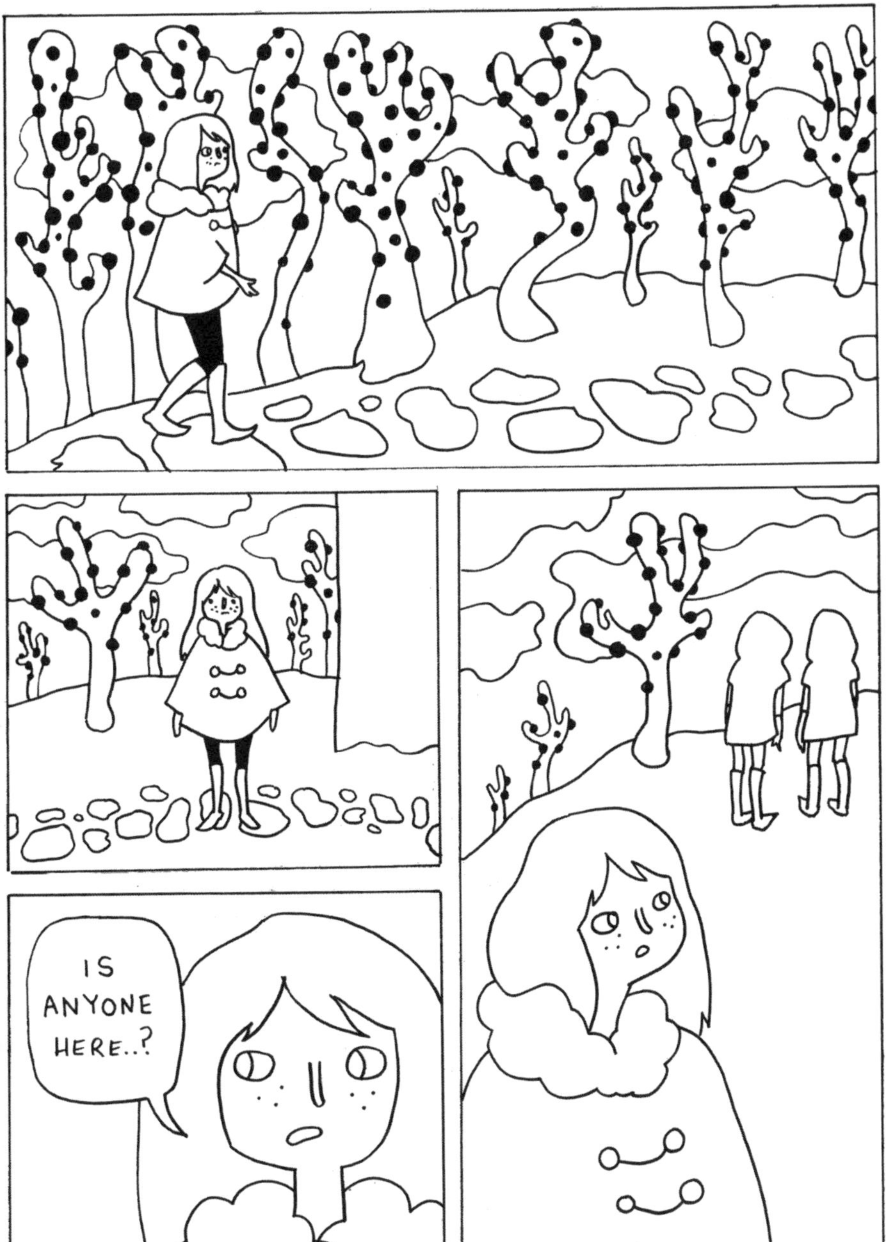
IS ANYONE HERE..?

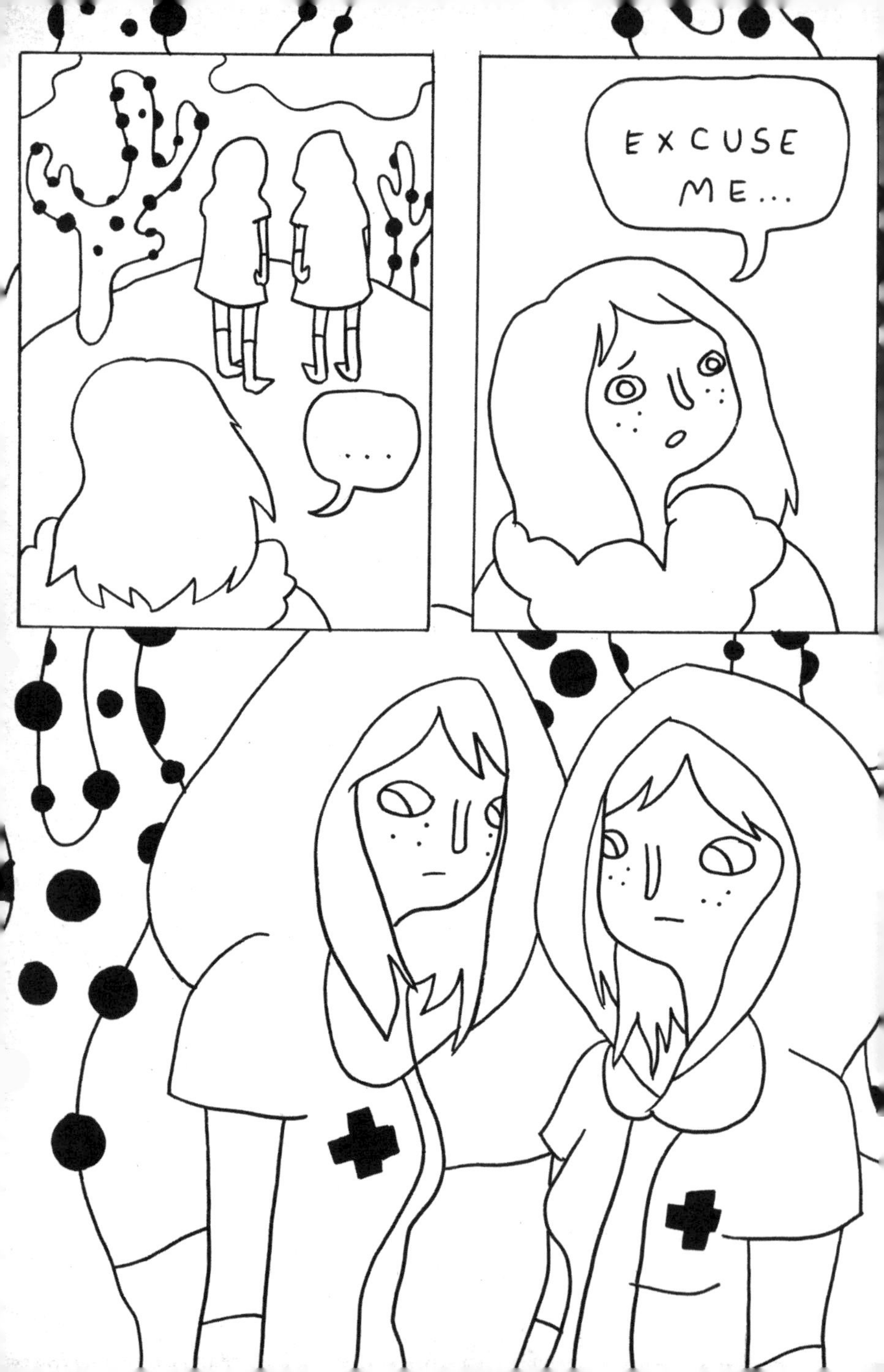
....
EXCUSE ME...

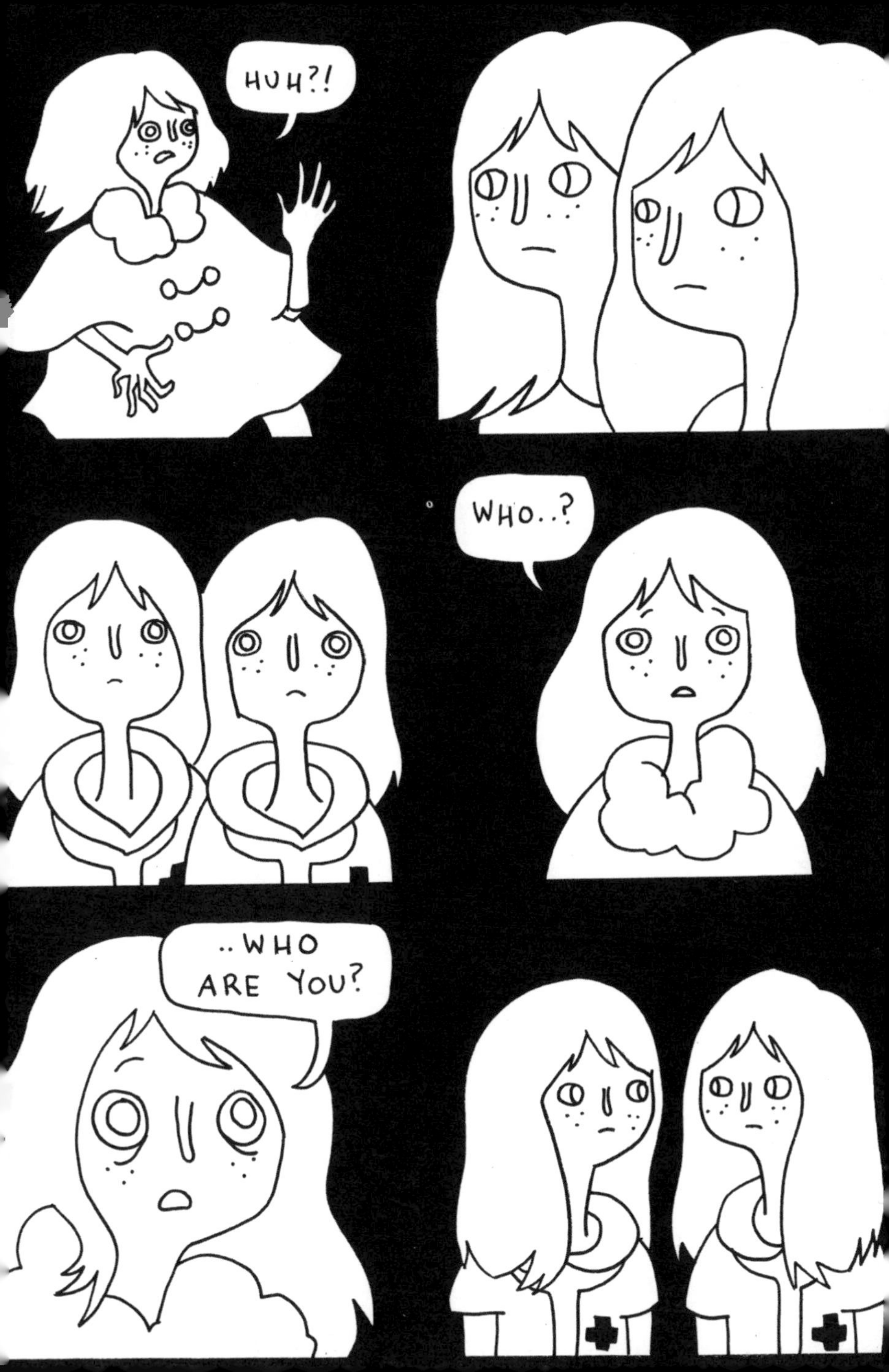
HUH?!
WHO..?
..WHO
ARE YOU?

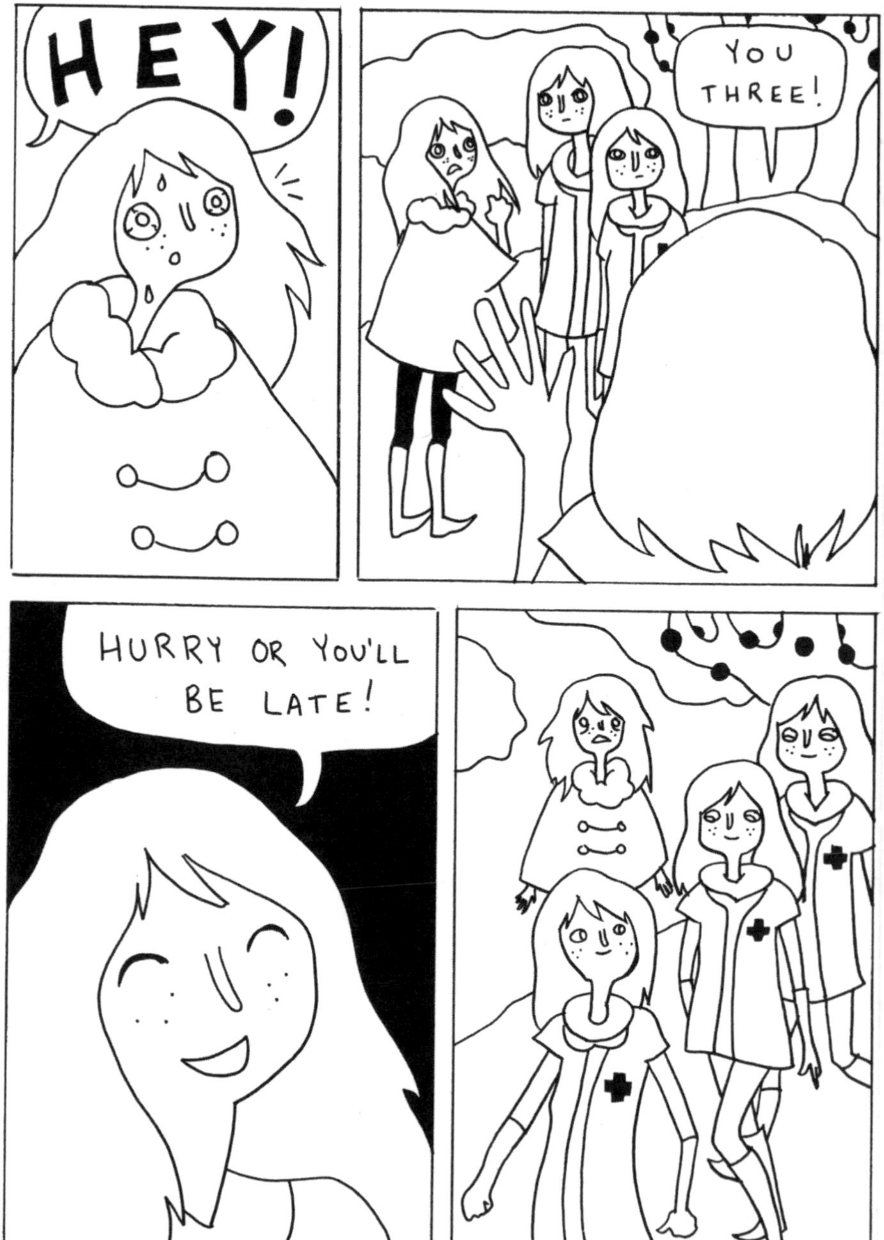
HEY!
YOU THREE!
HURRY OR YOU'LL BE LATE!

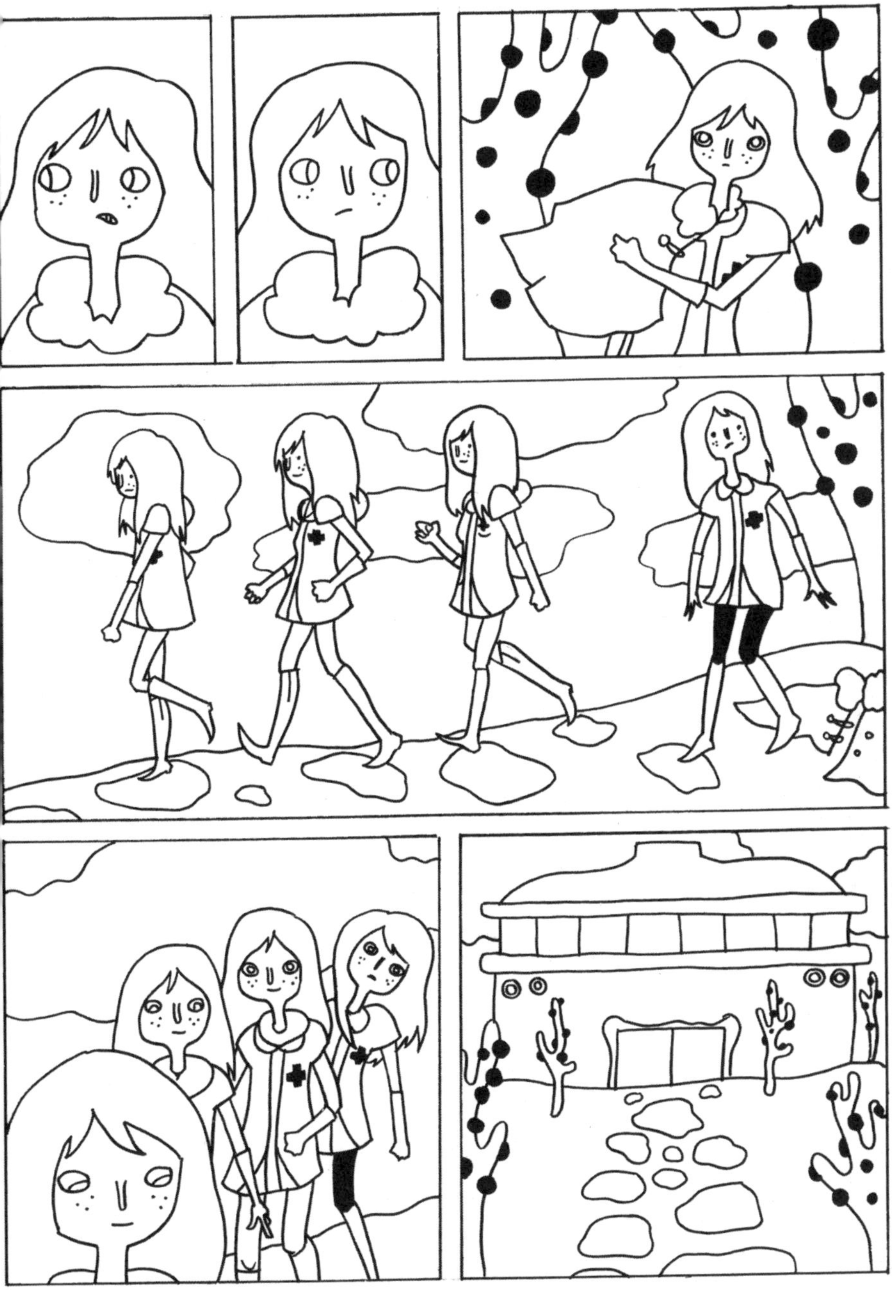

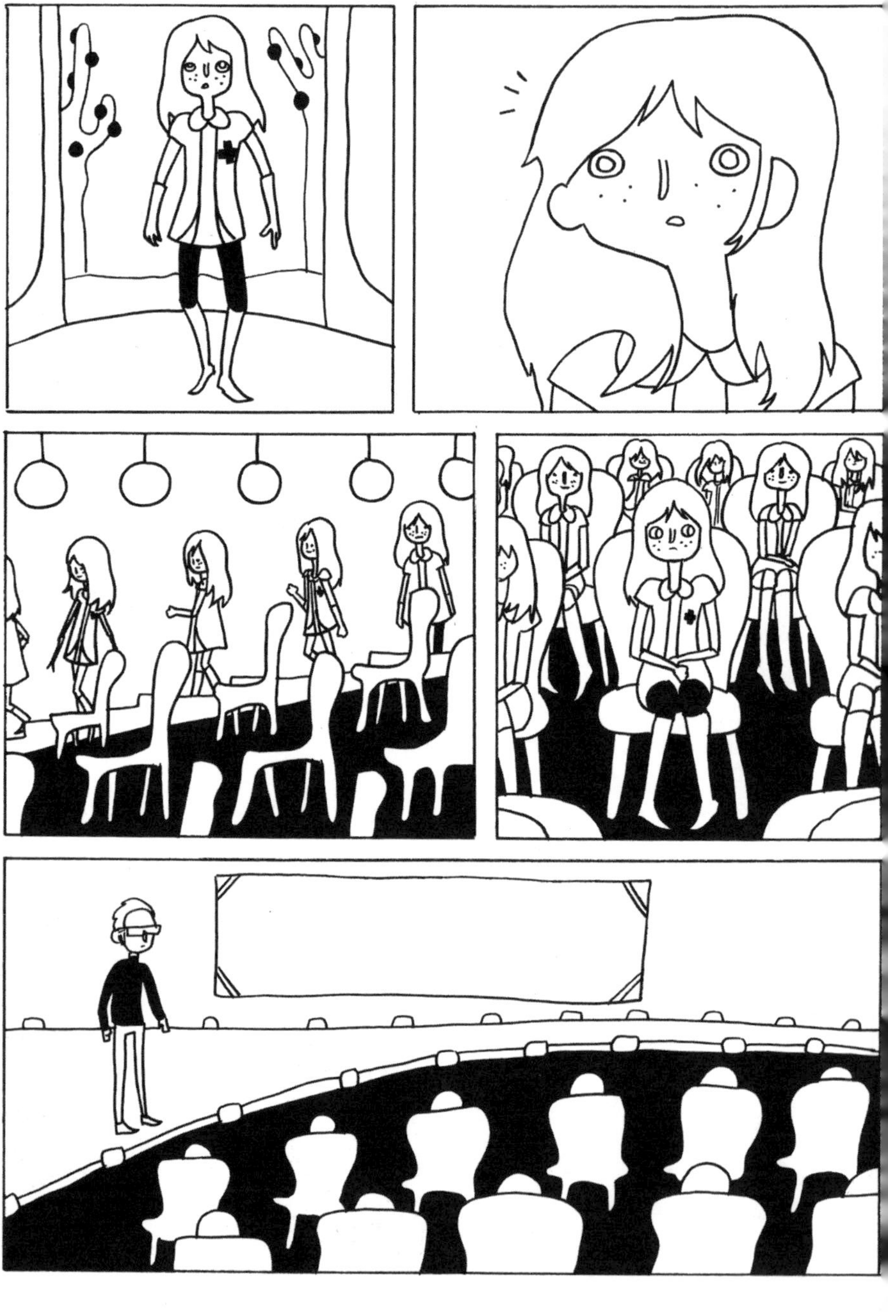

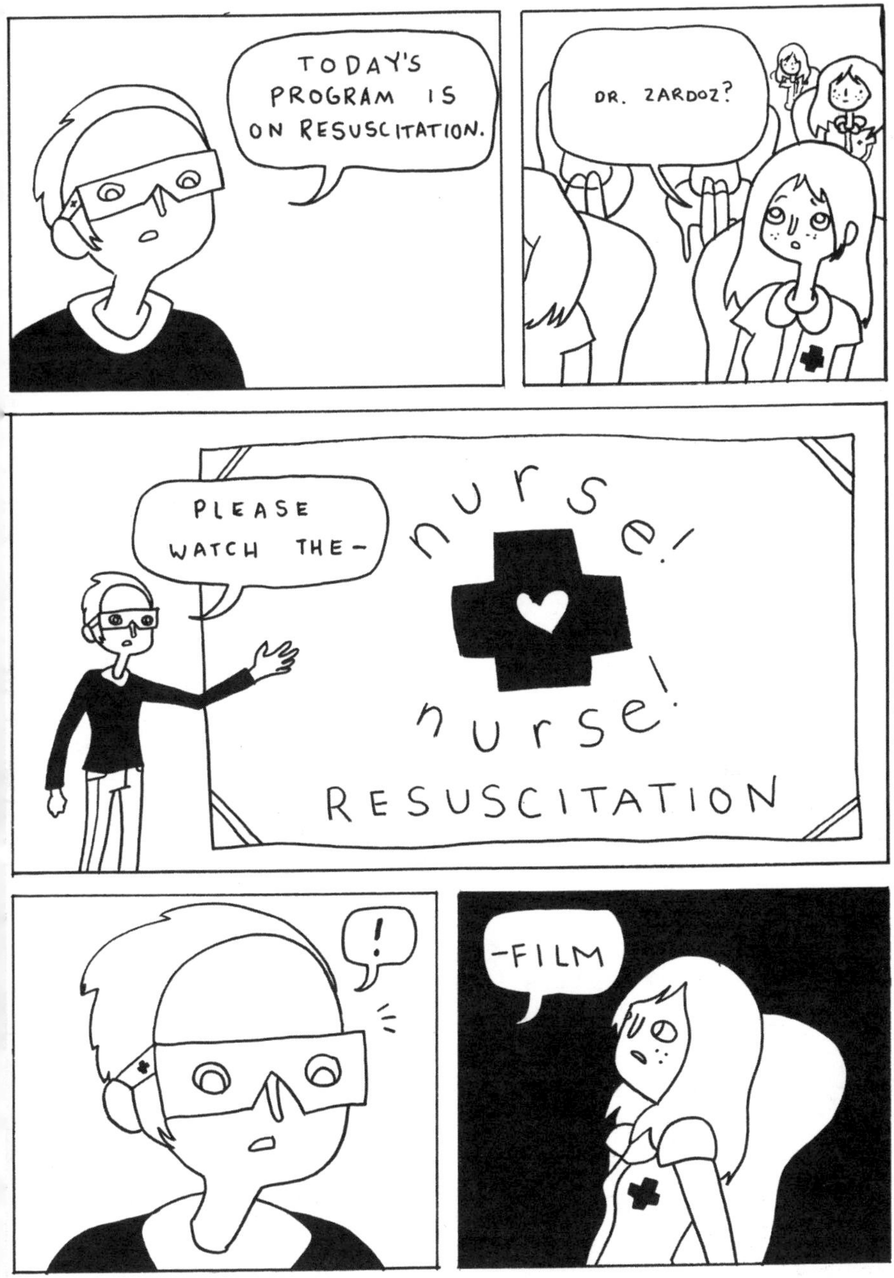
TODAY'S PROGRAM IS ON RESUSCITATION.
DR. ZARDOZ?
PLEASE WATCH THE-
nurse! nurse! RESUSCITATION
!
-FILM

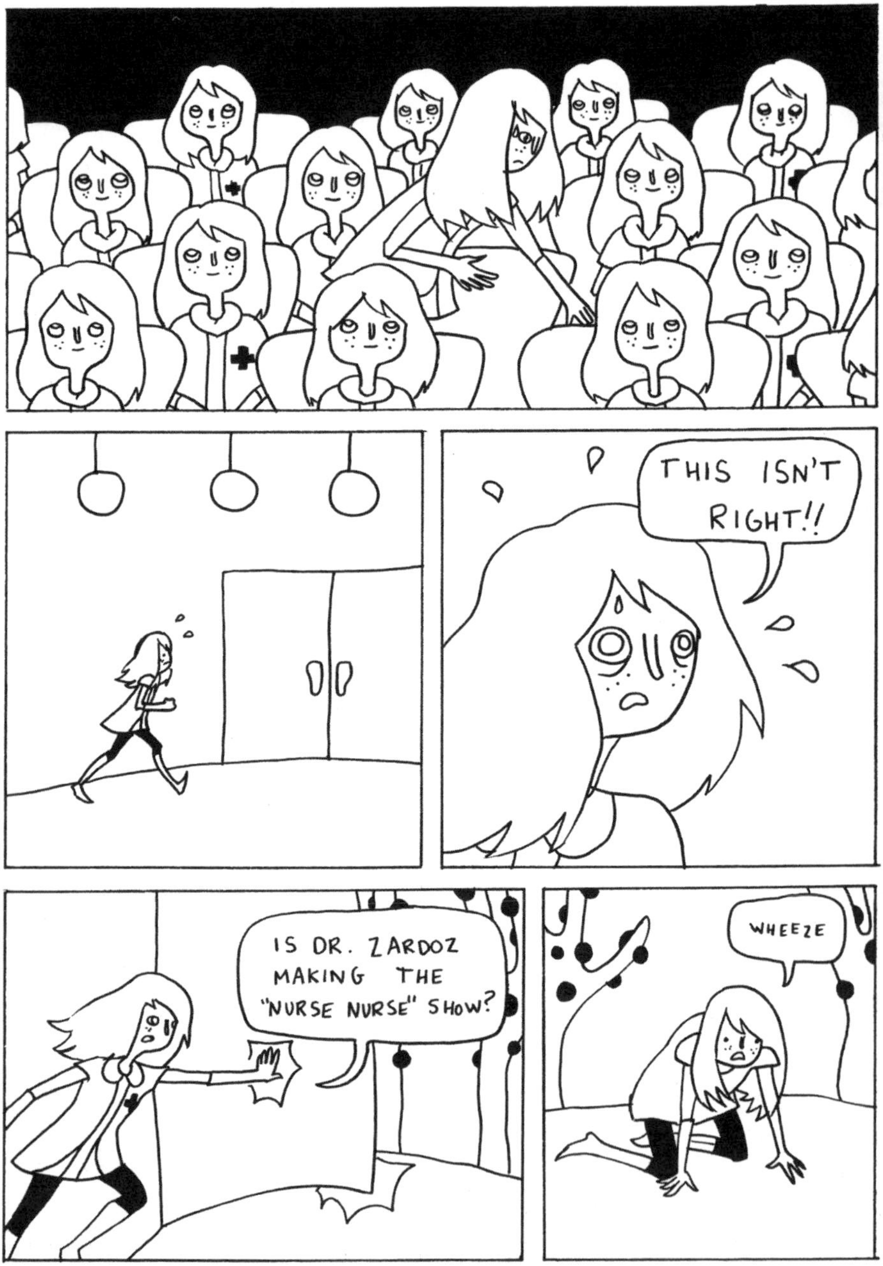
THIS ISN'T RIGHT!!
IS DR. ZARDOZ MAKING THE "NURSE NURSE" SHOW?
WHEEZE

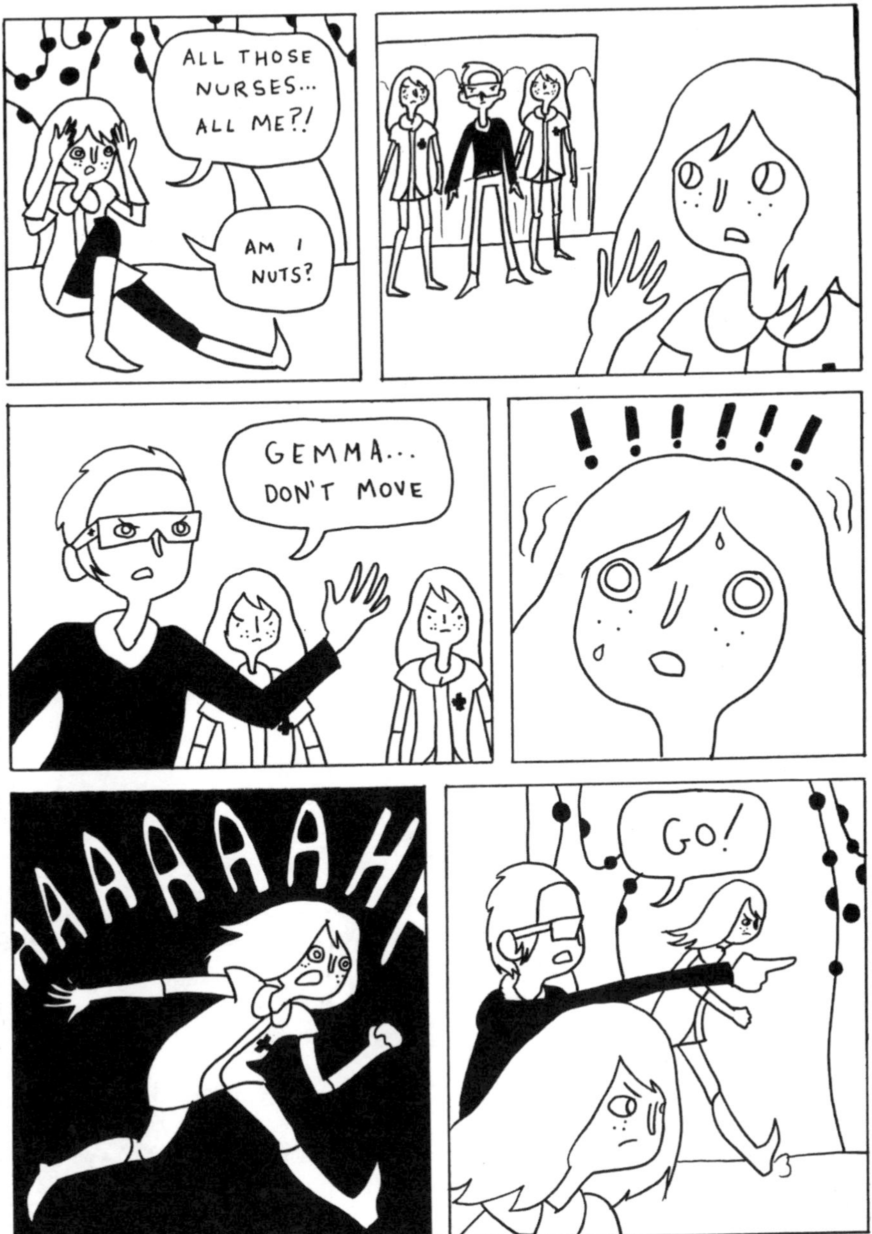
ALL THOSE NURSES... ALL ME?!
AM I NUTS?
GEMMA... DON'T MOVE
!!!!!!
AAAAAAH
GO!

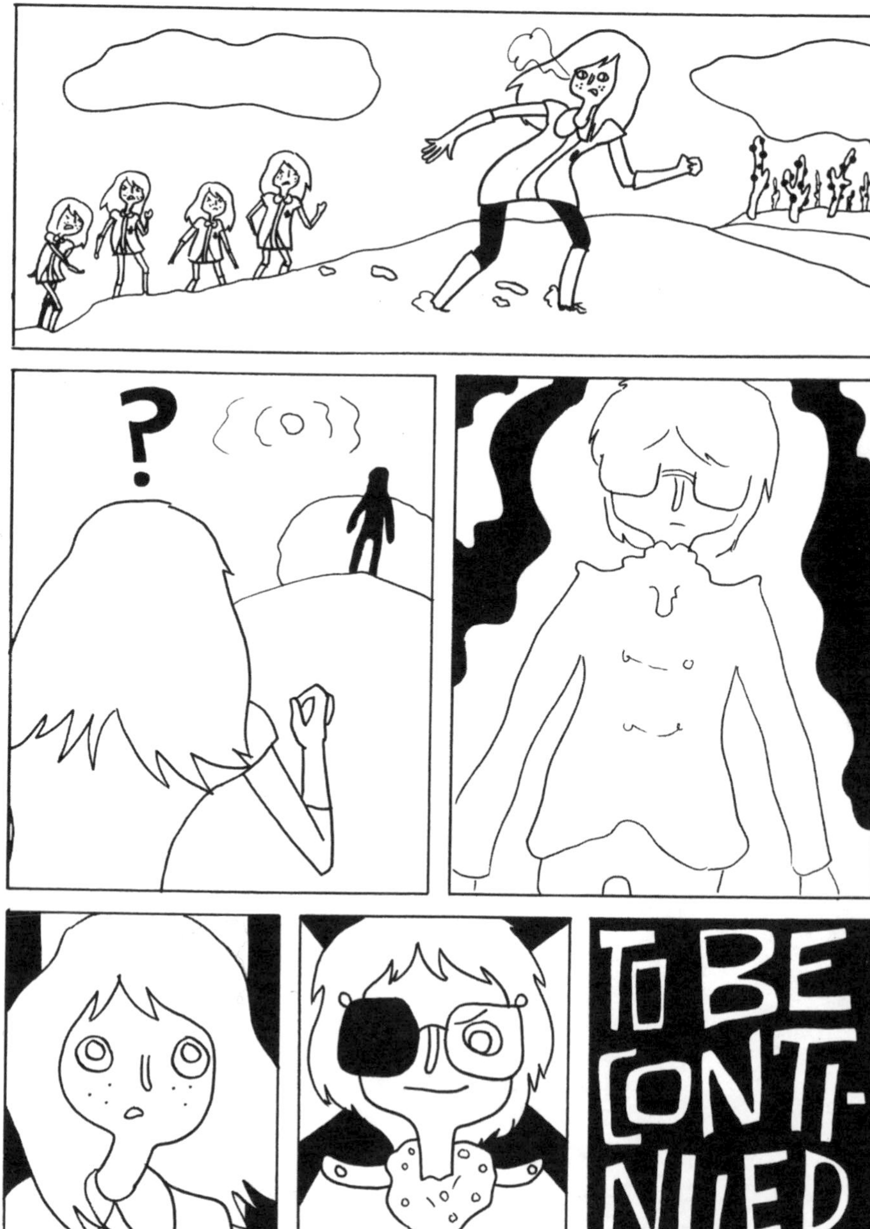
?
TO BE CONTI-NUED.

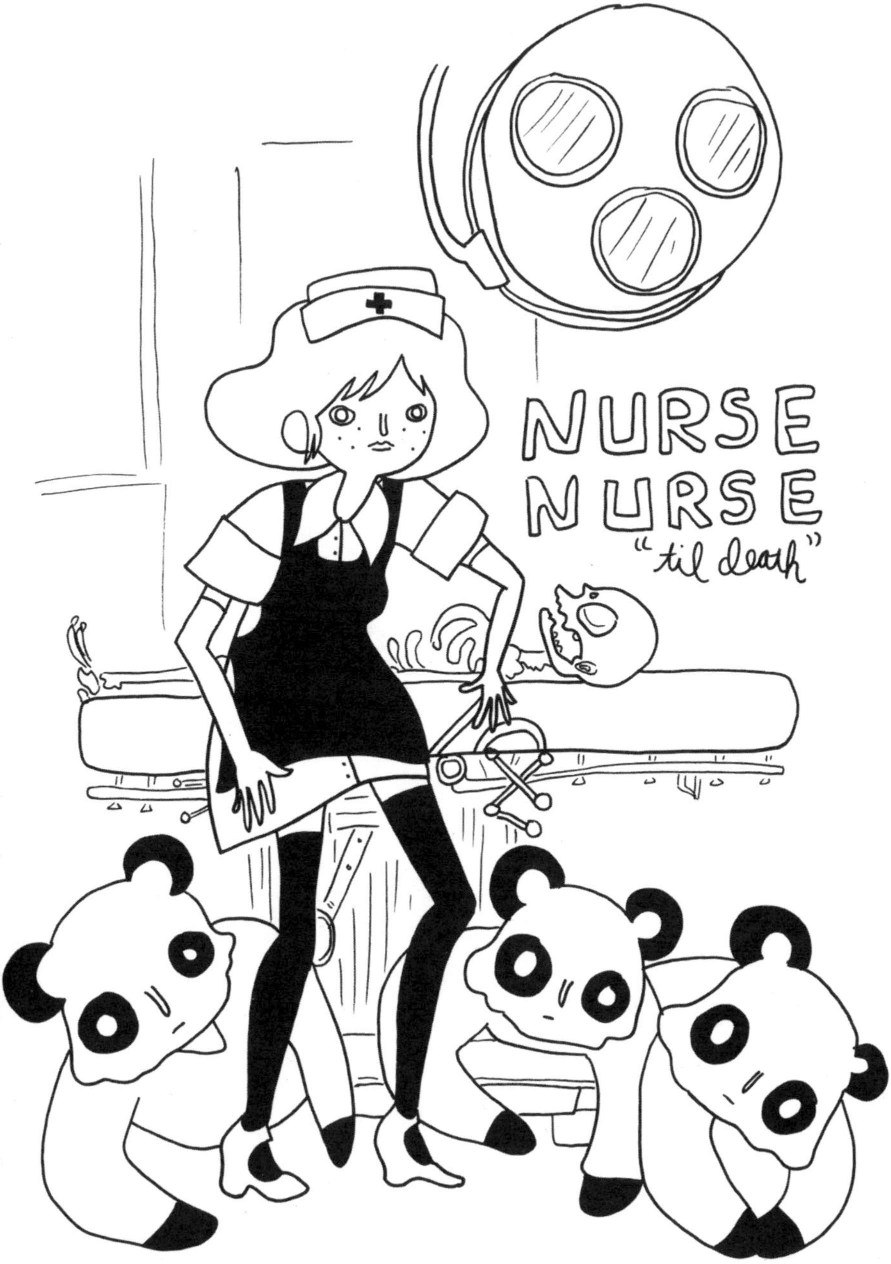
NURSE
NURSE
"til death"

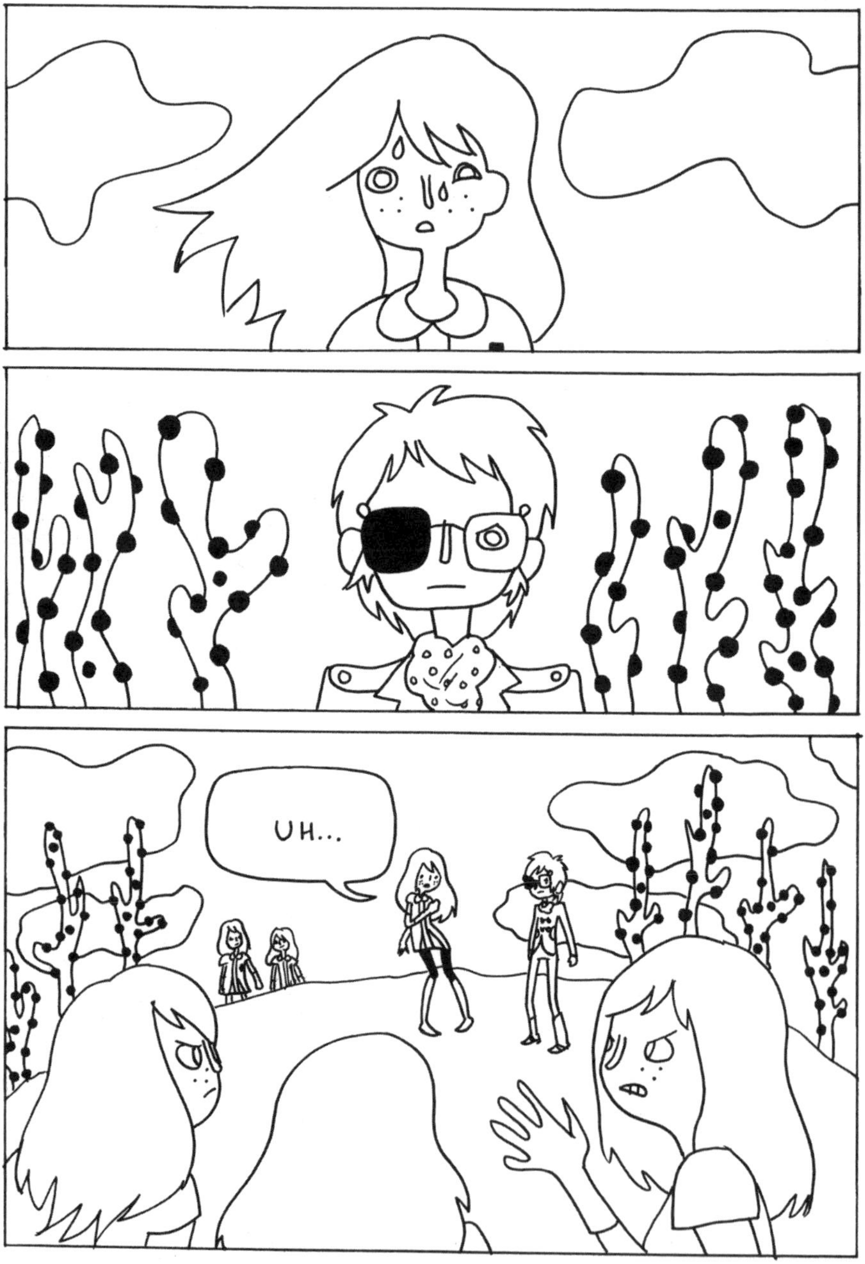
UH...

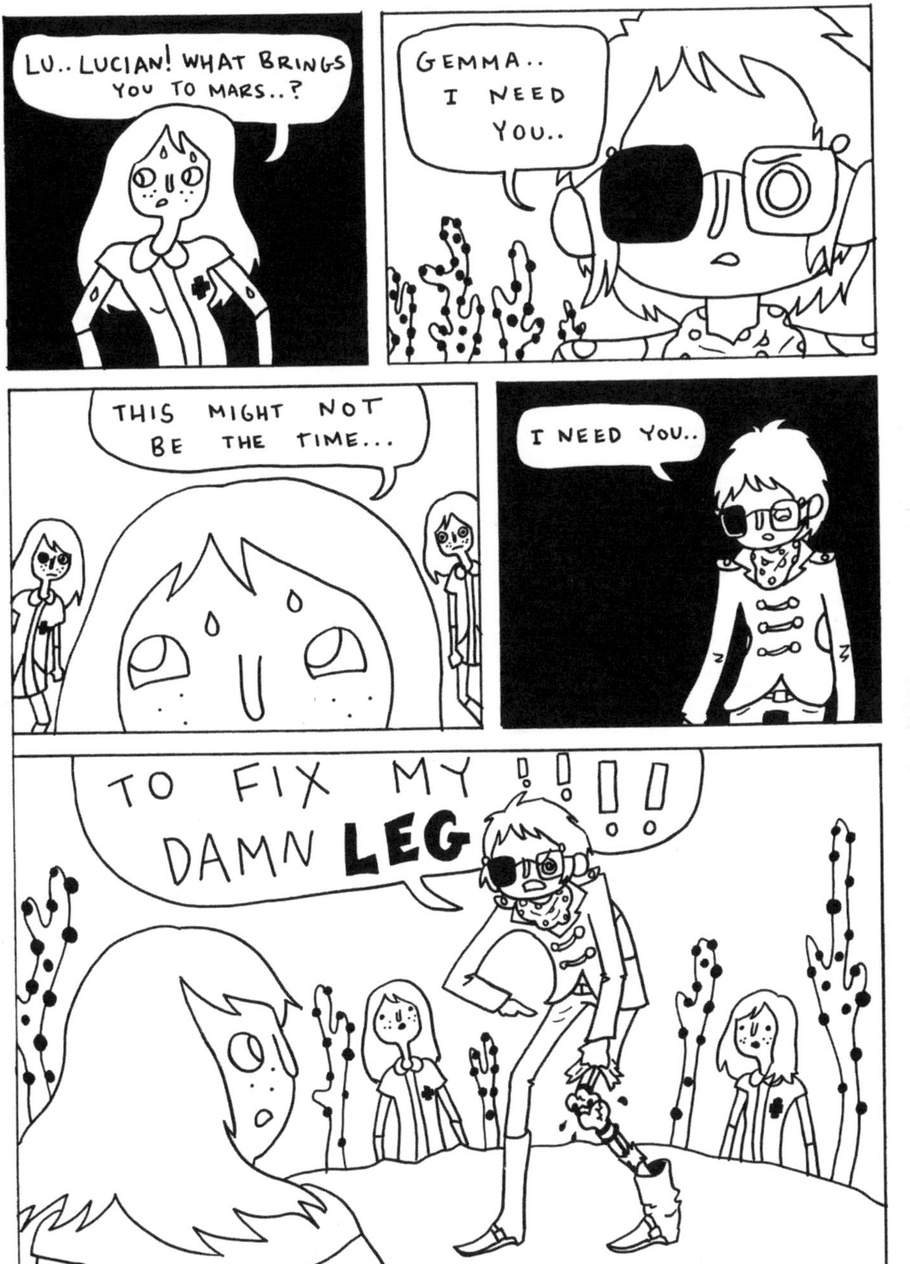
LU.. LUCIAN! WHAT BRINGS YOU TO MARS..?
GEMMA.. I NEED YOU..
THIS MIGHT NOT BE THE TIME...
I NEED YOU..
TO FIX MY DAMN LEG!!!!

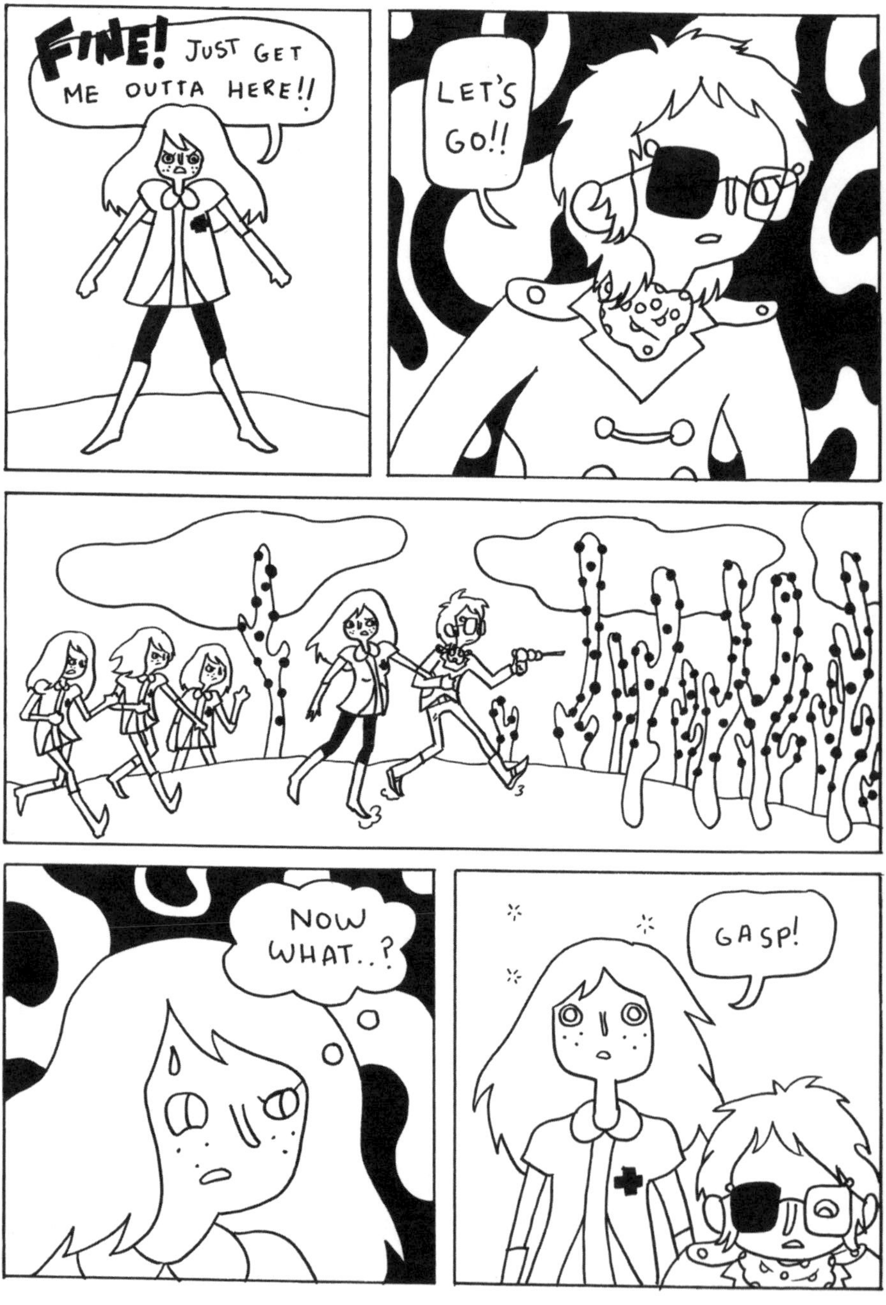
FINE! JUST GET ME OUTTA HERE!!
LET'S GO!!
NOW WHAT..?
GASP!

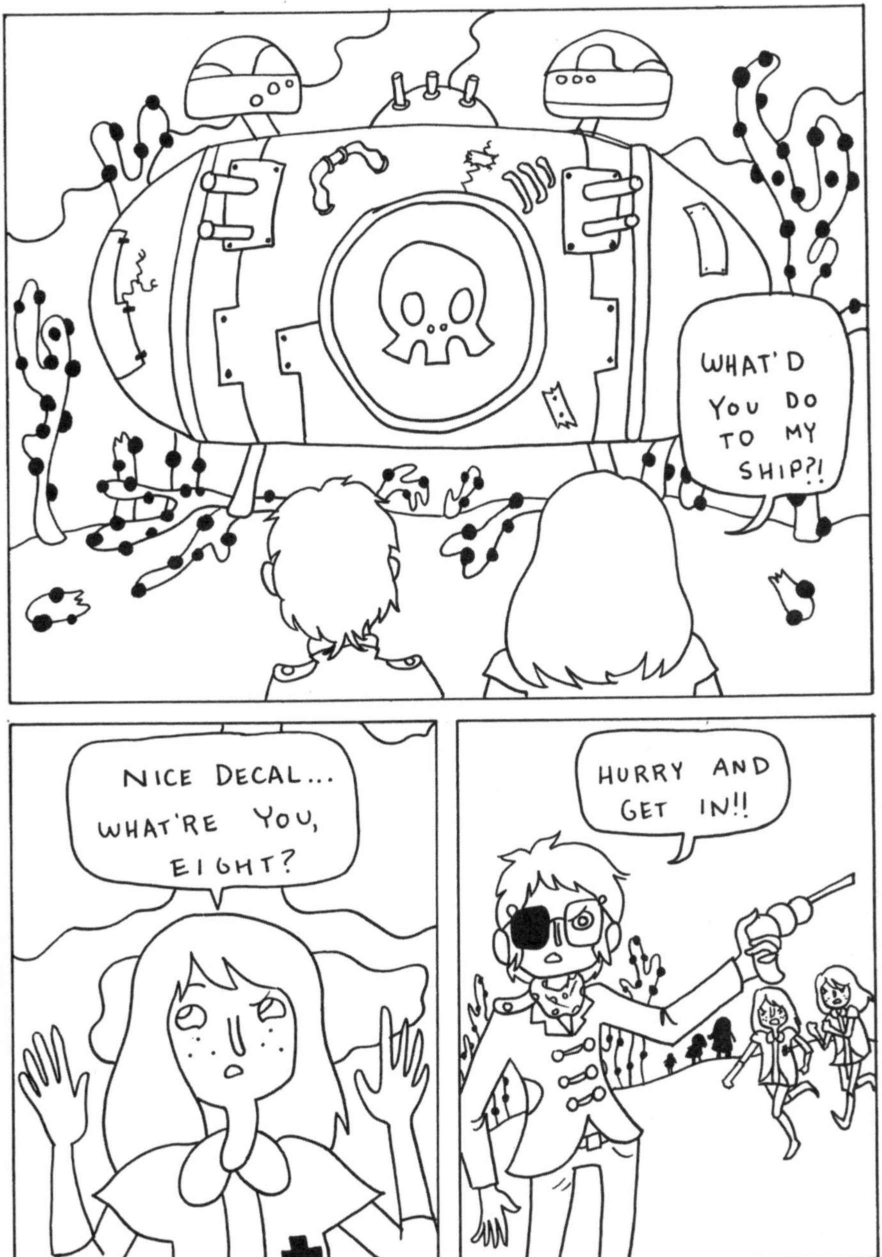
WHAT'D YOU DO TO MY SHIP?!
NICE DECAL... WHAT'RE YOU, EIGHT?
HURRY AND GET IN!!

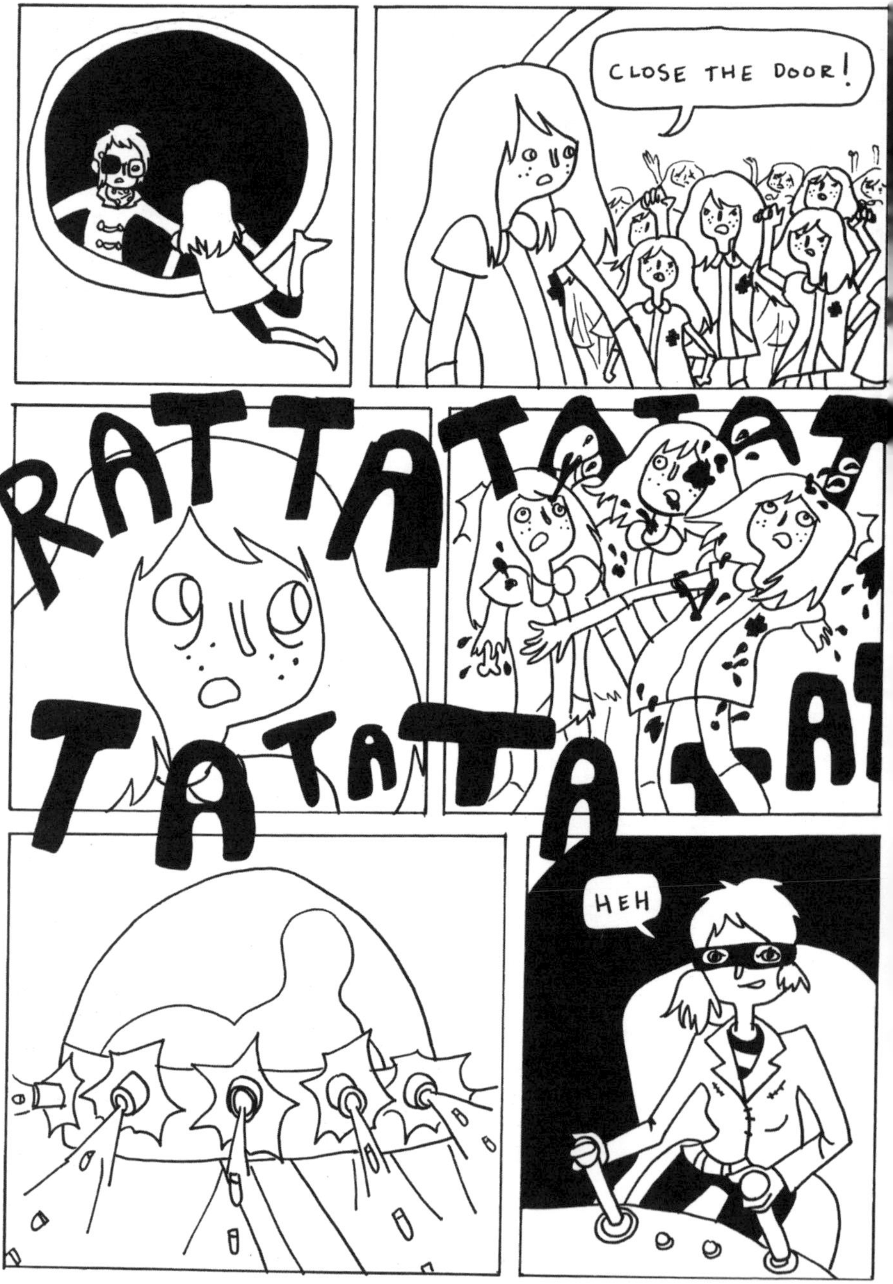
CLOSE THE DOOR!
RATTATATAT
TATATATAT
HEH

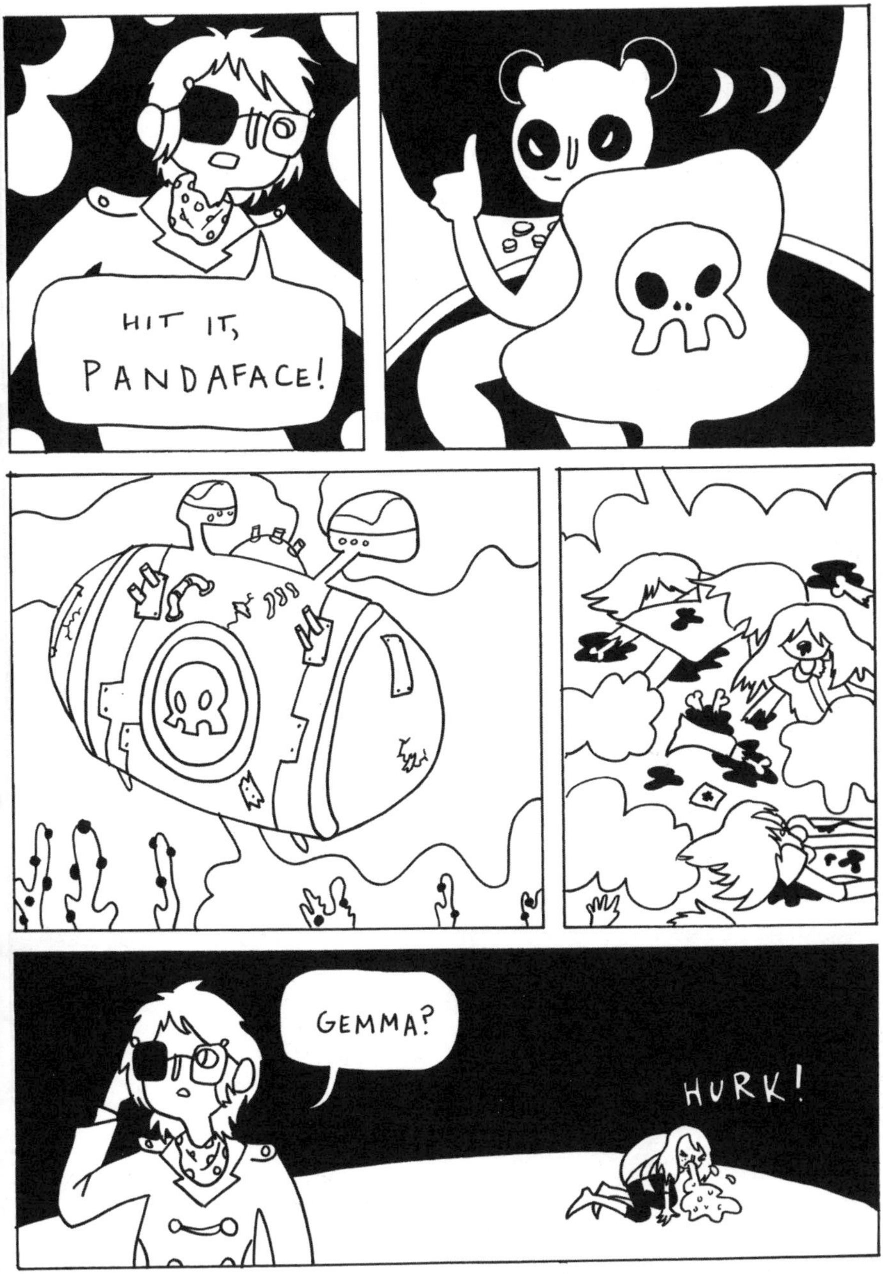
HIT IT,
PANDAFACE!
GEMMA?
HURK!

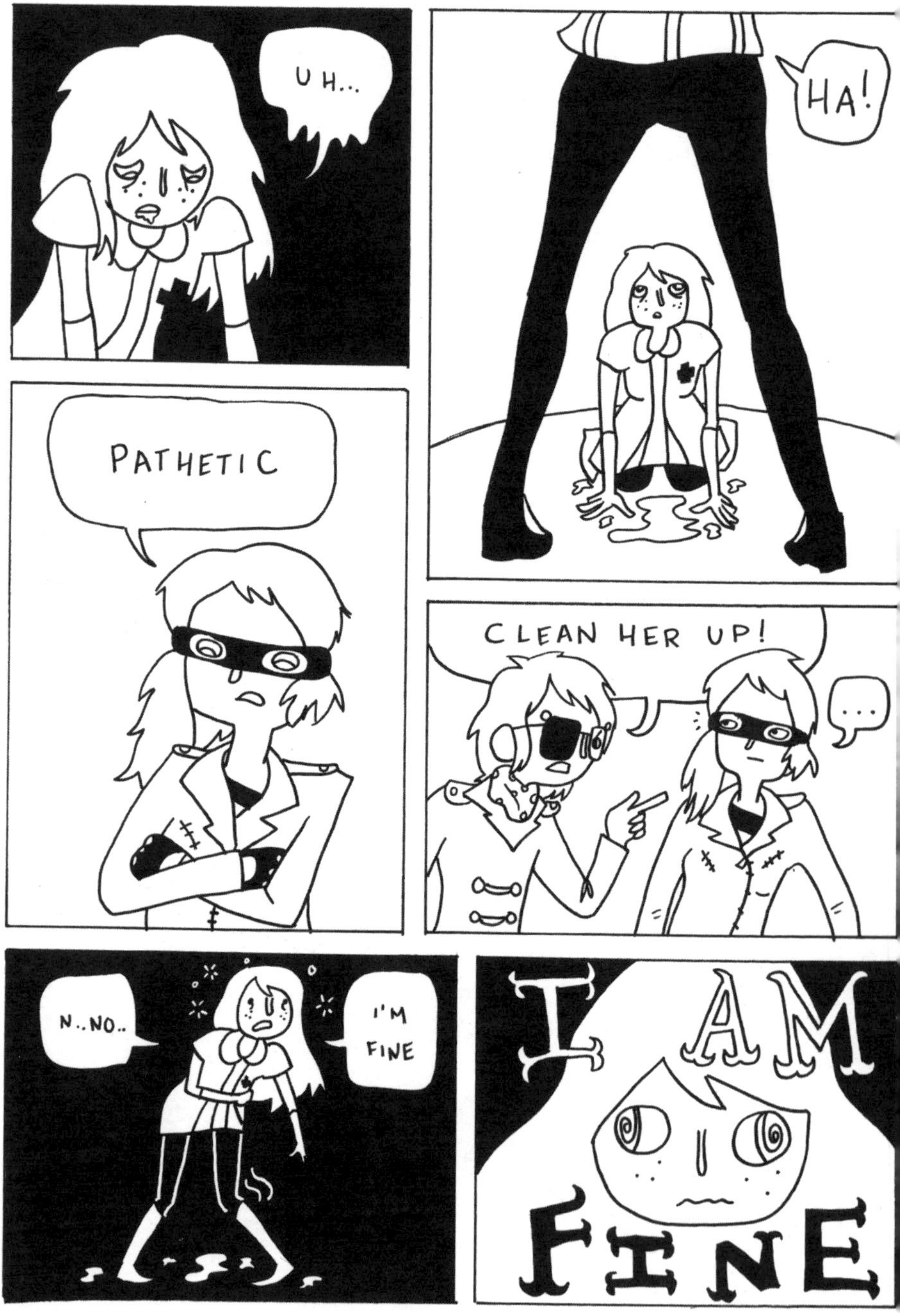
UH...
HA!
PATHETIC
CLEAN HER UP!
...
N..NO..
I'M FINE
I AM FINE

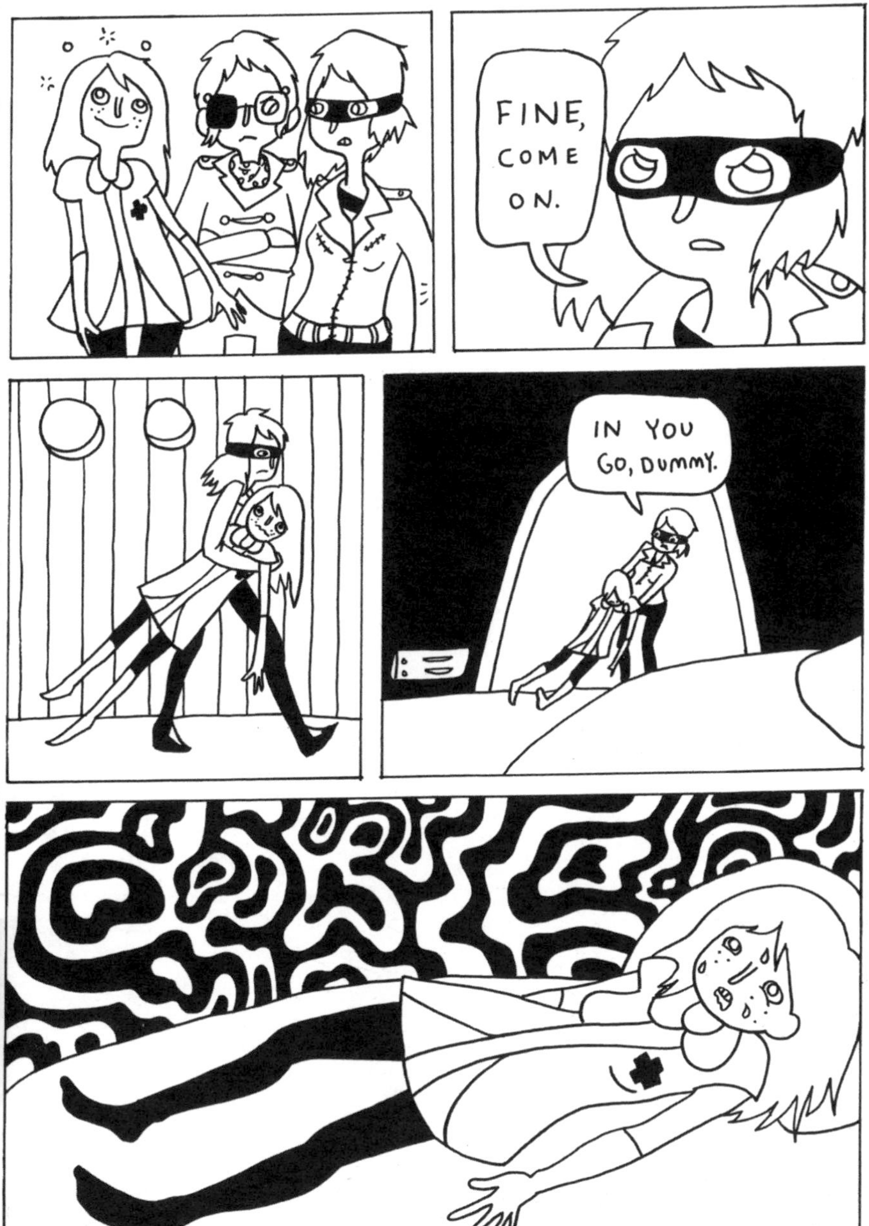
FINE, COME ON.
IN YOU GO, DUMMY.

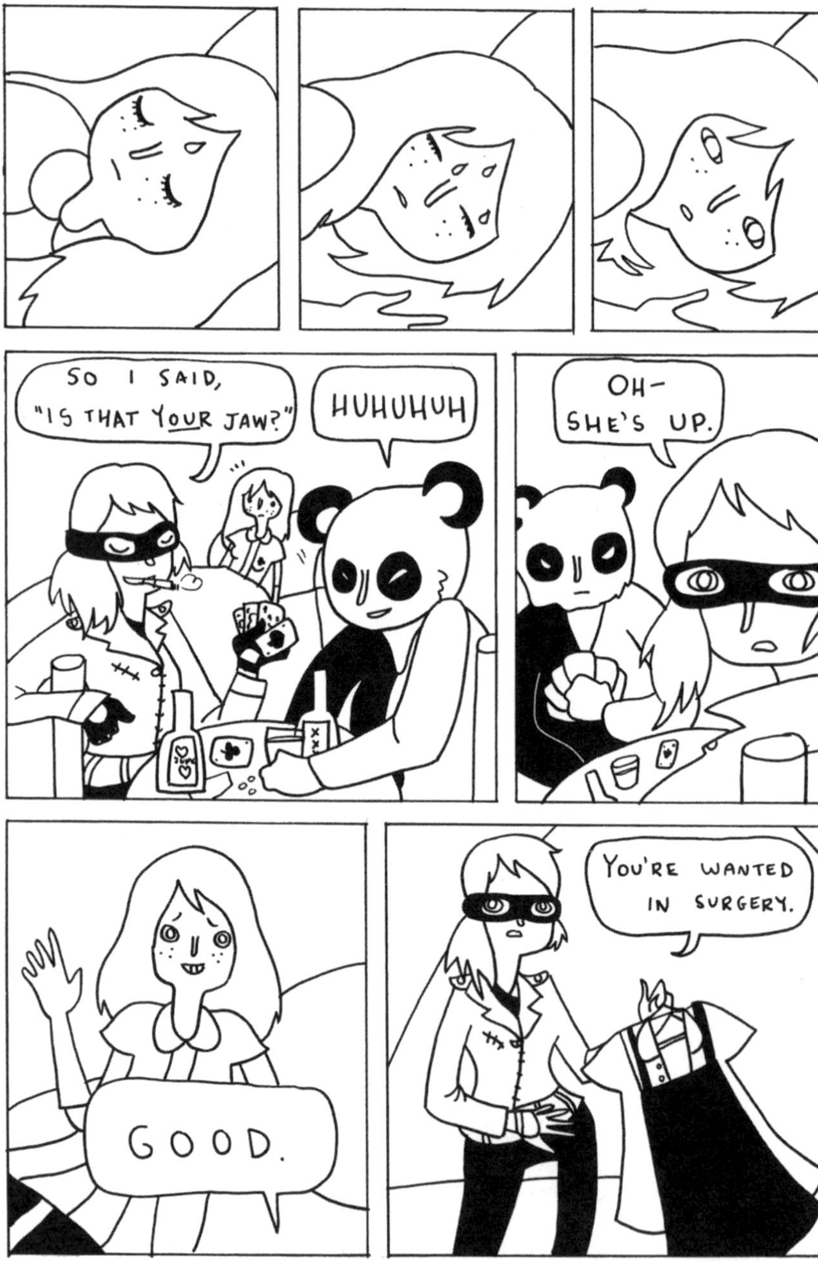
SO I SAID, "IS THAT YOUR JAW?"
HUHUHUH
OH- SHE'S UP.
GOOD.
YOU'RE WANTED IN SURGERY.

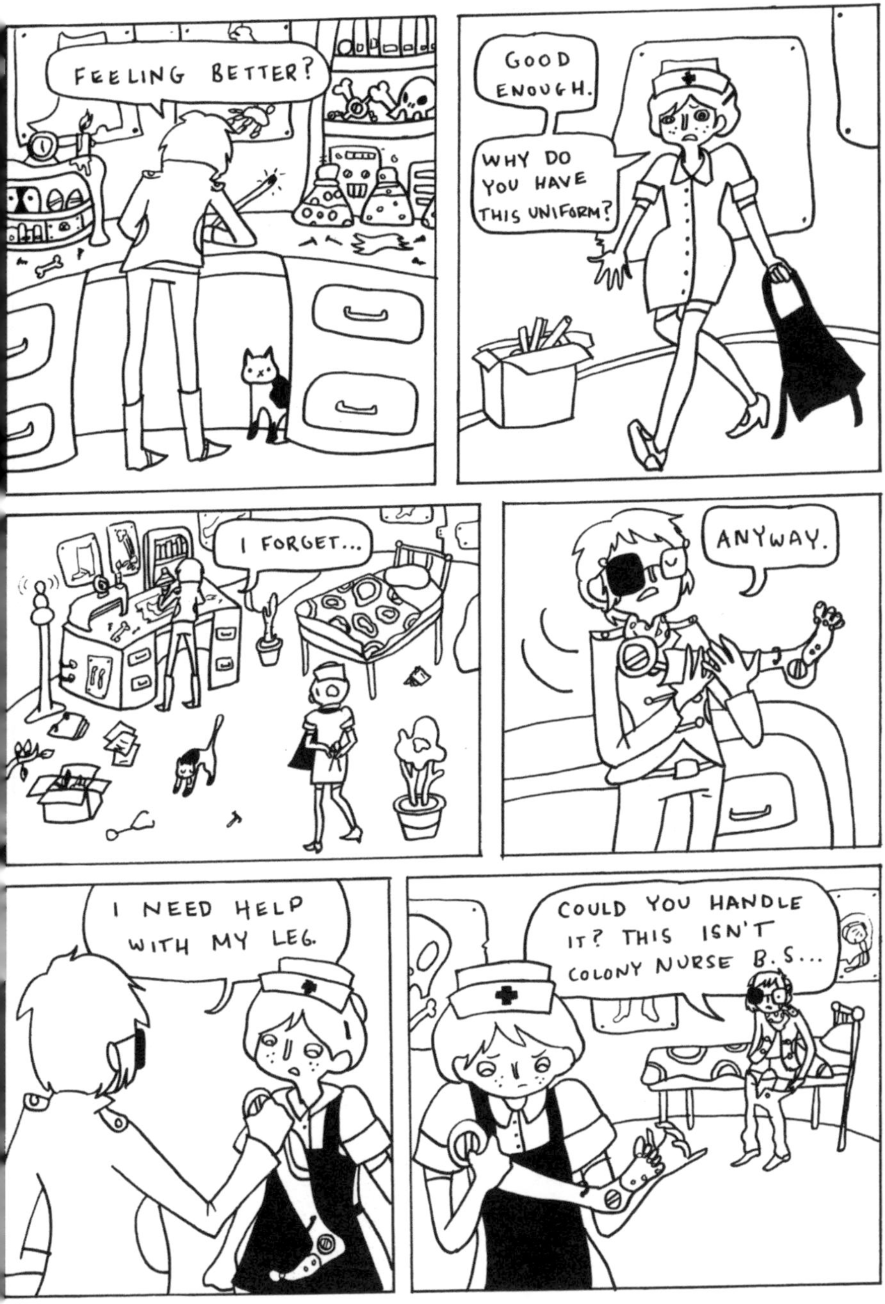
FEELING BETTER?
GOOD ENOUGH.
WHY DO YOU HAVE THIS UNIFORM?
I FORGET...
ANYWAY.
I NEED HELP WITH MY LEG.
COULD YOU HANDLE IT? THIS ISN'T COLONY NURSE B.S...

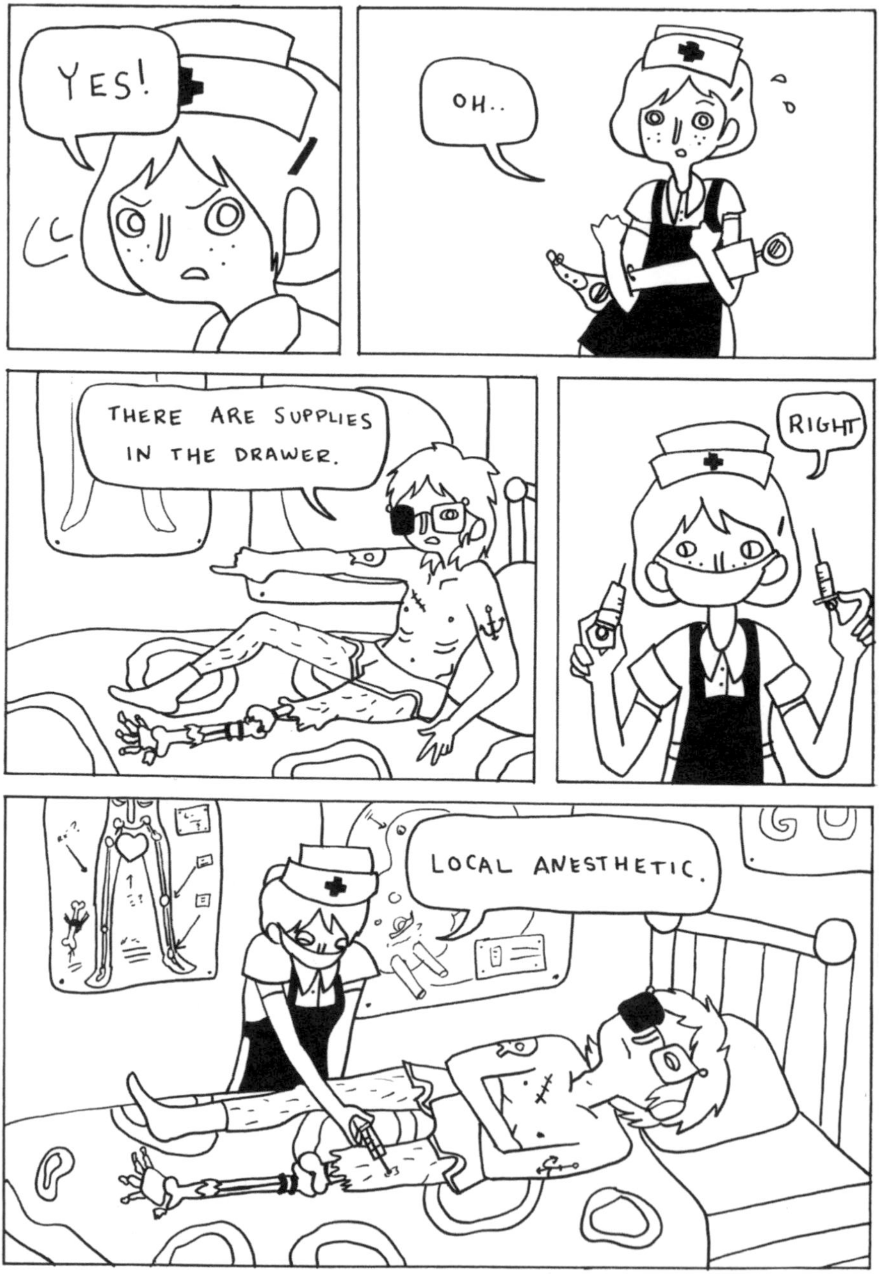
YES!
OH..
THERE ARE SUPPLIES IN THE DRAWER.
RIGHT
LOCAL ANESTHETIC.

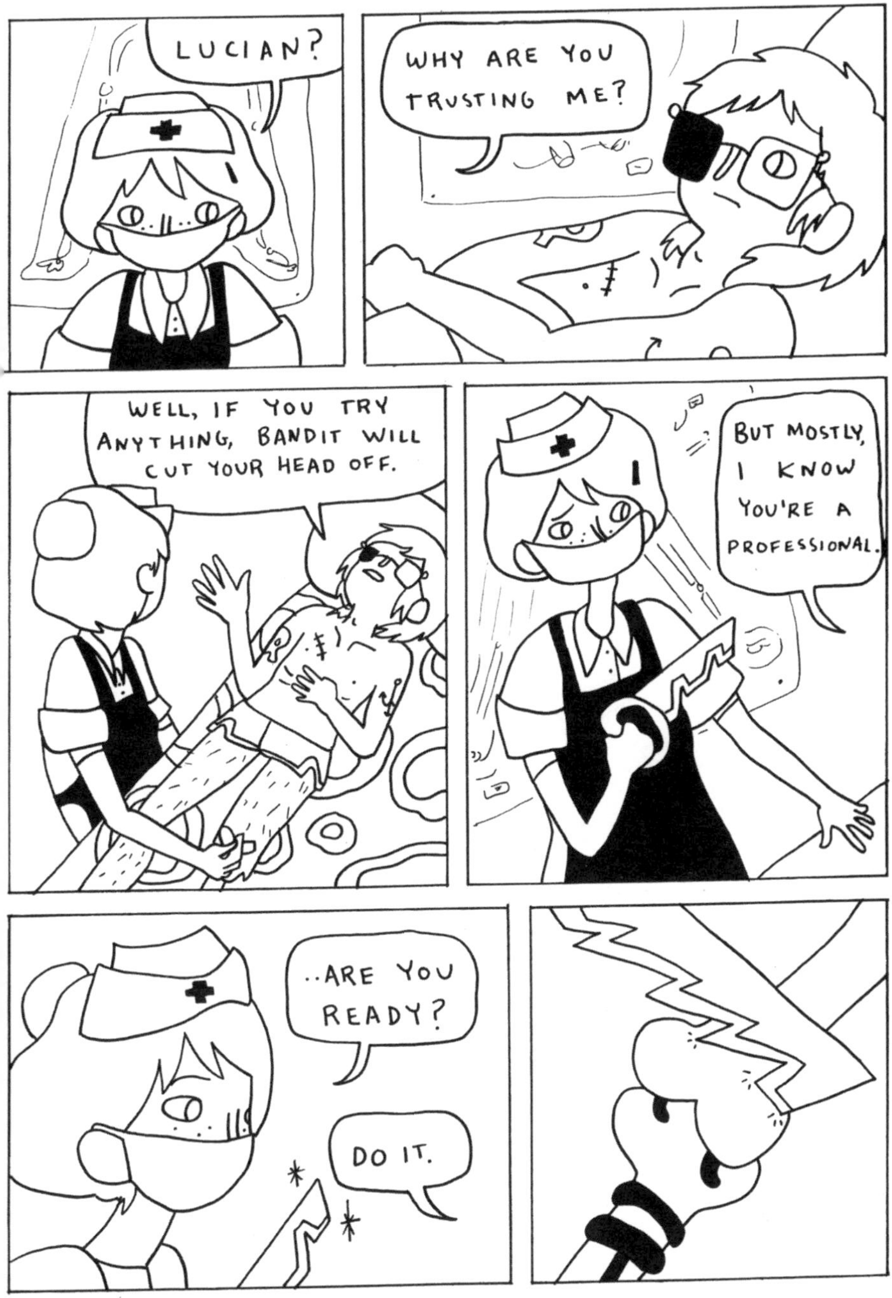
LUCIAN?
WHY ARE YOU TRUSTING ME?
WELL, IF YOU TRY ANYTHING, BANDIT WILL CUT YOUR HEAD OFF.
BUT MOSTLY, I KNOW YOU'RE A PROFESSIONAL.
..ARE YOU READY?
DO IT.

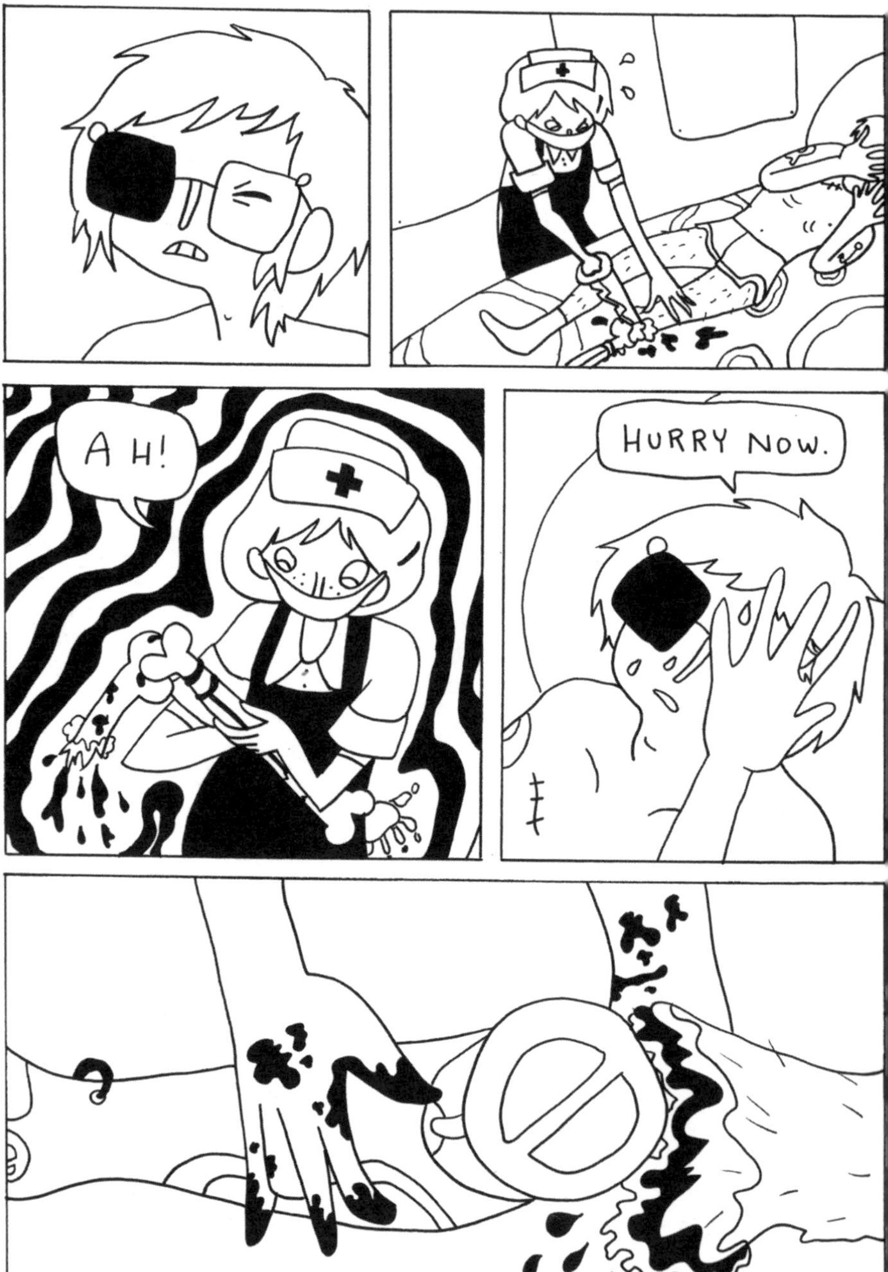
AH!
HURRY NOW.

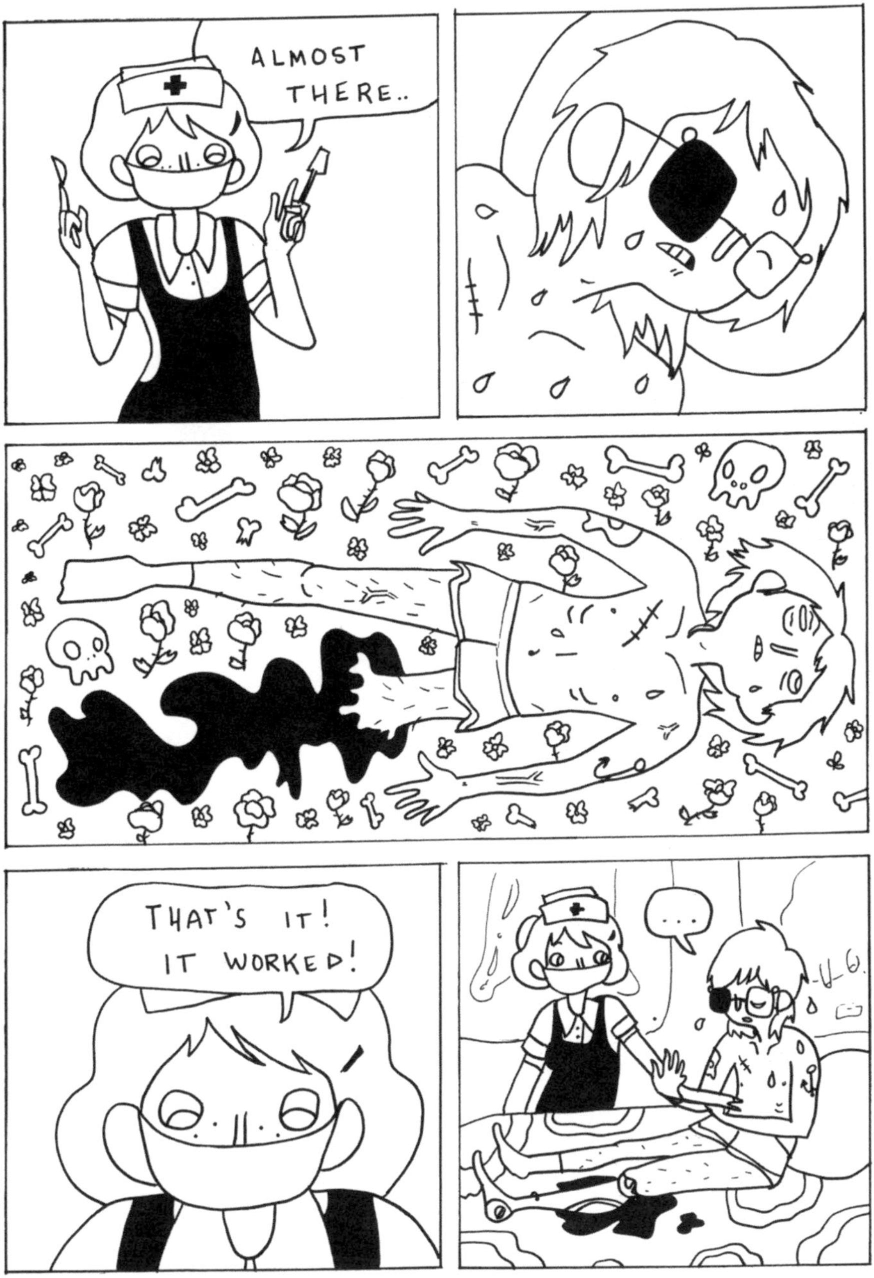
ALMOST THERE..
THAT'S IT! IT WORKED!
...

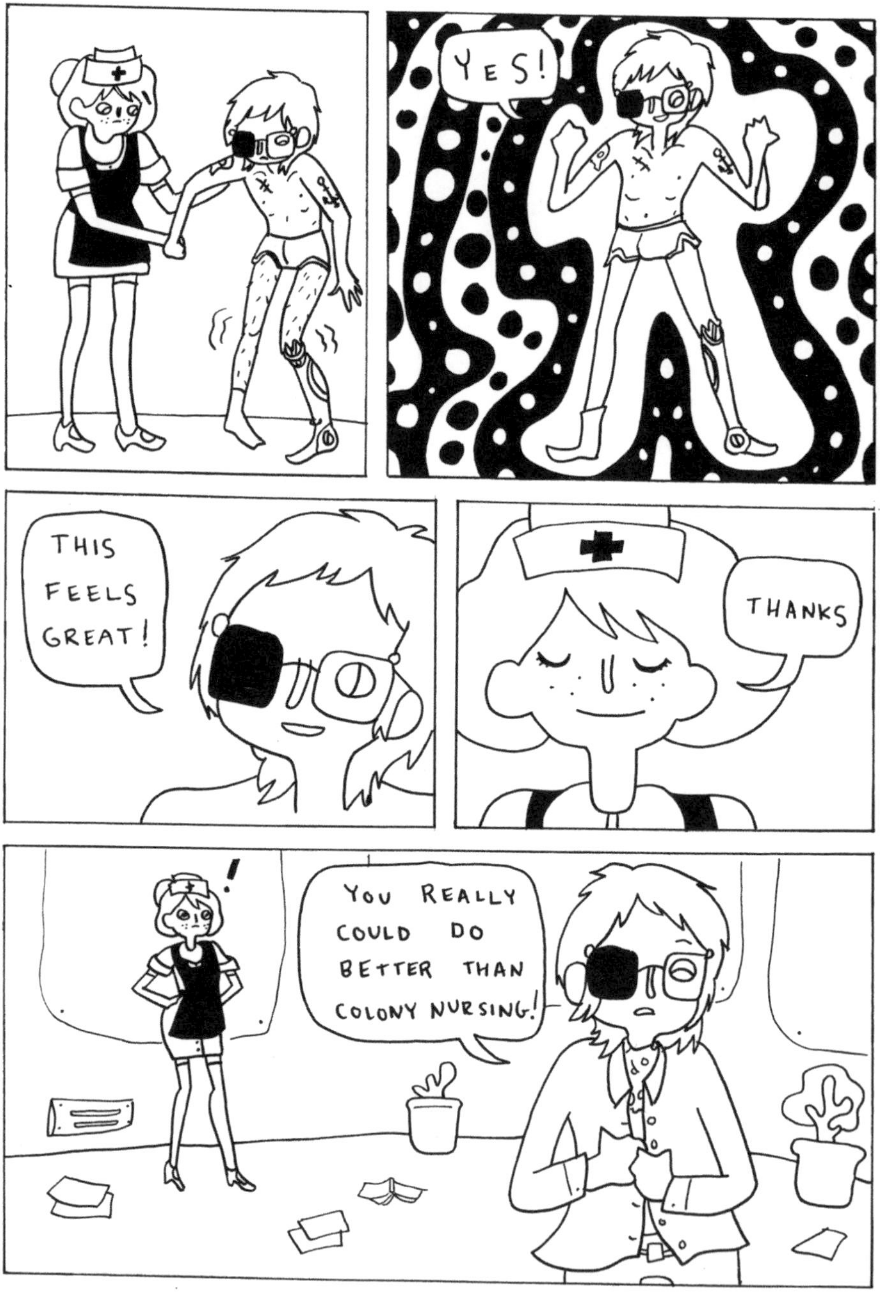
YES!
THIS FEELS GREAT!
THANKS
YOU REALLY COULD DO BETTER THAN COLONY NURSING!

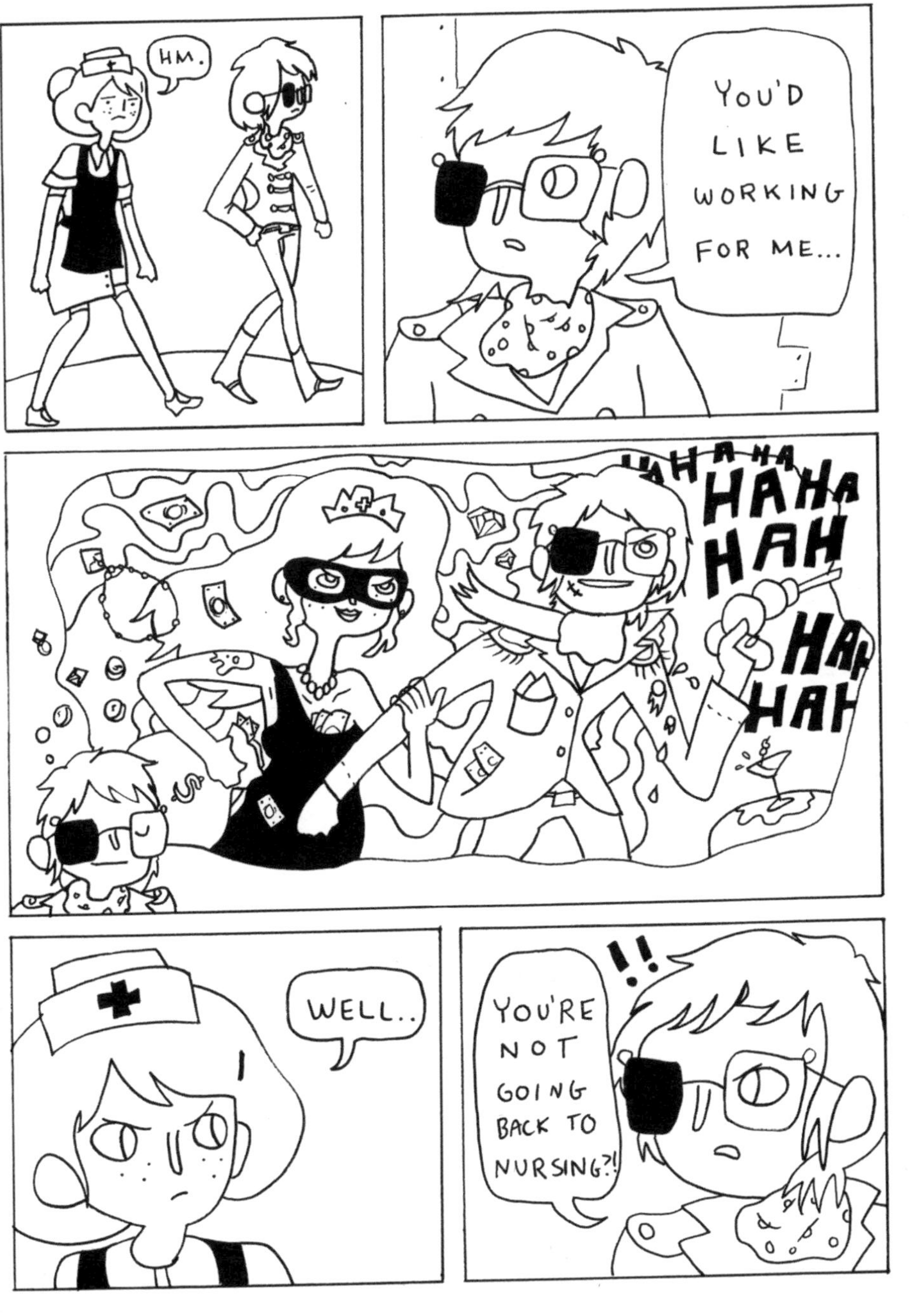
HM.
YOU'D LIKE WORKING FOR ME...
HAHAHA
HAHA
HAH
HAH
HAH
WELL..
!!
YOU'RE NOT GOING BACK TO NURSING?!

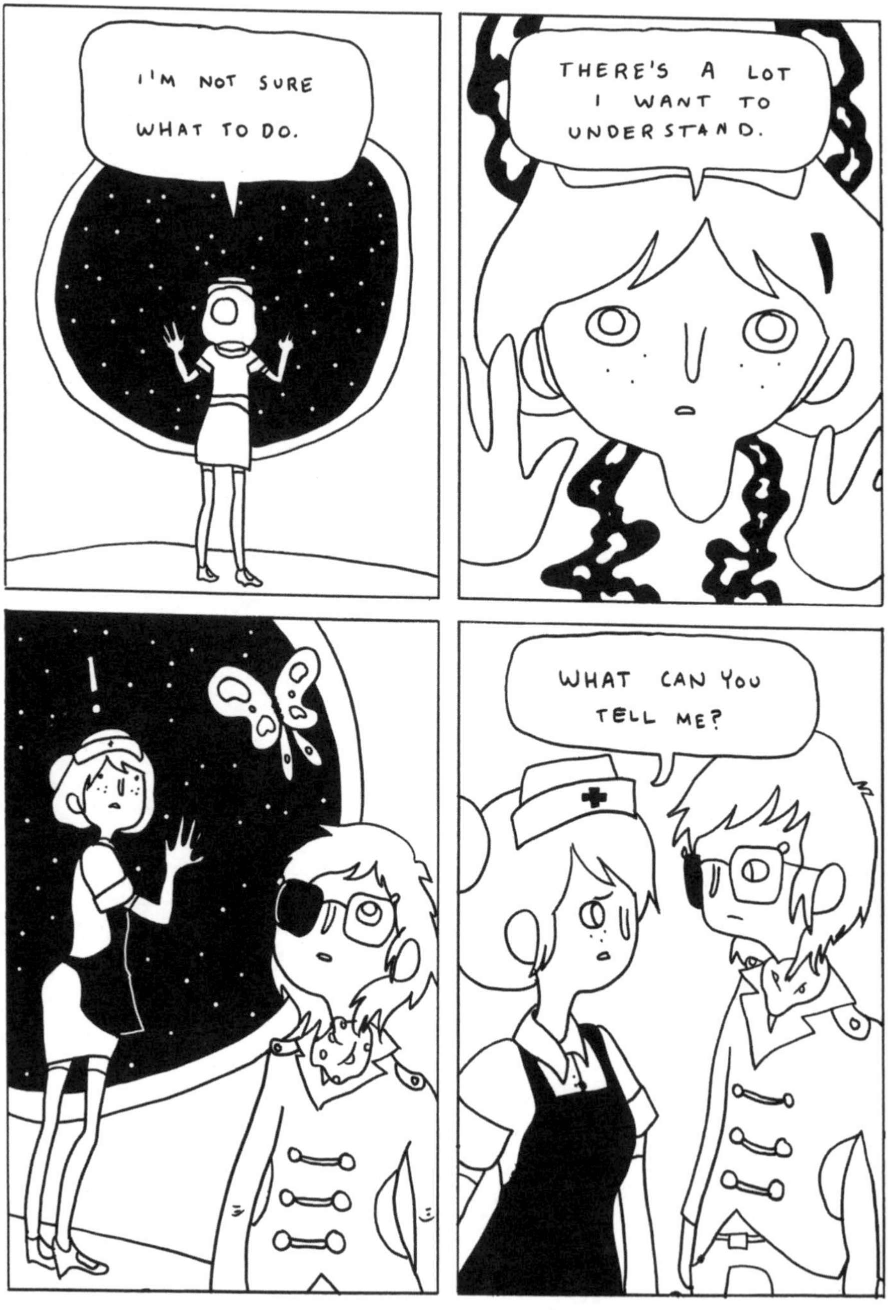
I'M NOT SURE WHAT TO DO.
THERE'S A LOT I WANT TO UNDERSTAND.
!
WHAT CAN YOU TELL ME?

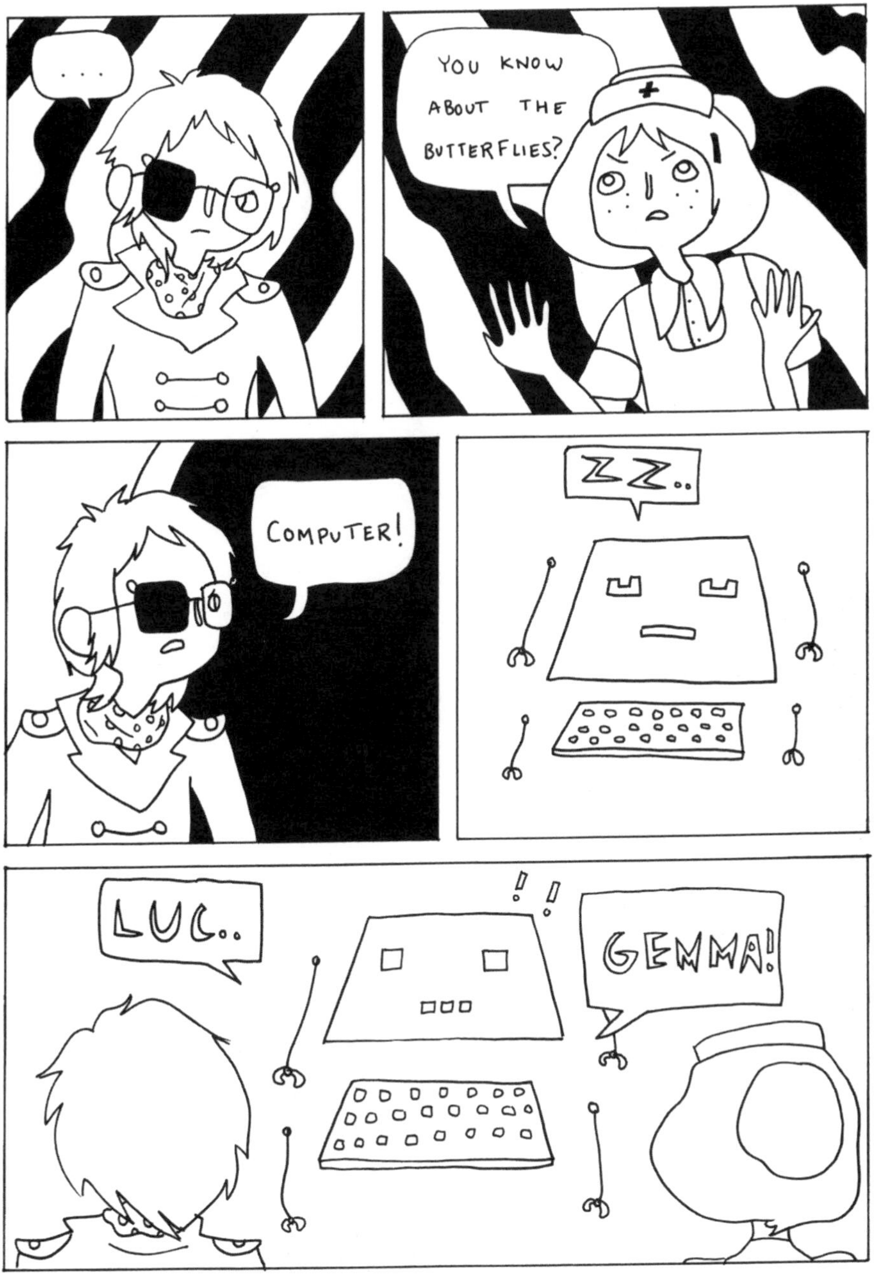
. . . .
YOU KNOW ABOUT THE BUTTERFLIES?
COMPUTER!
ZZ..
LUC..
!!
GEMMA!

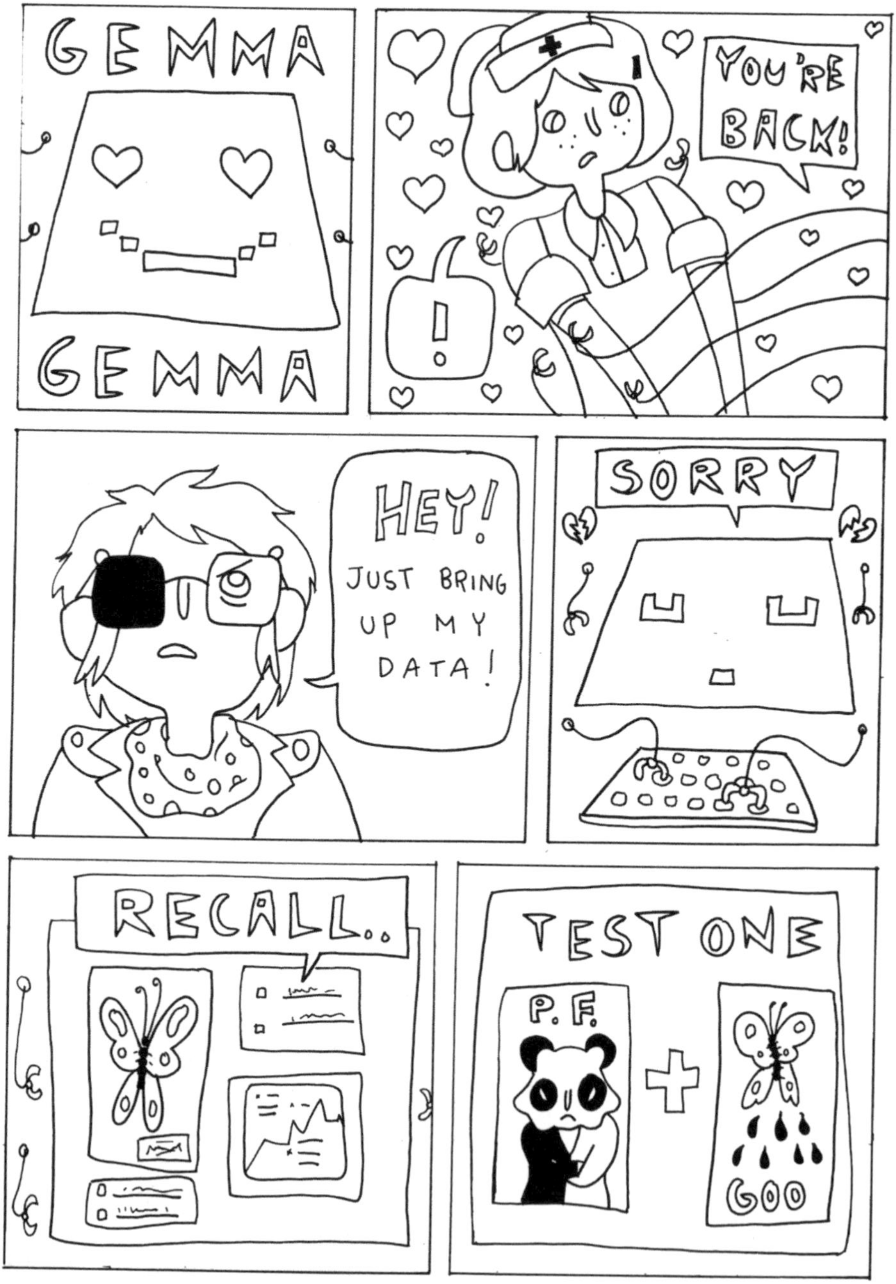
GEMMA
GEMMA
YOU'RE BACK!
!
HEY! JUST BRING UP MY DATA!
SORRY
RECALL..
TEST ONE
P.F.
GOO

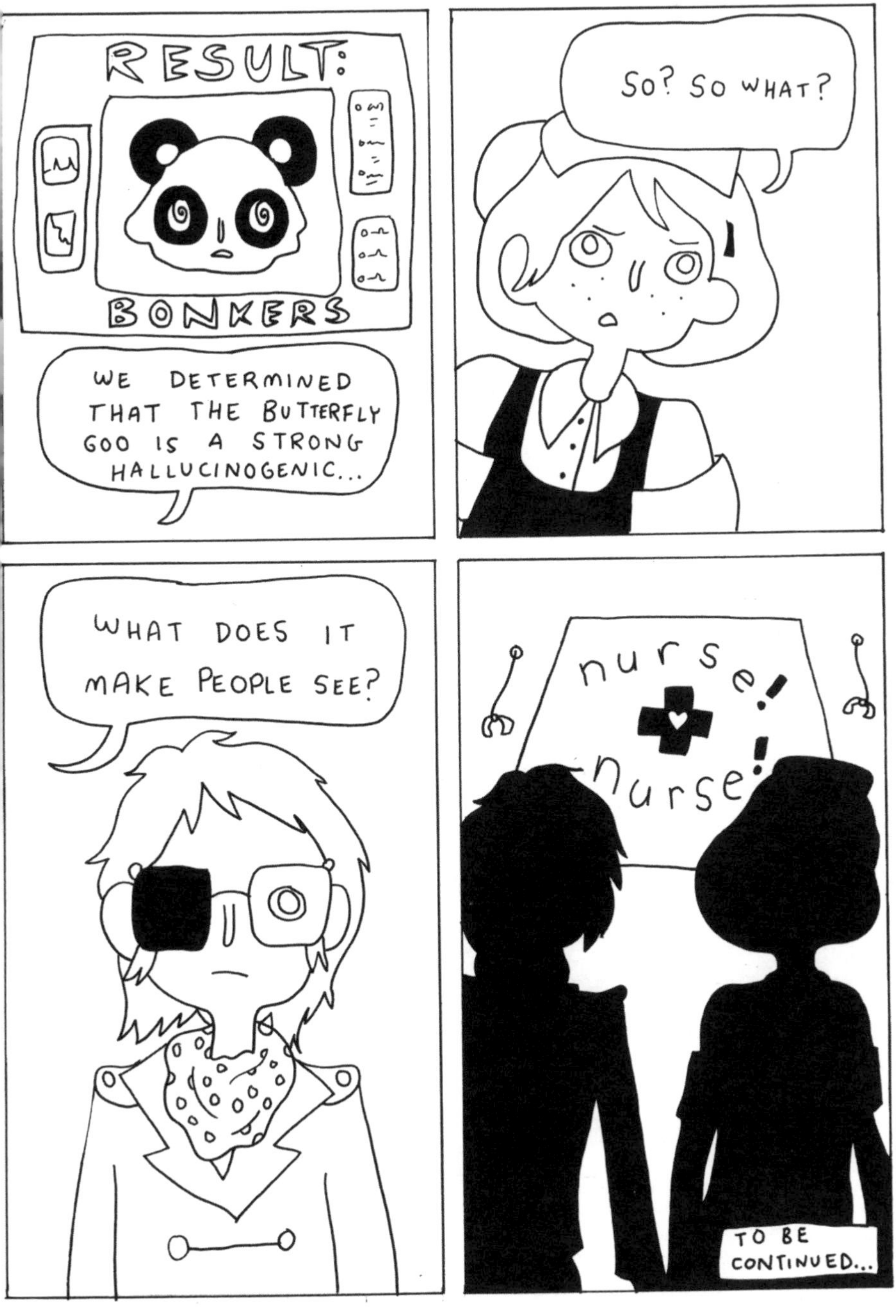
RESULT:
BONKERS
WE DETERMINED THAT THE BUTTERFLY GOO IS A STRONG HALLUCINOGENIC...
SO? SO WHAT?
WHAT DOES IT MAKE PEOPLE SEE?
nurse! nurse!
TO BE CONTINUED...

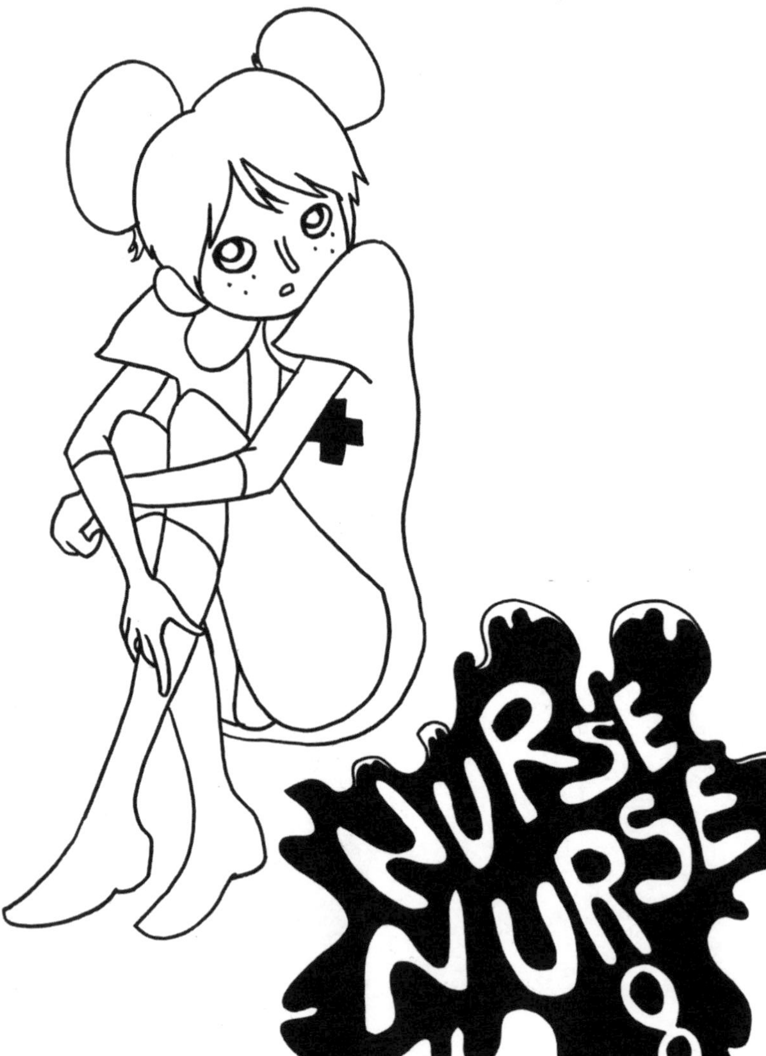
NURSE NURSE 8

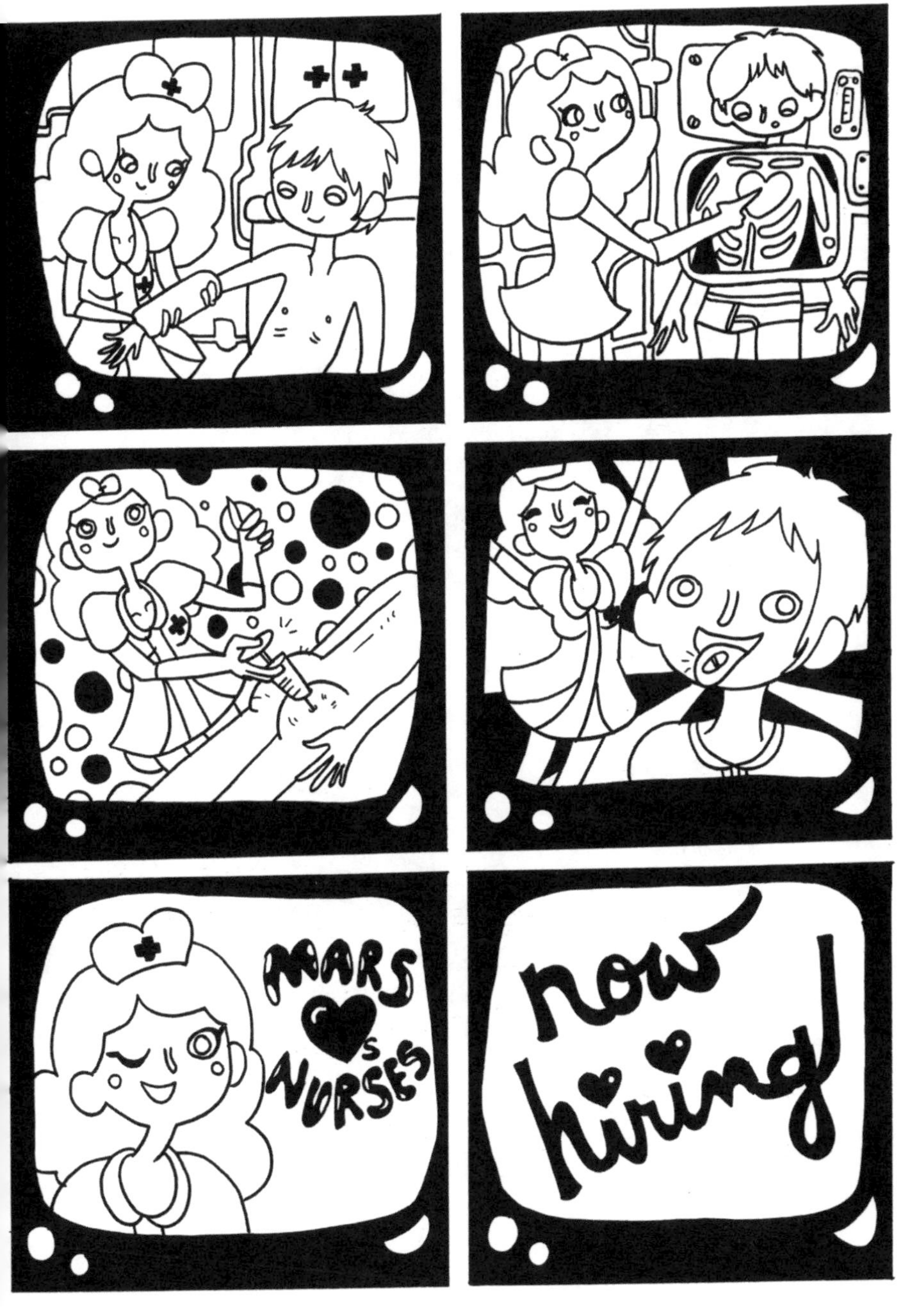
MARS ♥s NURSES
now hiring!

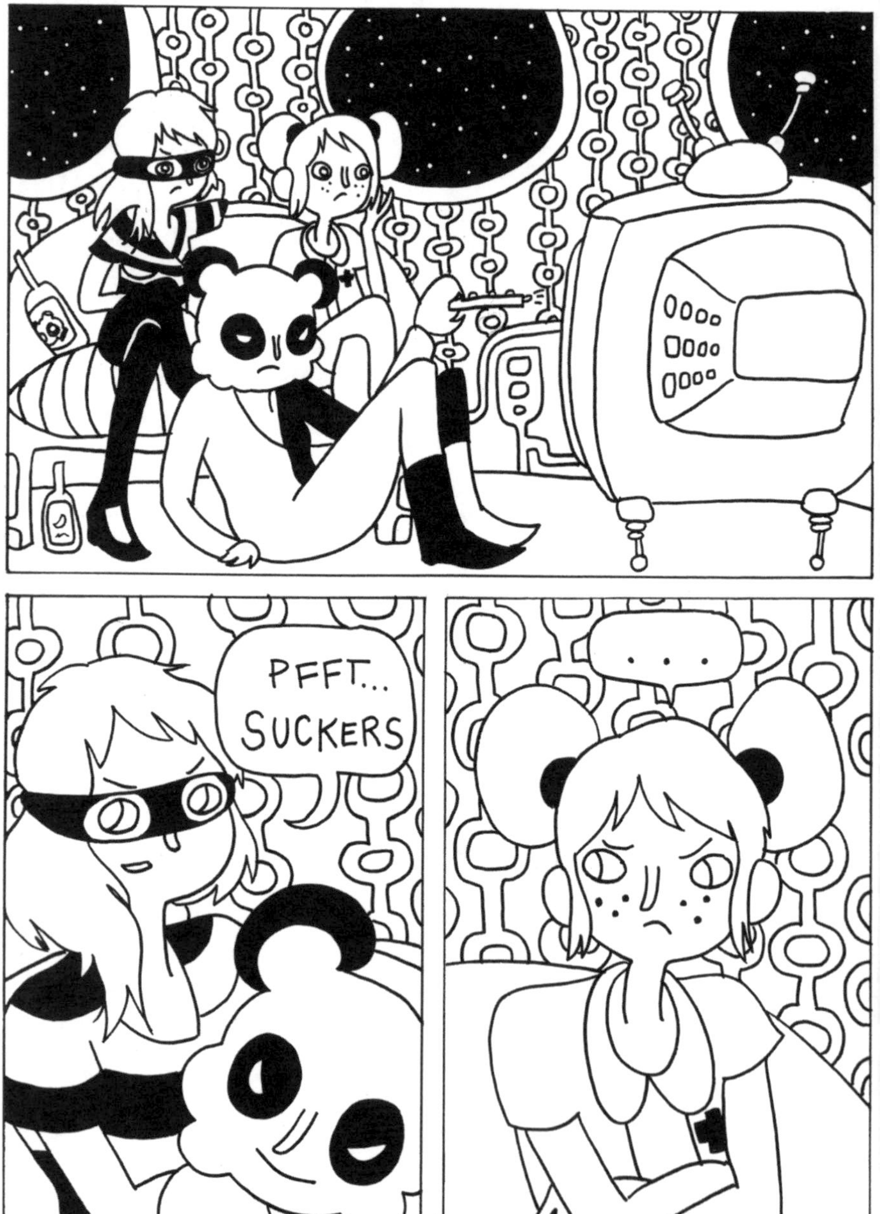
PFFT... SUCKERS
. . .

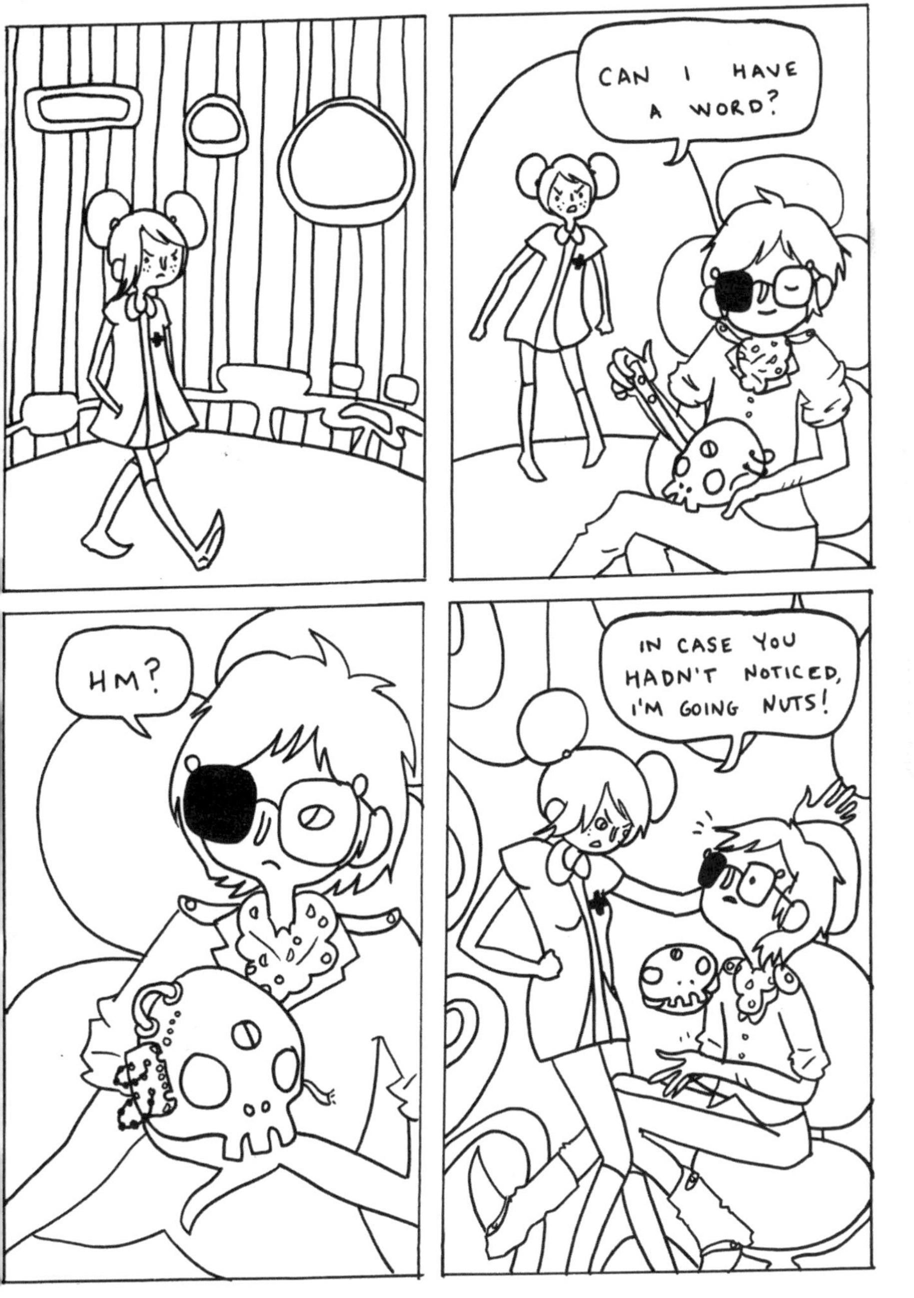
CAN I HAVE A WORD?
HM?
IN CASE YOU HADN'T NOTICED, I'M GOING NUTS!

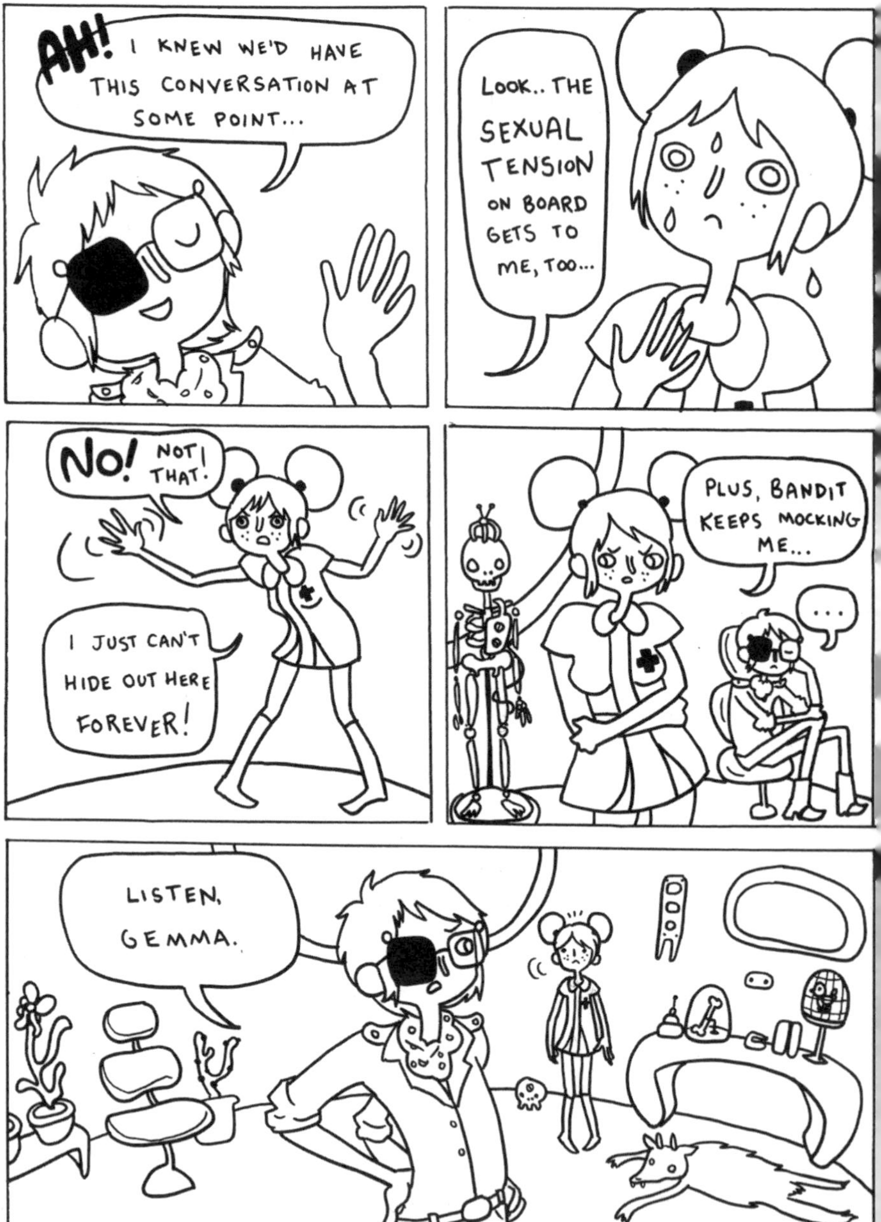
AH! I KNEW WE'D HAVE THIS CONVERSATION AT SOME POINT...
LOOK.. THE SEXUAL TENSION ON BOARD GETS TO ME, TOO...
NO! NOT THAT!
I JUST CAN'T HIDE OUT HERE FOREVER!
PLUS, BANDIT KEEPS MOCKING ME...
...
LISTEN, GEMMA.

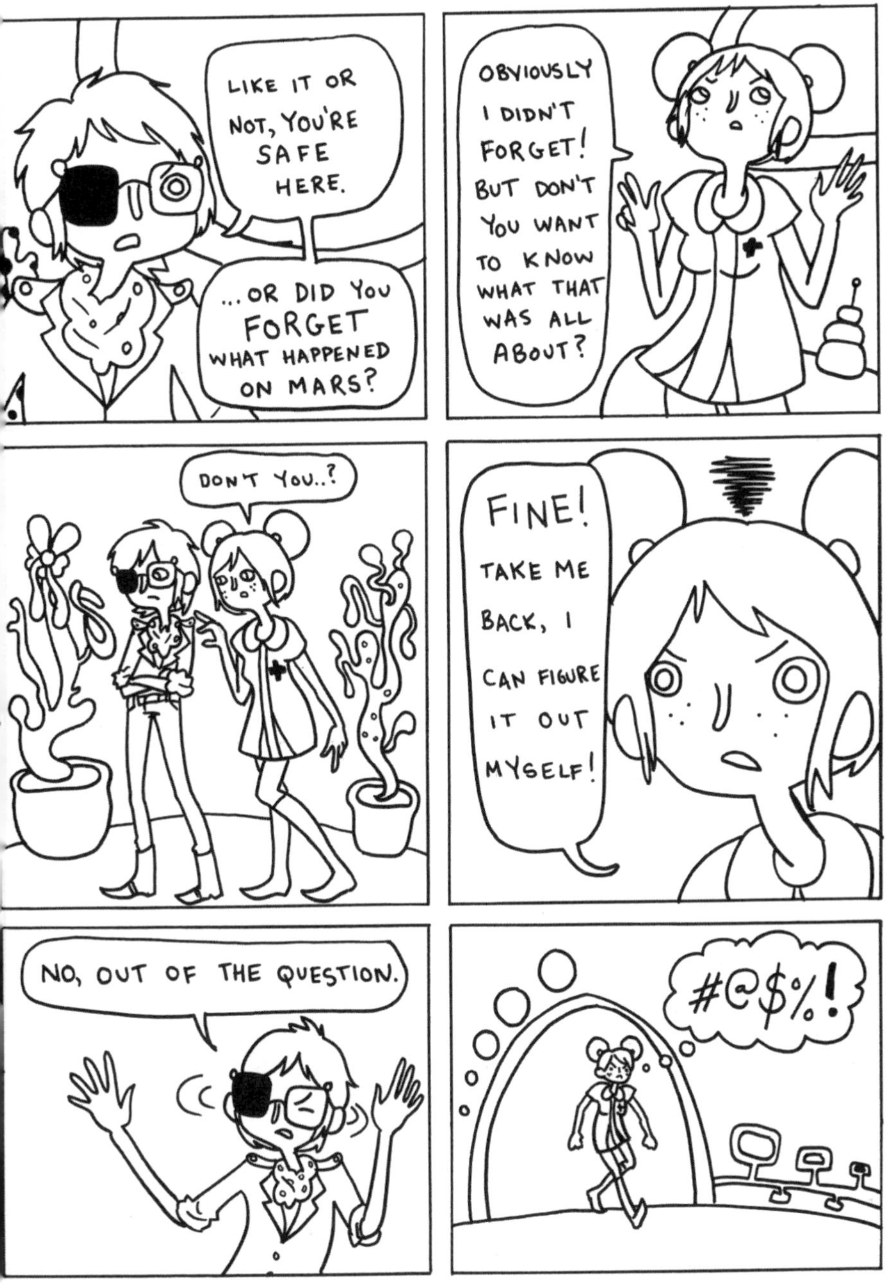
LIKE IT OR NOT, YOU'RE SAFE HERE.
...OR DID YOU FORGET WHAT HAPPENED ON MARS?
OBVIOUSLY I DIDN'T FORGET! BUT DON'T YOU WANT TO KNOW WHAT THAT WAS ALL ABOUT?
DON'T YOU..?
FINE! TAKE ME BACK, I CAN FIGURE IT OUT MYSELF!
NO, OUT OF THE QUESTION.
#@$%!

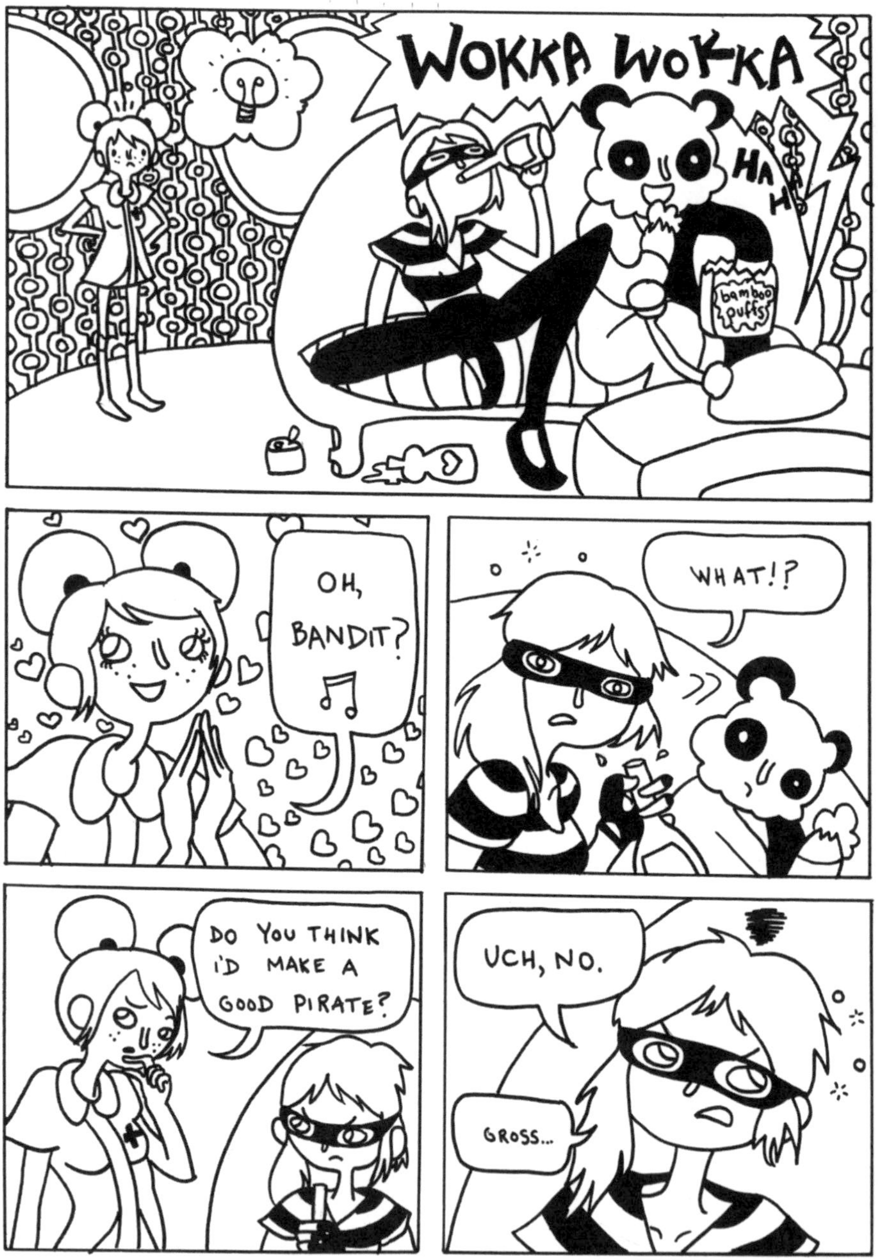
WOKKA WOKKA
HA HA H
bamboo puffs
OH, BANDIT?
WHAT!?
DO YOU THINK I'D MAKE A GOOD PIRATE?
UCH, NO.
GROSS...

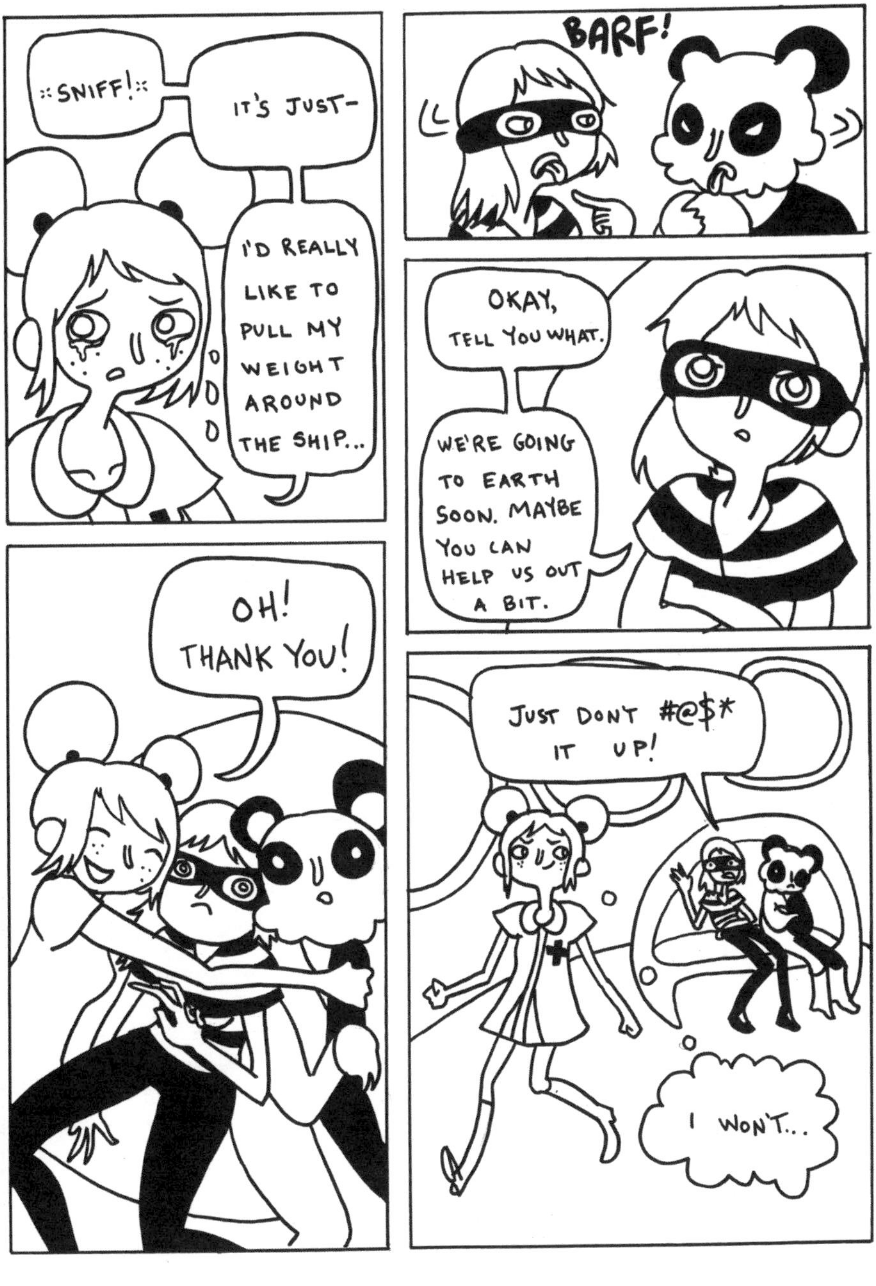

:: SNIFF! ::
IT'S JUST-
I'D REALLY LIKE TO PULL MY WEIGHT AROUND THE SHIP...
BARF!
OKAY, TELL YOU WHAT.
WE'RE GOING TO EARTH SOON. MAYBE YOU CAN HELP US OUT A BIT.
OH! THANK YOU!
JUST DON'T #@$* IT UP!
I WON'T...

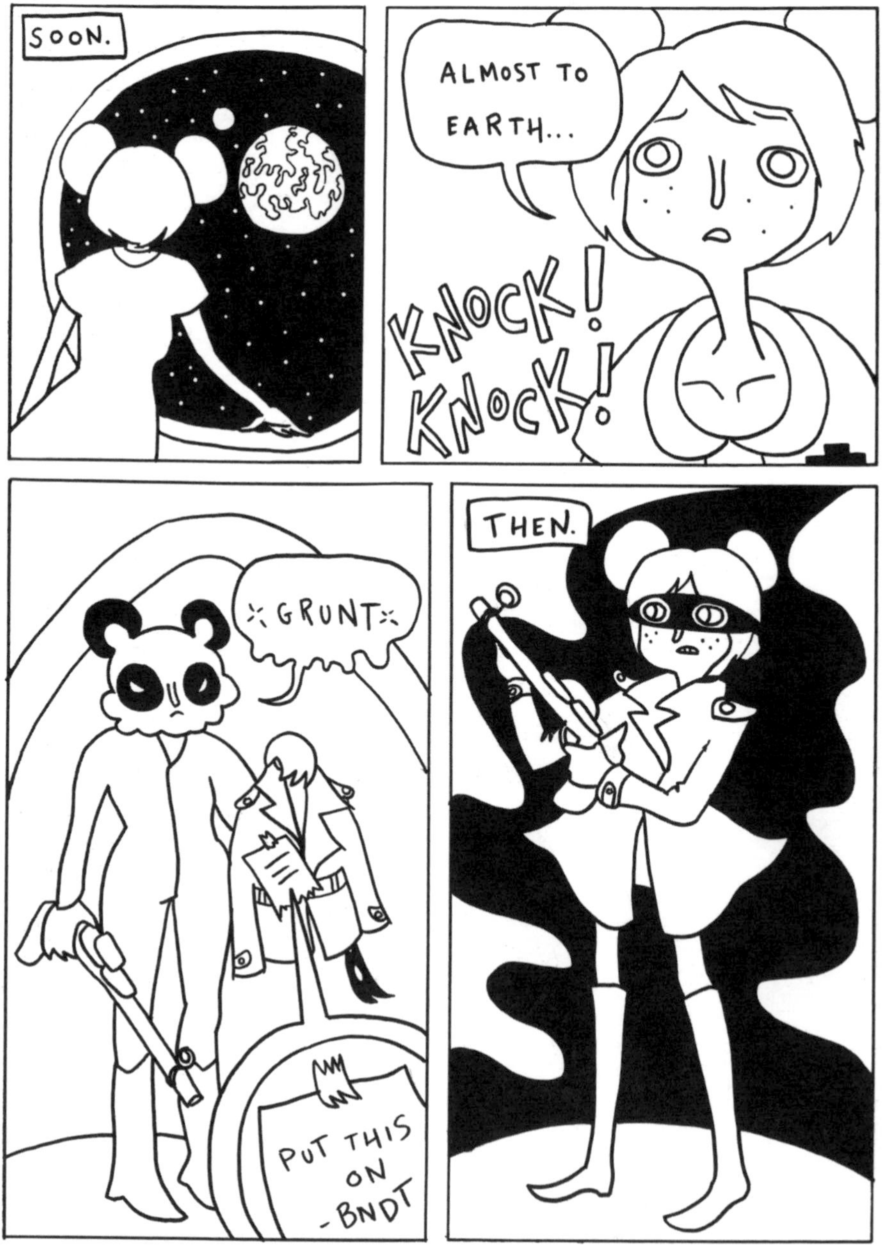
SOON.
ALMOST TO EARTH...
KNOCK! KNOCK!
GRUNT
PUT THIS ON -BNDT
THEN.

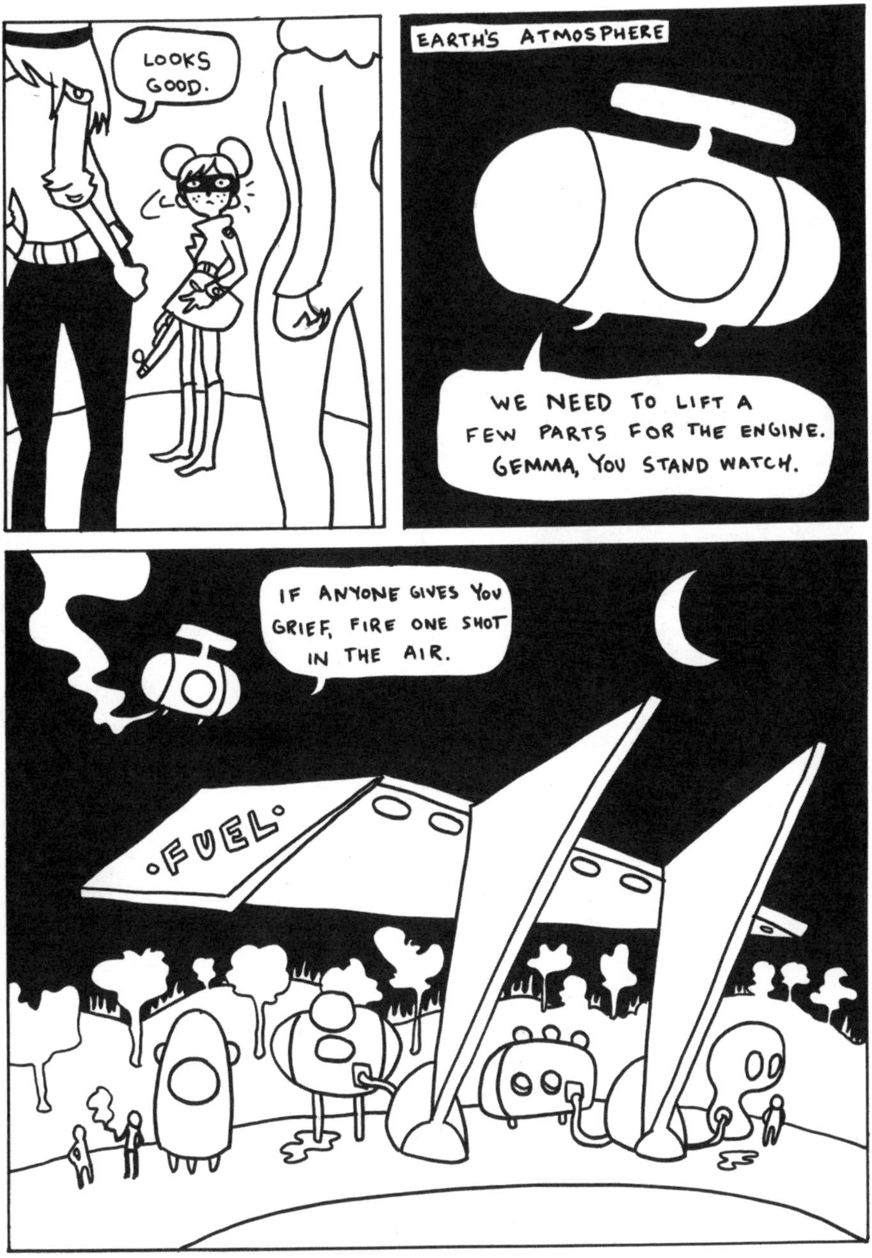
LOOKS GOOD.
EARTH'S ATMOSPHERE
WE NEED TO LIFT A FEW PARTS FOR THE ENGINE. GEMMA, YOU STAND WATCH.
IF ANYONE GIVES YOU GRIEF, FIRE ONE SHOT IN THE AIR.
FUEL

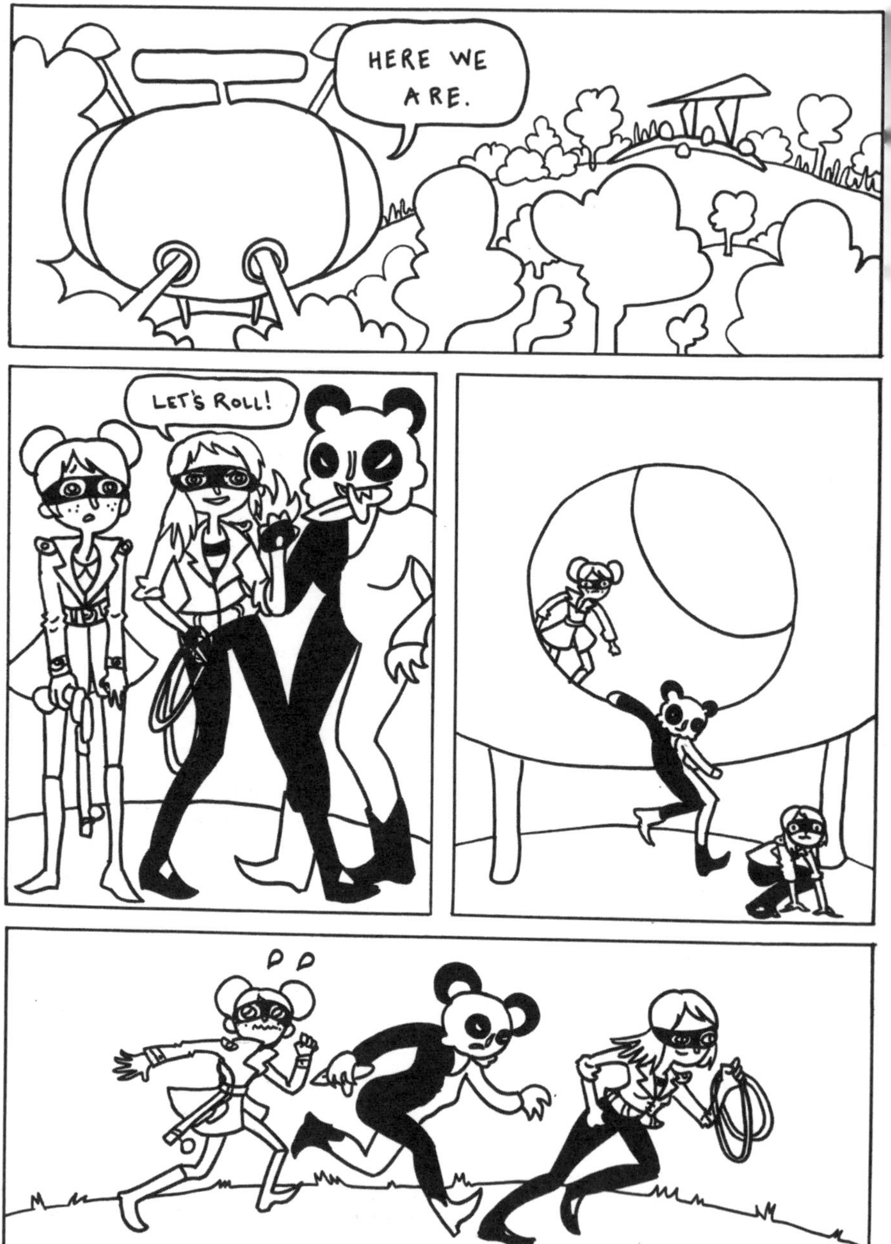
HERE WE ARE.
LET'S ROLL!

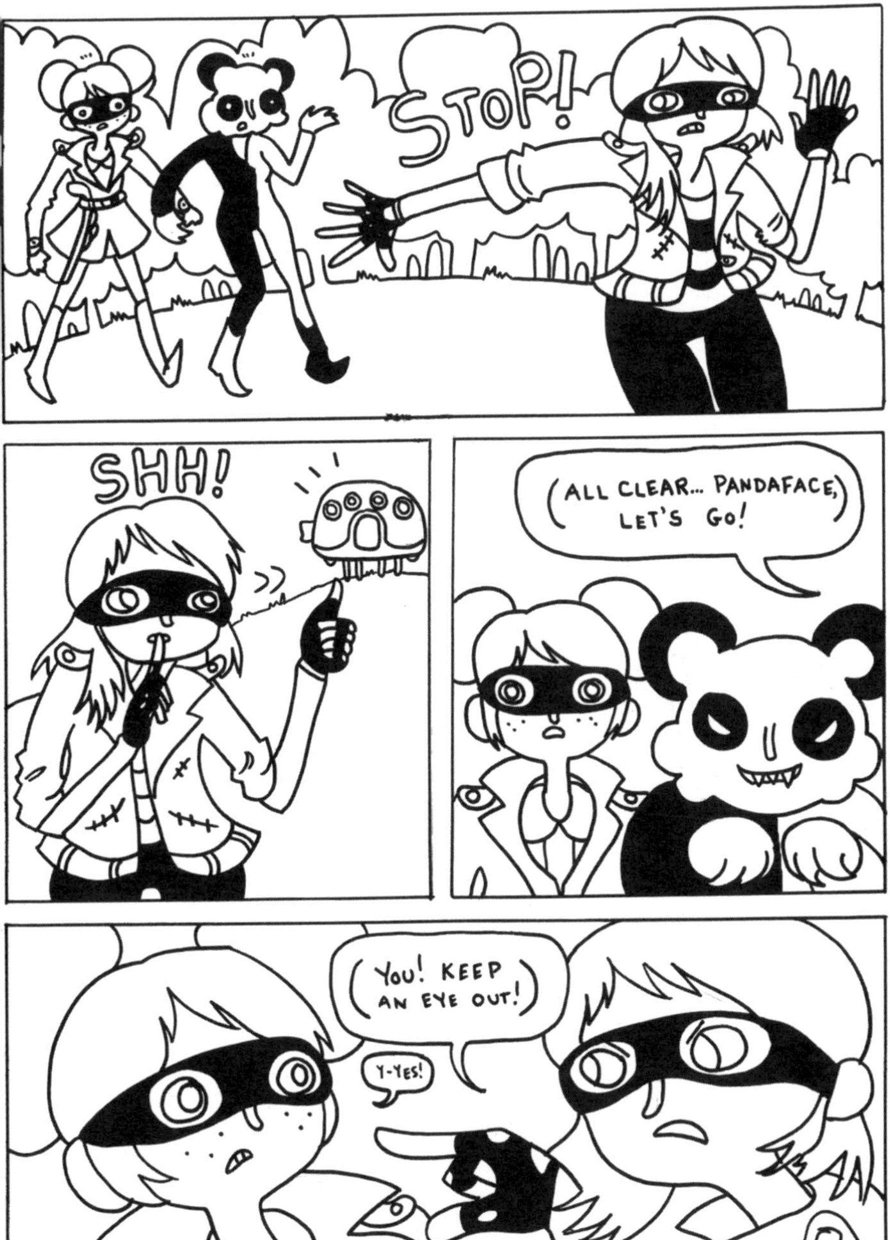
STOP!
SHH!
(ALL CLEAR... PANDAFACE, LET'S GO!)
(YOU! KEEP AN EYE OUT!)
Y-YES!

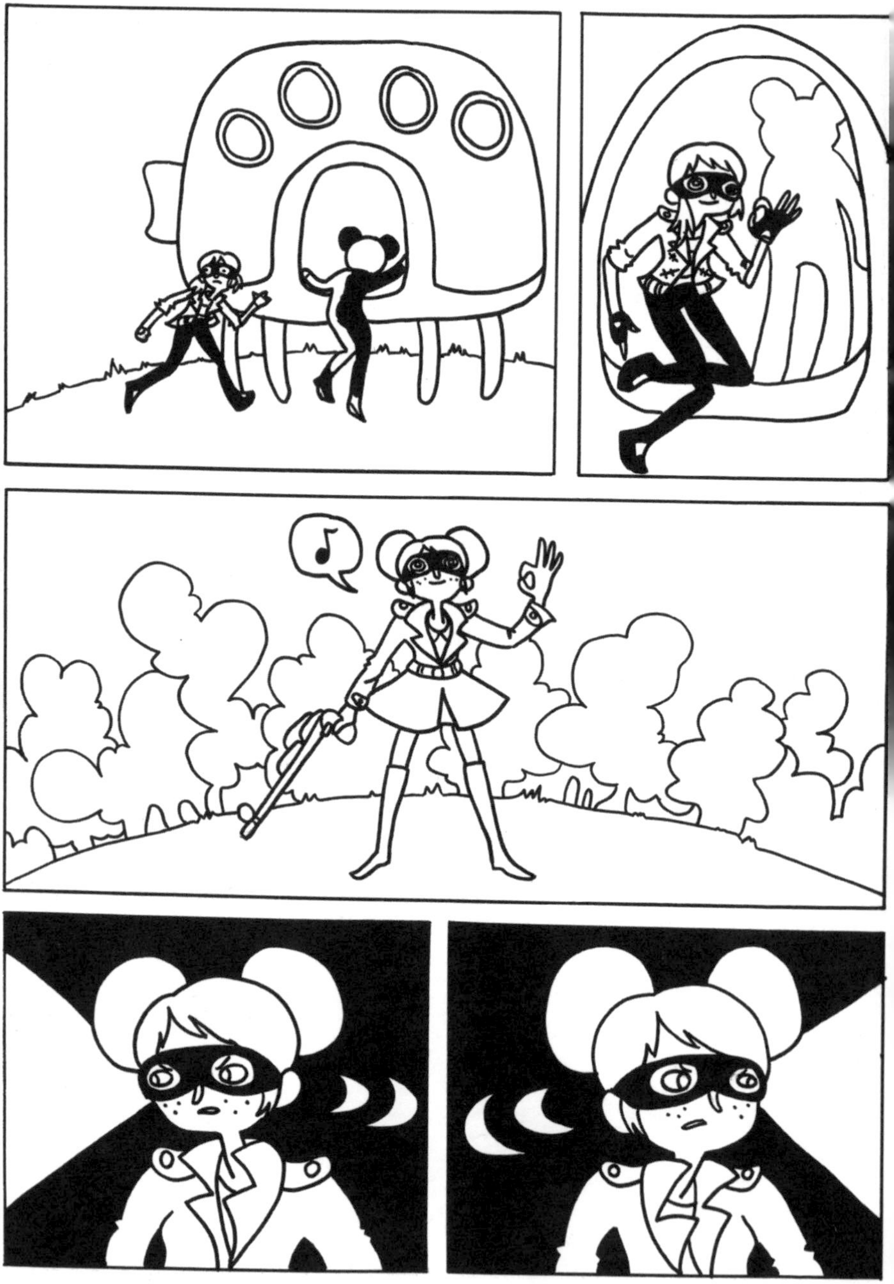

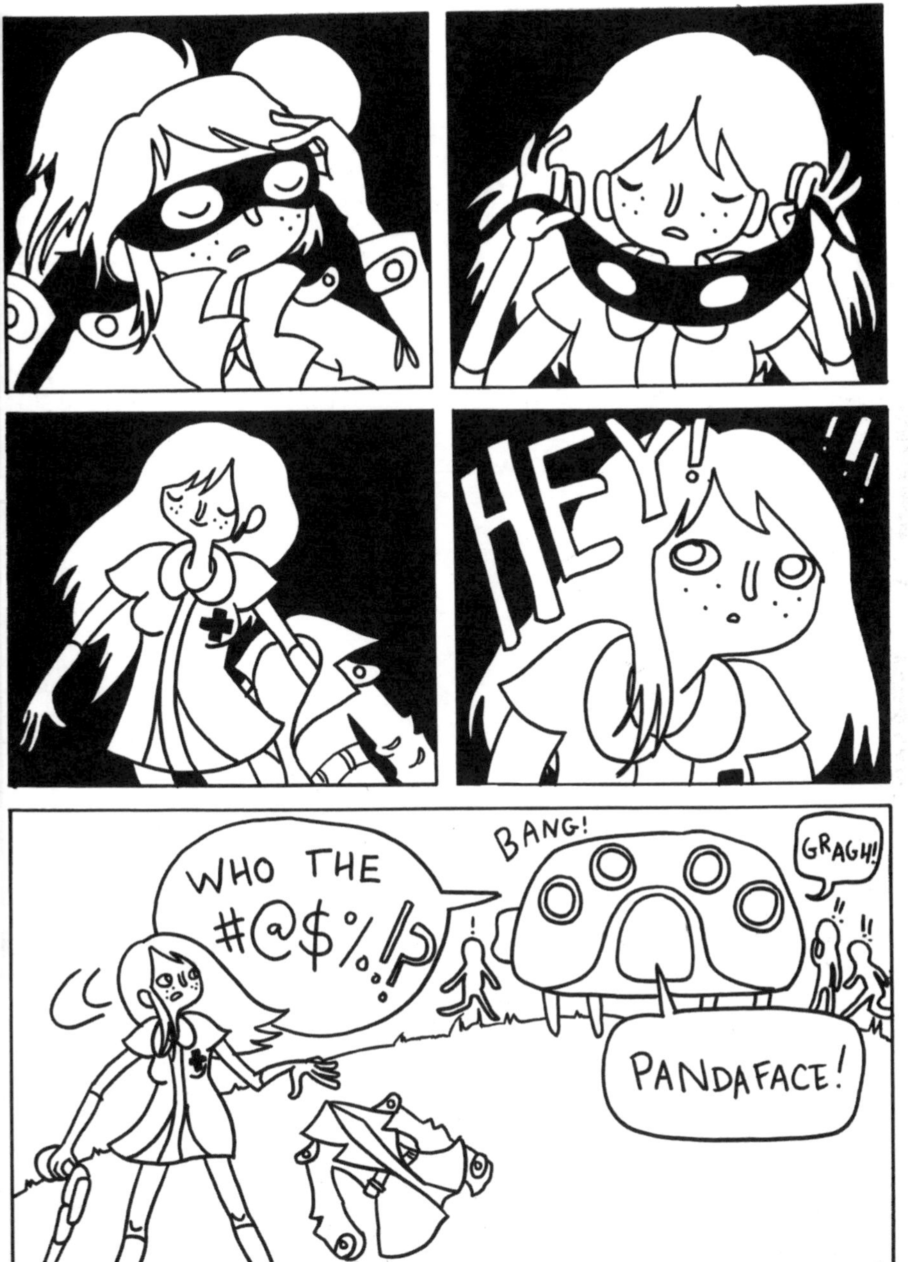
HEY!
!!
WHO THE #@$%!?
BANG!
GRAGH!
PANDAFACE!

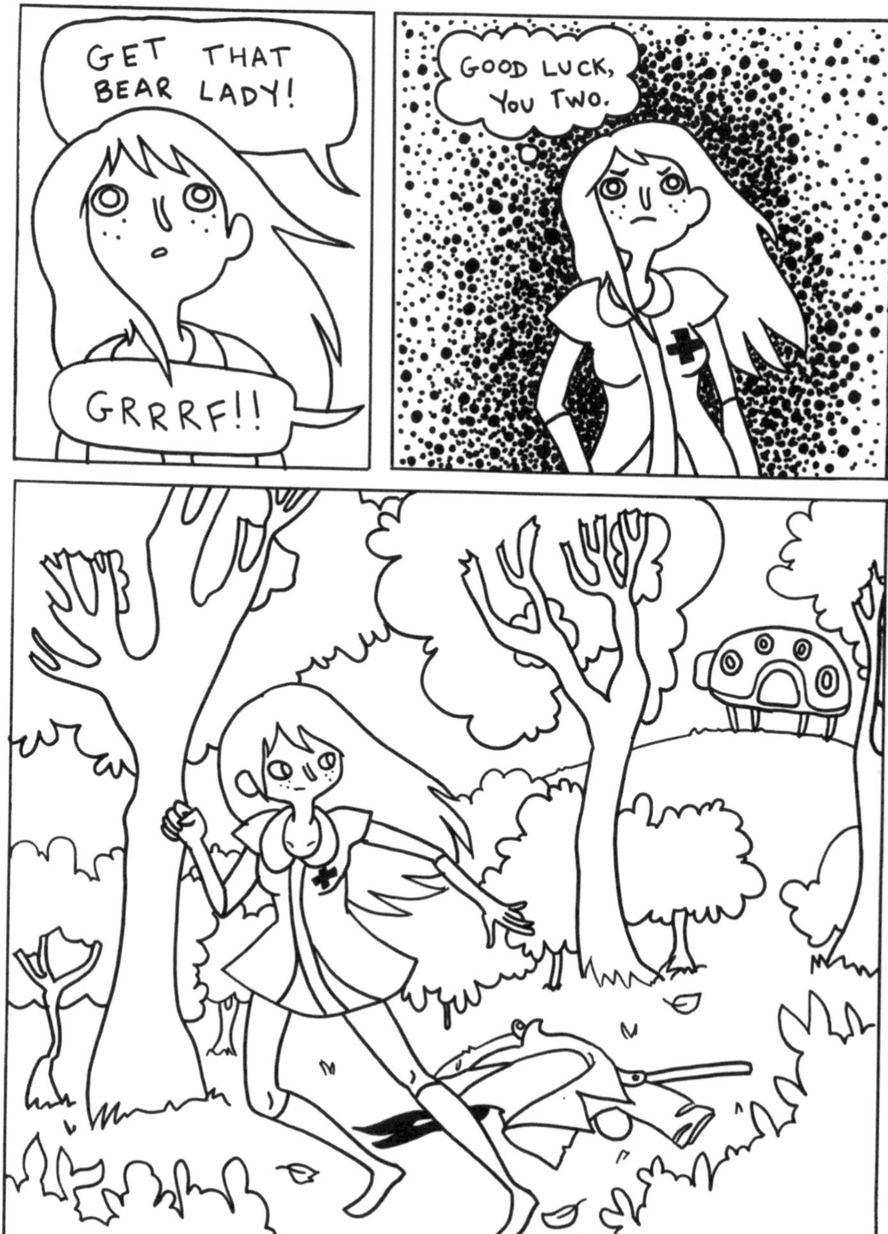
GET THAT BEAR LADY!
GRRRF!!
GOOD LUCK, YOU TWO.

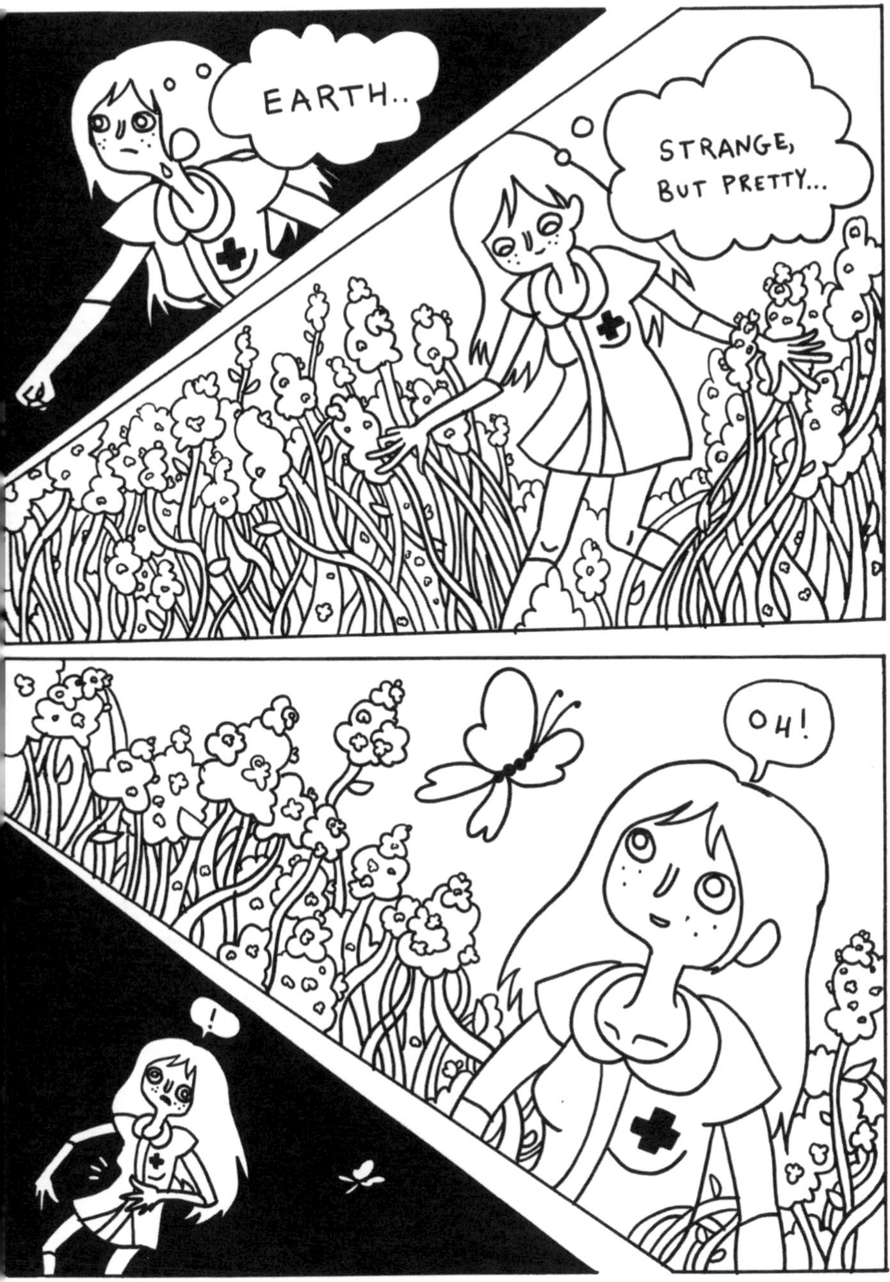
EARTH..
STRANGE, BUT PRETTY...
OH!
!

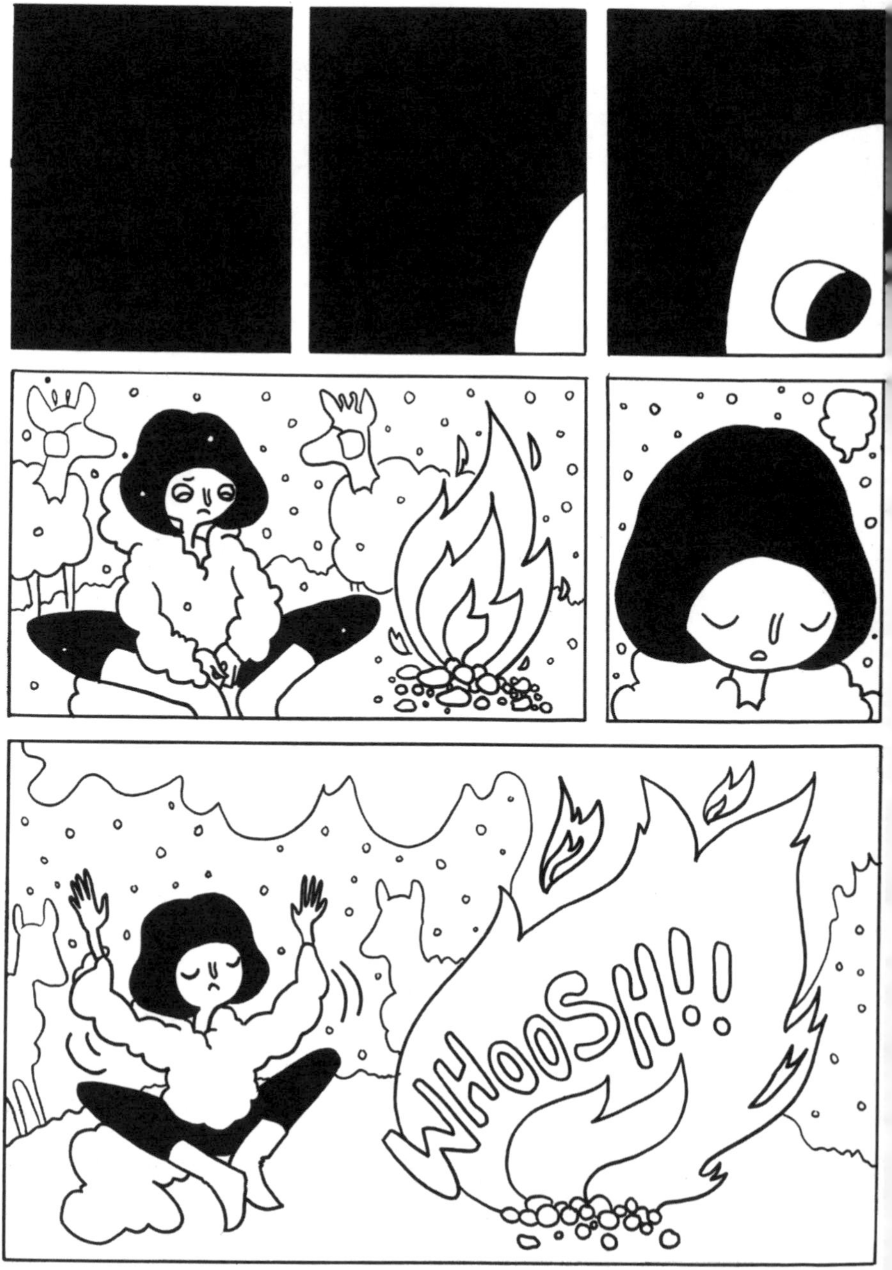
WHOOSH!!

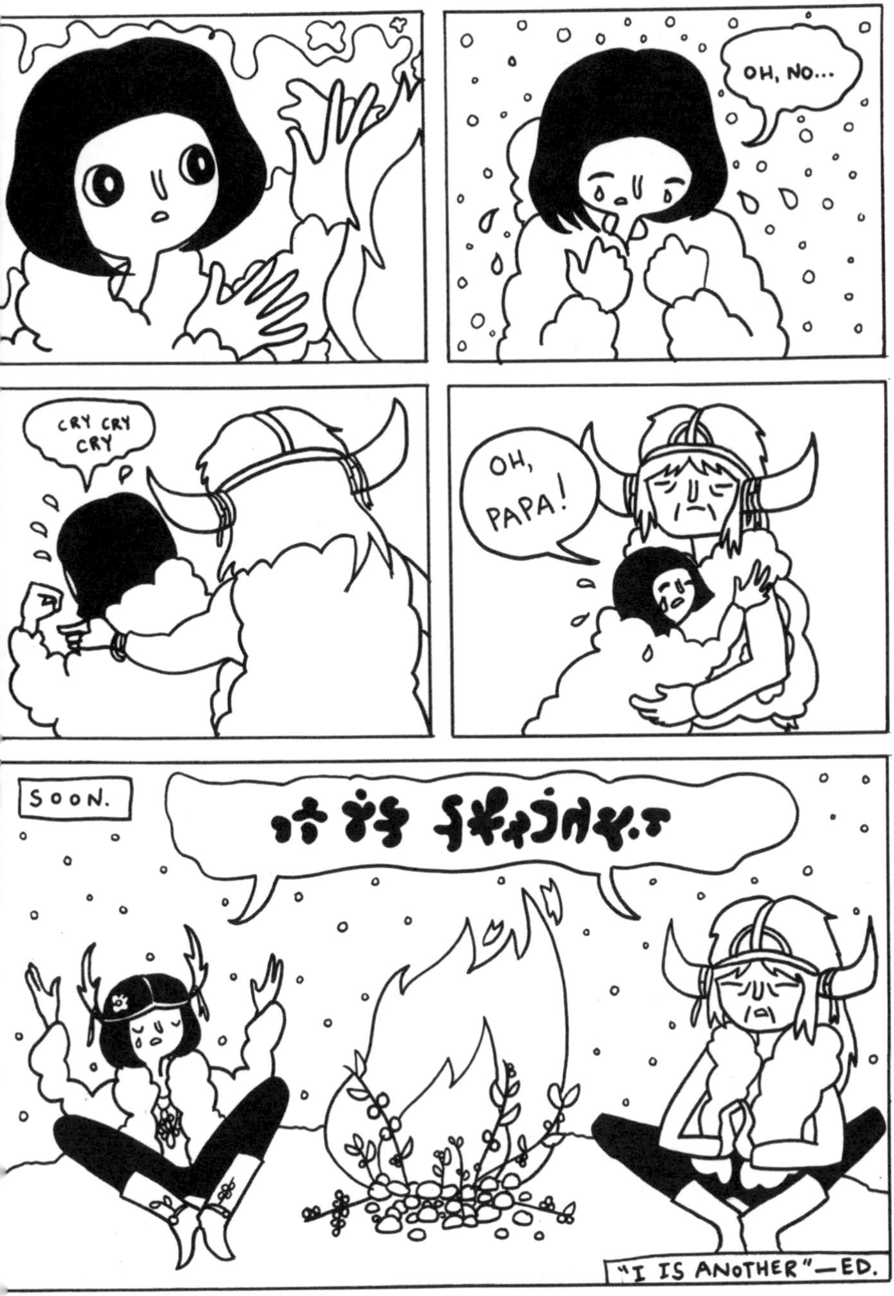
OH, NO...
CRY CRY CRY
OH, PAPA!
SOON.
"I IS ANOTHER"—ED.

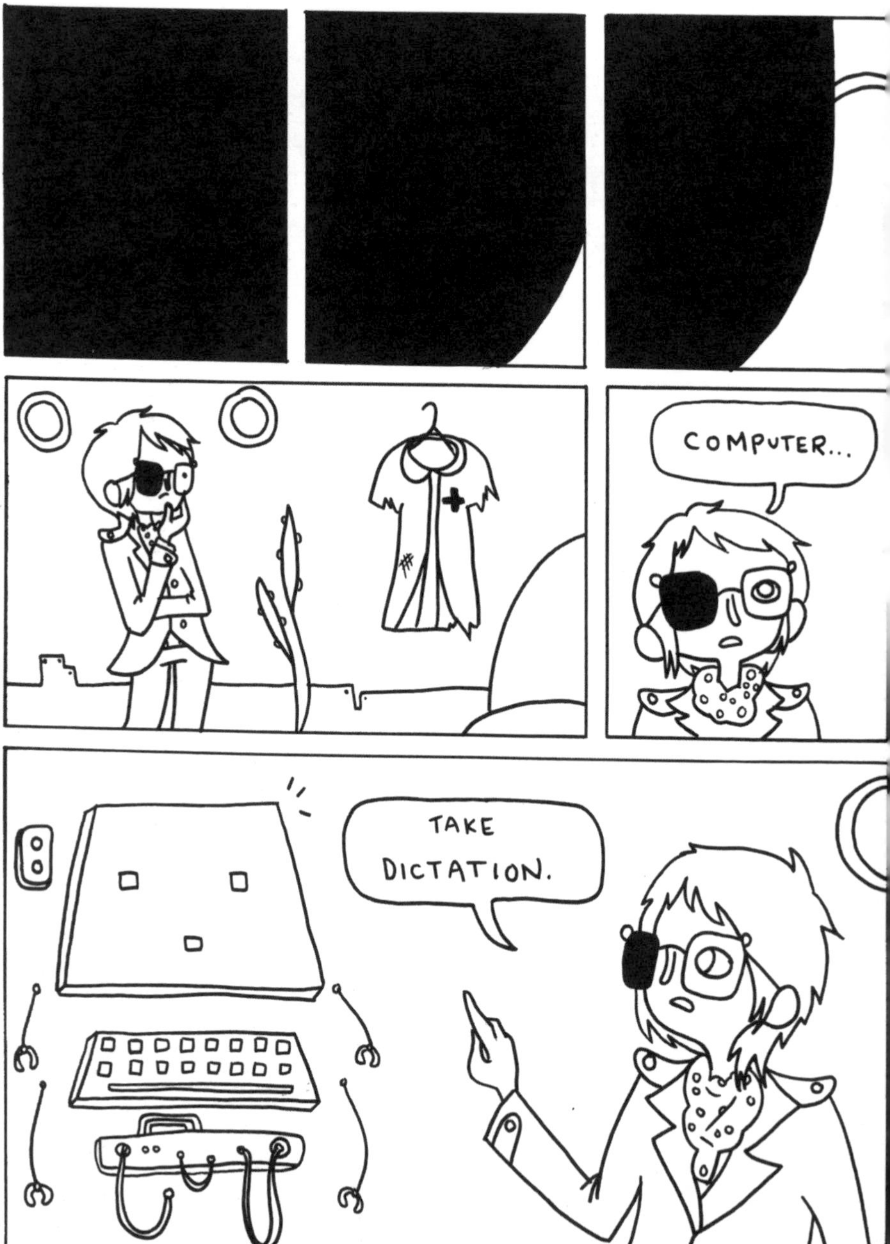
COMPUTER...
TAKE DICTATION.

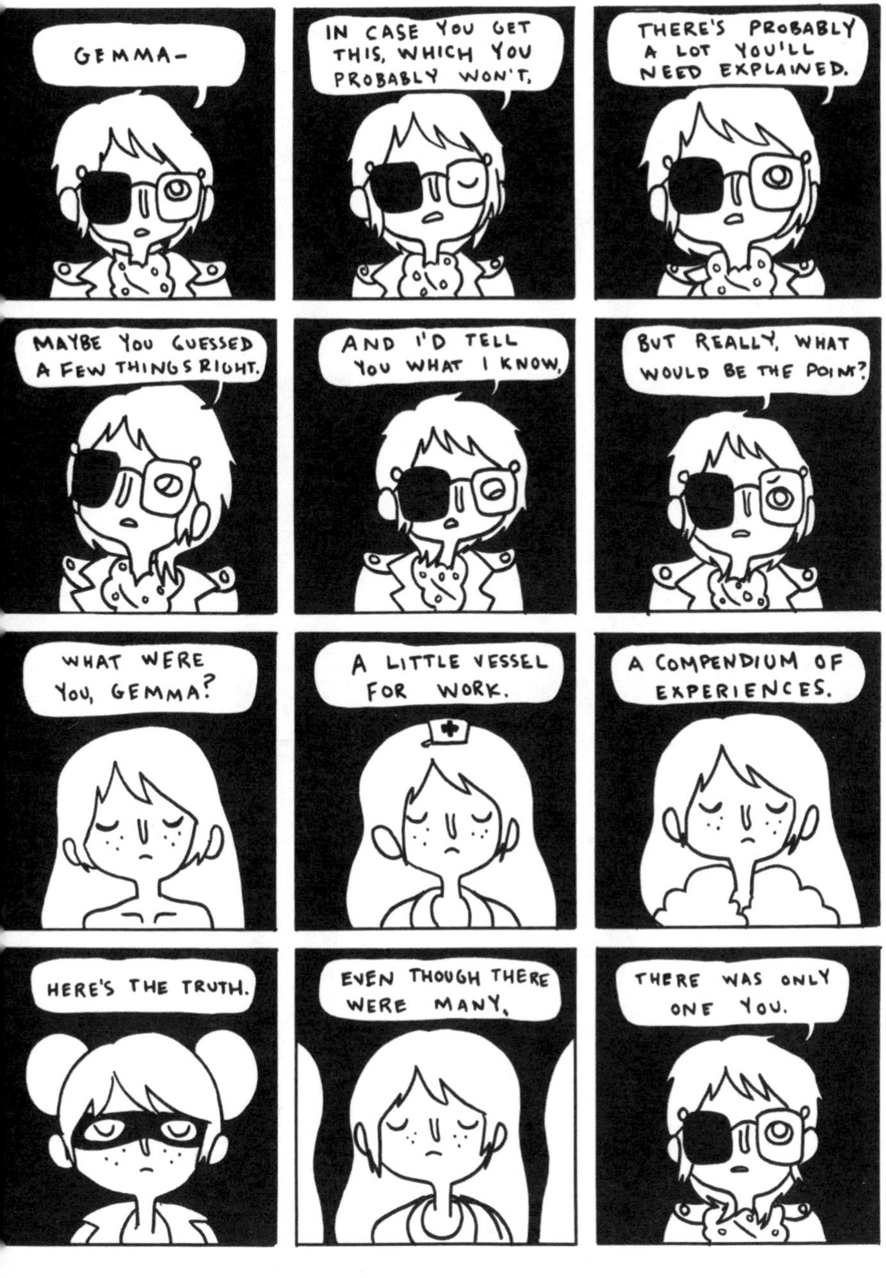
GEMMA-
IN CASE YOU GET THIS, WHICH YOU PROBABLY WON'T,
THERE'S PROBABLY A LOT YOU'LL NEED EXPLAINED.
MAYBE YOU GUESSED A FEW THINGS RIGHT.
AND I'D TELL YOU WHAT I KNOW,
BUT REALLY, WHAT WOULD BE THE POINT?
WHAT WERE YOU, GEMMA?
A LITTLE VESSEL FOR WORK.
A COMPENDIUM OF EXPERIENCES.
HERE'S THE TRUTH.
EVEN THOUGH THERE WERE MANY,
THERE WAS ONLY ONE YOU.

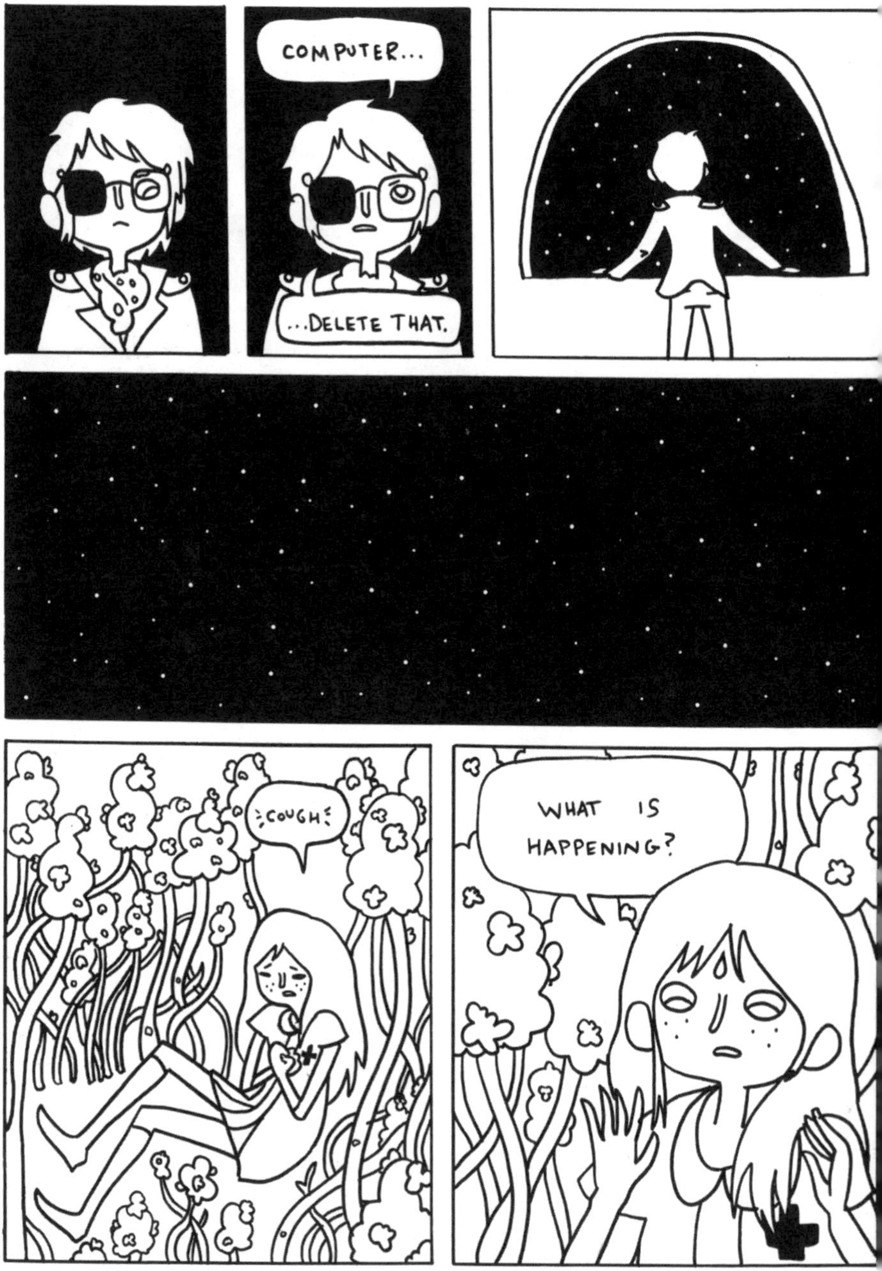
COMPUTER...
...DELETE THAT.
COUGH
WHAT IS HAPPENING?

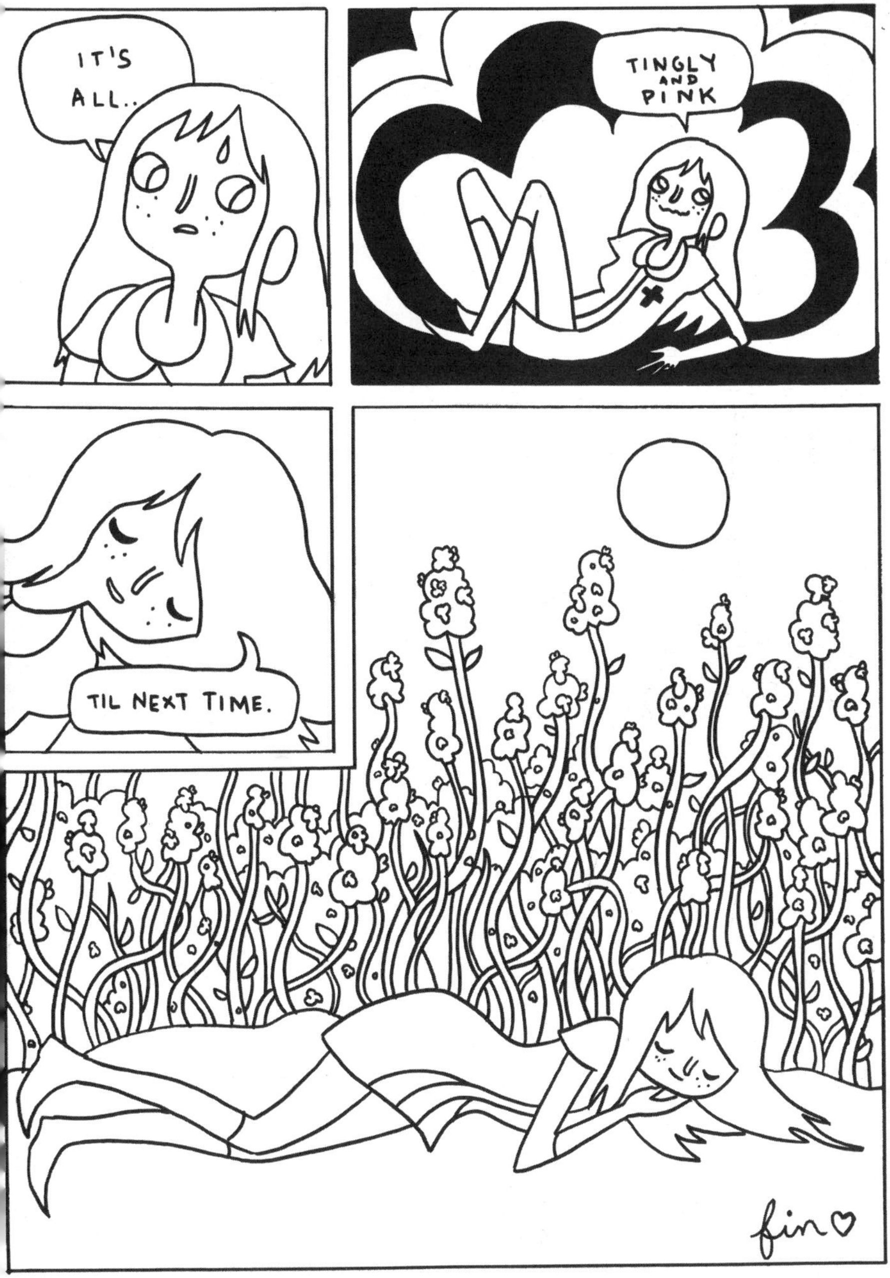
IT'S ALL..
TINGLY AND PINK
TIL NEXT TIME.
fin

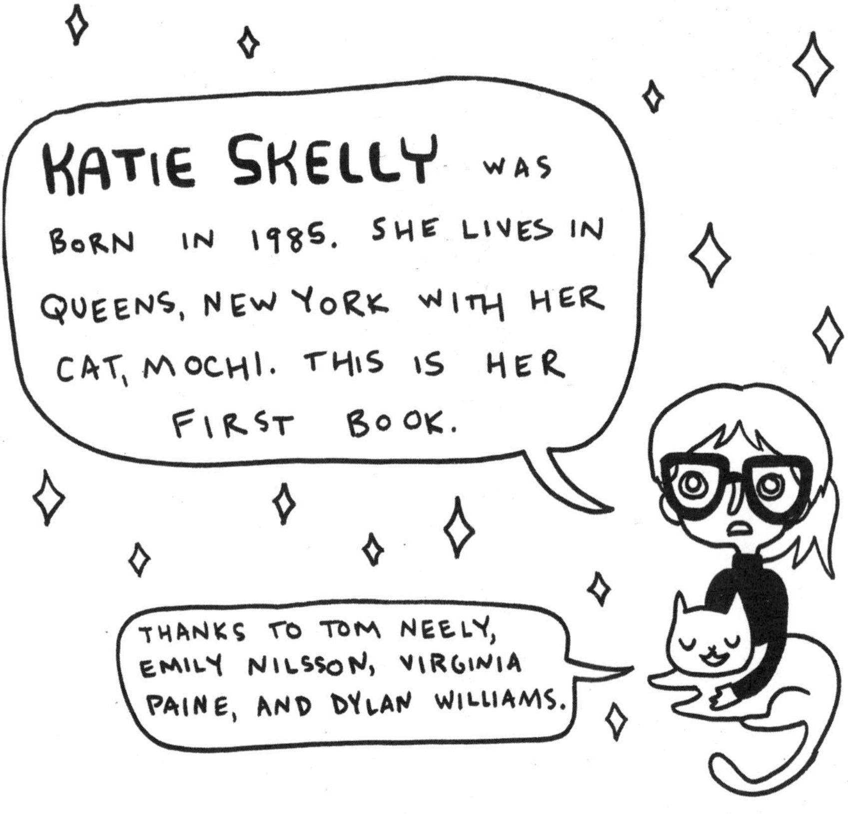
KATIE SKELLY WAS BORN IN 1985. SHE LIVES IN QUEENS, NEW YORK WITH HER CAT, MOCHI. THIS IS HER FIRST BOOK.
THANKS TO TOM NEELY, EMILY NILSSON, VIRGINIA PAINE, AND DYLAN WILLIAMS.

XTRA SPECIAL THANKS TO TALINE ALEXANDER, PAT LEWIS, SEAN McCARTHY, SALLY MADDEN, ALEXIS MEISELS, & THE SKELLYS.